CONTENTS

CHAP.		PAGE
	PREFACE	iii
I.	THE RANGE OF ARIEL MOTOR-CYCLES	1
II.	THE RUNNING COSTS OF AN ARIEL MOTOR-CYCLE	39
III.	THE LAW, LICENCES, INSURANCE	44
IV.	RUNNING-IN AND DRIVING HINTS	54
V.	WHEELS AND TYRES	64
VI.	THE ENGINE AND GEARBOX	71
VII.	LUBRICATION	86
VIII.	CARE OF THE ELECTRICAL EQUIPMENT	100
IX.	MAINTENANCE AND OVERHAULING	117
X.	CARE OF 1939 MODELS	168
	WAR-TIME RULES AND REGULATIONS	172
	INDEX	174

PREFACE

In this book the reader should find all he requires to enable him to keep his mount in perfect condition, and it is also hoped that he will derive considerable pleasure and interest from its perusal, for some of the recent Ariel models are obviously very clever engineering jobs, and a study of their design and construction is recommended to all interested in motor-cycling developments as well as to prospective buyers.

Special attention has been paid to that remarkably successful model known by its cylinder arrangement as the "Square Four," which was received with such enthusiasm at the 1935 Motor-cycle Show at Olympia. This machine has an exceptional turn of speed and marvellous acceleration, and its general performance is well above normal. Substantial improvements have recently been made to it, and it is now obtainable in 1,000 c.c. and 600 c.c. form.

In October, 1932, the production of Ariel motor-cycles came under new management. The new firm, which incidentally is known as *Ariel Motors Ltd.*, are continuing the manufacture of the "Square Four," but they have dropped the production of the characteristic "Sloper" models with longitudinal finning and also four-valve singles. Instead, they are marketing in various sizes three distinct vertical cylinder types, comprising a large capacity side-valve model, standard de luxe overhead models, and, lastly, the "Red Hunters," which have specially tuned engines and constitute ideal mounts for speed enthusiasts and all interested in competition events of various sorts. The largest "Red Hunter" possesses surging speed, and flat out will do an honest 90 m.p.h. Its cost, along with that of the other machines in the Ariel range, is very reasonable. Excellent value for money is, indeed, an outstanding feature of the latest Ariel range, as the reader will realize on glancing through the first chapter of this book. Those who want super-cheap motor-cycling on a snappy overhead-valve "two-fifty" will find two machines in the Ariel range worth serious contemplation. These machines, which, of course,

PREFACE

are licensed at only £1 2s. 6d. per annum, on account of their lightness should appeal strongly to novices.

For the benefit of the novice, the principles of the magneto, carburettor, and the four-stroke engine are fully explained in Chapter VI. The reader, be he novice or expert, will find the general notes on lubrication, adjustments, and overhauling of special value, and the various sub-headings should enable him to refer quickly to any special point about which he desires to obtain information or verification. While the present edition of this book deals mainly with 1933–9 models, earlier models have not been neglected, and owners of 1932 Ariels will find *full* maintenance and overhauling instructions included. There are still a great number of 1932 machines in use and on this account the author has retained in the present edition all essential information relating to them.

Owners of 1939 Ariel models are advised to read through Chapter X carefully before perusing the previous Chapters.

W. C. H.

INTRODUCTION

Welcome to the world of digital publishing ~ the book you now hold in your hand, while unchanged from the original edition, was printed using the latest state of the art digital technology. The advent of print-on-demand has forever changed the publishing process, never has information been so accessible and it is our hope that this book serves your informational needs for years to come. If this is your first exposure to digital publishing, we hope that you are pleased with the results. Many more titles of interest to the classic automobile and motorcycle enthusiast, collector and restorer are available via our website at **www.VelocePress.com.** We hope that you find this title as interesting as we do.

NOTE FROM THE PUBLISHER

The information presented is true and complete to the best of our knowledge. All recommendations are made without any guarantees on the part of the author or the publisher, who also disclaim all liability incurred with the use of this information.

TRADEMARKS

We recognize that some words, model names and designations, for example, mentioned herein are the property of the trademark holder. We use them for identification purposes only. This is not an official publication.

INFORMATION ON THE USE OF THIS PUBLICATION

This manual is an invaluable resource for the classic **ARIEL** enthusiast and a "must have" for owners interested in performing their own maintenance. However, in today's information age we are constantly subject to changes in common practice, new technology, availability of improved materials and increased awareness of chemical toxicity. As such, it is advised that the user consult with an experienced professional prior to undertaking any procedure described herein. While every care has been taken to ensure correctness of information, it is obviously not possible to guarantee complete freedom from errors or omissions or to accept liability arising from such errors or omissions. Therefore, any individual that uses the information contained within, or elects to perform or participate in do-it-yourself repairs or modifications acknowledges that there is a risk factor involved and that the publisher or its associates cannot be held responsible for personal injury or property damage resulting from the use of the information or the outcome of such procedures.

It is important that the reader recognizes that any instructions may refer to either the right-hand or left-hand sides of the vehicle or the components and that the directions are followed carefully. One final word of advice, this publication is intended to be used as a reference guide, and when in doubt the reader should consult with a qualified technician.

THE BOOK OF THE ARIEL

CHAPTER I

THE RANGE OF ARIEL MOTOR-CYCLES

ONE of the oldest firms in the motor-cycle industry, the Ariel manufacturers, have recently concentrated on the production of four-cylinder, overhead-valve models of unique design and quite exceptional performance, and a range of single-cylinder side-valve and overhead-valve models which are marketed at popular prices, and are designed to give trouble-free motor-cycling at its best for very long periods with a minimum of attention; in other words, performance plus reliability. As hitherto, attractive lines and superb finish characterize the whole Ariel range, which consists of eleven full "man-sized" machines —three more than last year. This sounds a large number and liable to confuse the prospective buyer, but it may be emphasized here that actually there are only, apart from the four-cylinder models, *three distinct types*, the other machines having specifications similar, except in regard to engine capacity, minor detail differences, and in certain cases the provision of somewhat more luxurious equipment, such as valanced mudguards, etc. The choice of an Ariel should not be difficult, the governing factors being the rider's power and speed requirements, and the price

ARIELS AVAILABLE FOR 1938

Model	c.c.	Bore and Stroke (mm.)	Lubrication	Valves	Gearbox Fitted	Tyres (ins.)	Tank Capacity (Petrol)
VB*	600	86·4 × 102	D.S.	S.V.	Burman 4F.	26 × 3·25	3¼ gal.
VG*	500	81·8 × 95	D.S.	O.H.V.	Burman 4F.	26 × 3·25	3¼ gal.
NG*	350	72 × 85	D.S.	O.H.V.	Burman 4F.	26 × 3·25	2¼ gal.
LG*	250	61 × 85	D.S.	O.H.V.	Burman 4F.	26 × 3·25 R	2¼ gal.
VH	500	81·8 × 95	D.S.	O.H.V.	Burman 4F.	26 × 3·25 R	3¼ gal.
NH	350	72 × 85	D.S.	O.H.V.	Burman 4F.	26 × 3·25 R	2¼ gal.
LH	250	61 × 85	D.S.	O.H.V.	Burman 4F.	26 × 3·25 R	2¼ gal.
4G	1000	65 × 75	D.S.	O.H.V.	Burman 4F.	27 × 4 R	3¾ gal.

* These are *de luxe* models with chromium and black tank finish and fully valanced mudguards.

he is prepared to pay. Prices, including electric lighting, automatic voltage control, horn, vary from £53 10s. to £89 10s., so that there is a machine suitable for those with large and small financial resources. If a buyer wishes, he can obtain possession of a brand new current model on payment of a small deposit, and most agents will make an allowance on a used machine.

Hire-purchase Terms. Nowadays a great number of motorcyclists take advantage of the hire-purchase system, and pay for their machines in instalments while riding. Any of the eight Ariel models tabulated on page 1 can be immediately supplied by Ariel dealers on payment of a 25 per cent deposit plus an amount to cover full comprehensive insurance. The balance is payable in twelve equal monthly instalments.

Electric Lighting Equipment. The prices of Ariel models given elsewhere include electric lighting. This comprises a 6-volt Lucas M.S. type "Magdyno" (with automatic voltage control) substituted in place of the magneto; a Lucas battery mounted on a strong steel platform in a readily accessible position below the saddle; an 8-in. improved pattern headlamp (type DU142) with built-in centre-zero ammeter and rotary switch; tail light; dimming switch; and the Ariel-designed instrument panel light. It will be found that the latest Lucas electrical equipment is, if reasonable care of the battery and dynamo is taken, 100 per cent reliable. Moreover, the 8-in. diameter headlamp, which is neatly mounted on a bracket attached to the forks, is capable of converting the darkest road into a blaze of light, so enabling the night rider to travel fast with absolute safety.

The instrument panel is protected against vibration and road shocks by means of rubber insulation interposed between the panel and the fuel tank on which it is mounted. As may be seen in Fig. 1, the panel houses at the rear the oil pressure gauge, to the left the quick release cam-operated filler cap, and to the right the speedometer where fitted. Provision is also made at the front for fitting a Smith 8-day clock, as well as the gearbox-driven speedometer. In the centre, a panel light is provided, and this can be detached for use as an inspection light.

Present Ariel Features. Before giving fairly detailed specifications of the Ariel range, it is perhaps as well to inquire as to what are the chief features of present Ariel design. There are so many good points about Ariels that it is impossible to do more than hurriedly run through some of the more obvious ones.

Ariel designers have always considered the comfort of the average rider, and high performance has not blinded them to riders' needs in other directions. A recent detail improvement,

THE RANGE OF ARIEL MOTOR-CYCLES

which is incorporated on all models, is an extraordinarily simple, yet very effective, device for reducing riding fatigue. Why no one adopted it before is a mystery that defies explanation. Wrist fatigue after several hours in the saddle when riding over poor roads is a common and unpleasant experience. The new method

Fig. 1. The Ariel Instrument Panel

of mounting the Ariel handlebars (see Fig. 2) entirely eliminates this nuisance, and renders long cross-country journeys considerably less tiring. The handlebars are no longer in metal-to-metal contact with the lugs, but are passed through enlarged lugs clamped to the fork spindle bearing. Rubber washers are clipped over the handlebars and pushed up into recesses in the lugs. A firm grip of the handlebars, which ensures no deterioration in steering, is obtained by means of taper-faced gland nuts screwed into the lugs.

Comfortable riding is assured by the provision of footrests having a wide range of adjustment (the handlebars are also adjustable), a low elastic top saddle position, central spring front forks with hand adjustment for the shock-absorber. The new forks, which closely resemble the Webb type, have considerably improved the Ariel road-holding qualities, and there is less tendency for bucking on bad roads. Stiff cradle frames are used on all models, and these have a four-point engine attachment. Four-speed Burman gearboxes with pivotal mounting are now standardized on

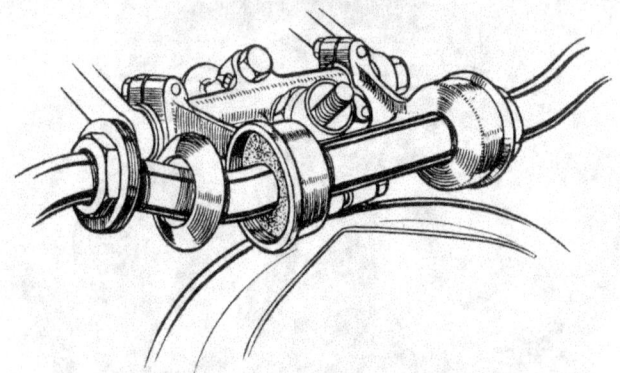

(*From " The Motor Cycle"*)

FIG. 2. AN AID TO RIDING COMFORT—THE RUBBER-MOUNTED HANDLEBARS

For the sake of clarity, the steering damper knob is omitted and the locking plug and bevelled washer on the handlebars have been unscrewed.

all of the eleven models, and in every single instance the gear ratios are well chosen. Multi-plate clutches of the shock-absorber type are used throughout the range. The transmission also includes an engine-shaft shock-absorber, and in the case of all models the primary chain runs in an oil-bath chain-case. Foot-gear control is standard on all models, and hand control has completely disappeared. With foot control the right hand need not be removed from the handlebars when making a gear change, and it is therefore to be preferred to the tank quadrant type, especially on the faster Ariel models and those used for competition work. Experience has shown that some riders have difficulty in selecting "neutral" with the foot type of gear change, and it is thus satisfactory to note that on all Ariel four-speed models a "neutral" indicator is provided. The location of "neutral" is thus no longer a matter of guesswork. The indicator, which is shown in Fig. 3, should prove particularly welcome to those using foot-gear control for the first time, and those who are rather heavy-footed.

Other commendable features in the Ariel specification include polished oil-bath chain-cases (Fig. 4), handsome saddle tanks of sensible capacity, with large knee-grips and built-in instrument panel, wheels having taper roller bearing hubs, 7-in. brakes with fulcrum adjustment for the rear, handlebar controls adjustable for position (except in regard to the throttle, which has twist-grip), and unusually good mudguarding. The rear mudguard has a detachable tail-piece which greatly facilitates wheel removal.

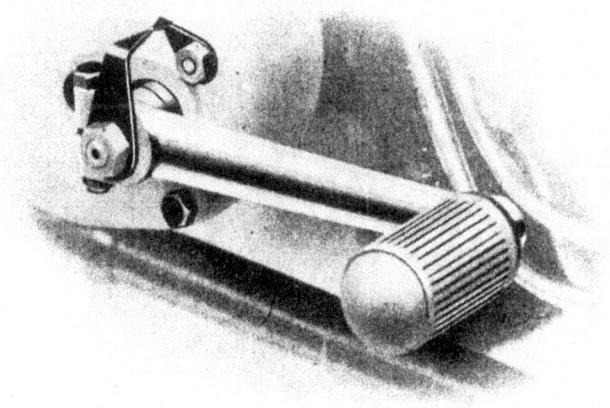

Fig. 3. The Ariel "Neutral" Indicator
Provided on all four-speed Burman gearboxes with foot control.

The two-port exhaust system deserves a word of praise. It is neither too quiet nor too noisy, and the exhaust note should satisfy the type of rider who, for certain psychological reasons, attaches considerable importance to this point. All models except four have tubular silencers with tail pipes, and back-pressure is almost negligible. The other seven models have equally effective streamlined fish-tail silencers. Downswept or upswept competition exhausts are available at the rider's option on the Red Hunter models.

As regards the 1939 single-cylinder power units, cleanliness of design is the outstanding feature, and, as already mentioned, all eight engines are built on very similar lines. Actually, many of the components are interchangeable, and it is due largely to this that Ariel production costs are kept at a low figure. All the engines, which have vertical cylinders, incorporate dry sump lubrication, detachable cylinder heads (also side-valve), rear

"Magdynos," totally-enclosed valve gear, steel connecting rods, aluminium pistons, ball-bearing mainshafts, double roller bearing big-ends, single camwheel timing gear, and large bore downdraught carburettors. On the side-valve engine a detachable cylinder head is now provided, and the valve gear, which is, of course, housed in the usual valve chest is noteworthy in that tappet guides are again fitted, with consequently better wear of the valves and springs. On the de luxe overhead-valve models the alloy steel valve rockers are housed in die-cast aluminium rocker-boxes, and the enclosure now extends to the valve springs

FIG. 4. THE ARIEL CLUTCH AND REAR BRAKE PEDAL

The clutch shown is fitted to all singles and is designed to eliminate "oil drag" and improve accessibility. It has a separate cover and the load capacity is increased by 40 per cent. Note the impoved brake pedal mounting.

themselves, quickly detachable caps being used. Automatic lubrication is utilized for the rockers, which are provided with drilled shafts and valve-clearance adjuster screws. Both valve guides are automatically lubricated. The "Red Hunter" high-compression engines are similar in general design to the standard engines, but various internal parts are polished, special cams and valve springs are used, 14 mm. plugs and racing pistons are fitted, and the crankcases are stiffened. There are also various other detail modifications designed to obtain an abnormally high power output, and these engines are specially tuned and bench-tested to deliver a definite brake-horse-power. Either a single- or two-port head may be specified (no extra charge) on the Red Hunters which are also obtainable with special competition equipment, including a crankcase undershield, racing magneto, racing mudguards, nail catchers, etc.

Finish. All non-plated parts are first coslettized to make them

THE RANGE OF ARIEL MOTOR-CYCLES

rust-proof. They are then given three coats of finest black enamel. All bright parts are heavily chromium-plated. Fuel tanks are beautifully finished according to specification, and embody a new black transfer with name badge in permanent vitreous enamel.

THE 1935 RANGE

The Side-valve Models. There are three side-valve models, all in the 550 c.c. class. They are models VA3, VA4, and VB, and these powerful models are excellent for general purposes, especially for long distance touring and heavy passenger work. It is no exaggeration to say that with a sidecar attached one of these models will make light work of any gradient where the rear wheel can obtain a grip. Special features of these machines are their high cruising speeds, their silky running, quiet tick-over, and utter dependability. Running and maintenance costs are also extremely small and, of course, decarbonizing is a matter of about 20 min. with the detachable cylinder head.

Models VA3 and VA4 are the standard side-valve models, and have an identical specification, except that the latter model has a four-speed gearbox instead of a three-speed gearbox. The four-speed gearbox is preferable for sidecar work. Model VB is the side-valve *de luxe* model, and is identical to the standard side-valve model VA4, except that in addition to the four-speed gearbox it has fully valanced mudguards, a polished aluminium oil-bath chain-case, and a fuel tankage ¾ gal. greater. The tank also is chromium-plated.

The Standard Overhead-valve Models. These comprise seven machines, three in the 500 c.c. class, two in the 350 c.c. class, and two in the 250 c.c. class. All of them possess lightning acceleration and high maximum speeds (i.e. according to engine capacity), and those who love the invigorating sensation and thrill of high-speed motor-cycling should find in this range the machine to suit them. What finer sensation is there than to feel a 60–70 m.p.h. gale lashing past one's ears, listen to the hum of a high revving engine, and watch the scenery approach and disappear behind one? All these, and a thousand other pleasures, await the buyer of an overhead-valve Ariel. Of course, if a man wants phenomenal speed and acceleration he is advised to go in for a "Red Hunter" or a "Square Four." It should be mentioned here, because some people do not realize it, that although the modern overhead-valve machine is extremely fast and has almost vicious acceleration, it can also, unlike its predecessor of a few years ago, be driven in a very docile manner, and with proper carburettor adjustment its tick-over leaves nothing to be desired. Push-rod breakages are now of rare occurrence, and there is little to choose as far as reliability is concerned between the side-valve and overhead-valve types.

The three 500 c.c. standard overhead-valve Ariels are models VF3, VF4, and VG. Driven solo, these machines will easily exceed 70 m.p.h., and very high average speeds can be maintained due to the exceptionally powerful brakes provided. With suitable gear ratios all three models constitute ideal fast passenger outfits. They are recommended for the sportsman as well as the tourist. Models VF3 and VF4 are identical, except that model VF4 has a four-speed gearbox instead of a three-speed one. Model VG is a *de luxe* model and is similar to the four-speed model VF4, except that the fuel tank is chromium-plated and holds ¾ gal. more fuel, streamlined fish-tail silencers are used in place of the tubular type, fully valanced mudguards are provided, and the primary chain runs in an oil-bath chain-case.

The two standard 350. c.c. models are models NF3 and NF4, and they have a very excellent performance. Except that the engine capacity is smaller, the general specification of these two machines is very similar to that of the 500 c.c. models. They are considerably lighter and should appeal strongly to those who prefer the 350 c.c. class. Both models have a high turn of speed, and sufficient power reserve for undertaking hard work for prolonged periods. They are also quite powerful enough for passenger work, but when a rider intends to drive long distances regularly with a sidecar attached the 500 c.c. class of machine is undoubtedly preferable. Models NF3 and NF4 are exactly the same, except that the former has a three-speed gearbox and the latter a four-speed gearbox.

The two models in the 250 c.c. class, and taxed at only 30s. per annum, are models LF3 and LF4. Both are smaller replicas of the larger models, and have an equally complete specification. Their performance is also extraordinarily good, and when riding them it is difficult to realize that they are not three-fifties. Maximum speeds are over 65 m.p.h. and acceleration is of a high order. On a gallon of petrol these machines will run 95 to 100 miles at a good average speed. A three-speed gearbox is fitted to model LF3, and a four-speed gearbox to model LF4. In other respects the specifications are the same.

The " Red Hunters." These comprise models VH, NH, LH. The general specification of all three models is very similar to that of the standard overhead-valves, but they incorporate many special features required for competition work, and, as already stated on page 6, the engines, which have high compression pistons, are specially tuned and bench-tested. To ensure stability at speed, backrests are provided, and studded rear and ribbed front tyres of slightly smaller section are fitted. Foot-gear control of the four-speed gearboxes is provided, and, of course, the exhaust systems are upswept to prevent damage when riding in trials. Downswept exhausts are, however, available without extra charge, and these are slightly more efficient as far as the elimination of back-pressure is concerned.

Model VH is the 500 c.c. "Red Hunter," and is a machine of which any sportsman can be justifiably proud, and a machine on which a clever rider can pit himself against all comers with a reasonable chance of success. With its chromium and red tank and clean lines it is a real "good looker." With a 7·5 to 1 high compression piston fitted it is tuned to give a road speed of 87–90 m.p.h.—enough for anywhere, except possibly Brooklands or the Isle of Man. By further skilled tuning its maximum speed could probably be raised still higher.

Model NH is a similar machine to model VH, but has an engine of 350 c.c., bench-tested and tuned to give a road speed of 75–78 m.p.h. with a 7 to 1 high compression piston. Apart from engine capacity, the only other appreciable difference in specification is the provision of a slightly smaller fuel tank and, of course, different gear ratios.

Model LH is the "baby" "Red Hunter," the second of the overhead-valve two-fifties, and qualifies for a 32s. 6d. per annum tax. It, nevertheless, has a specification similar to that of its larger brothers, except that the primary chain does not run in a polished aluminium chain-case, a smaller fuel tank is provided, and smaller tyres are fitted. It is tuned to attain 67–70 m.p.h., a performance equal to that of any other motor-cycle of this capacity, and has a fuel consumption of 95–100 m.p.g. It is a wonderful little bus and ideal for those who require a light and easily-handled competition and sports mount.

The Four-cylinder Overhead Camshaft Model. This 500 c.c. machine, officially known as model 4F, but dubbed from its birth in 1930, on account of its characteristic cylinder arrangement, the "Square Four," and by some people the "Squariel," is the most interesting and in many ways unique model of the 1935 Ariel range. It is also one of the few really successful monobloc types of multi-cylinder models. The principal features in its design are the casting of the cylinders *en bloc* in square formation, the use of a self-tensioning chain-driven overhead camshaft, and the twin gear-coupled crankshafts. The principal features in its running are the flexibility of the engine, the extraordinarily easy starting, the acceleration akin to that of a fighting scout which can be obtained, the complete absence of vibration, and the exceptionally high maximum speed (over 80 m.p.h.). Decarbonizing and tappet adjustment can be carried out very easily, as accessibility has been most carefully studied. The makers rightly refer to this machine as "the world's most exclusive motor-cycle." The author envies any reader who has a "Square Four" in his backyard! As regards the general specification, excluding the engine, this closely follows that of the *de luxe* overhead-valve model, but a special carburettor is fitted. Needless to say, a "Square Four" and sidecar make a superb passenger outfit. A four-speed gearbox with these ratios and foot control, and a very light clutch, enable rapid silent changes to be made, but it is worthy of note that on the solo model such is the pick up and flexibility of the engine that the gearbox can be completely ignored for miles on end. It is, in fact, possible to accelerate from a crawl to 80 m.p.h. using the throttle only without the slightest tendency for pinking, and this with the magneto on full advance; 83 m.p.h. is probably about the maximum speed, and this represents about 5,600 r.p.m. An experimental supercharged "Square Four" has, however, lapped Brooklands at over 100 m.p.h. Stability and braking are excellent.

A 500 c.c. version of the "Square Four" is no longer marketed, but the 600 c.c. model incorporates, in addition to the new features common to the whole Ariel range, such as shock-proof handlebars, new forks, improved tank, re-designed frame with single front down tube, and a gearbox with internal dog gear engagement; several important modifications. For instance, the seat-tube toolbox has been scrapped, and primary chain adjustment is much more easily effected; twin-gear type oil pumps are replaced by a large single plunger pump, and a fabric oil filter is mounted below the camshaft chain-case; the oil is now contained in the engine sump.

1935 MODELS VA3, VA4 (550 c.c. S.V.)

The specification of the two large capacity standard side-valve Ariels applies in general to the other machines, and will accordingly be described in considerable detail. It is as follows—

The 5·50 h.p. Side-valve Engine. This is a particularly clean looking orthodox, vertical, four-stroke, single-cylinder unit having a bore and stroke of 86·4 mm. and 95 mm. respectively, giving a cubic capacity of 550 c.c., and a large number of its components are interchangeable with those of other engines.

The crankcase is a massive aluminium casting ribbed in several places to ensure rigidity, and a circular hollowed projection on the off side constitutes the timing case to which is screwed the timing-case cover, which is integral with the rearwardly-inclined magneto chain-case. At the crankcase end of the chain-case cover

THE RANGE OF ARIEL MOTOR-CYCLES 11

is a flat-faced projection housing the oil pump and oil pressure regulator. A ball type crankcase breather is used to prevent generation of pressure in the crankcase, and also to lubricate the secondary chain with oil mist. The oil sump is detachable.

Within the crank-case is the very carefully balanced crankshaft assembly, comprising two webbed cast-iron flywheels with their keyed and tapered mainshafts running in ball bearings, and a shouldered crankpin to receive the big-end of the connecting rod, which is of high-tensile steel and has a double row of rollers.

FIG. 5. FULCRUM ADJUSTMENT FOR REAR BRAKE.

The small-end has a phosphor-bronze bush, and takes a $1\frac{3}{16}$ in. diameter fully-floating gudgeon pin secured with spring circlips.

The piston itself is a self-compensating aluminium alloy type, but the skirt is not split. It provides a compression ratio of 5 to 1, and is peculiarly free from that annoying malady known as "piston slap." Two narrow width compression rings are provided, but no scraper rings, and the correct gap at the ring slots is .006 in. The piston reciprocates in a well-finned cylinder which has a detachable head with the valves below the level of the head, and, consequently, the ports are cast integral with the cylinder barrel, which has an unusually thick base flange. A cylinder gasket is fitted between the barrel and head which has a 7-bolt fixing, and the design of the combustion chamber and ports is such as to provide good gas turbulence and freedom from detonation of the explosive mixture which enters *via* a downswept inlet port, and after combustion is ejected into a heavily plated and large diameter downswept exhaust pipe terminating in a large streamlined silencer. The exhaust pipe locking ring is finned to provide additional cooling in the neighbourhood of the exhaust port.

The valves, which are of nickel-chrome steel, are contained in

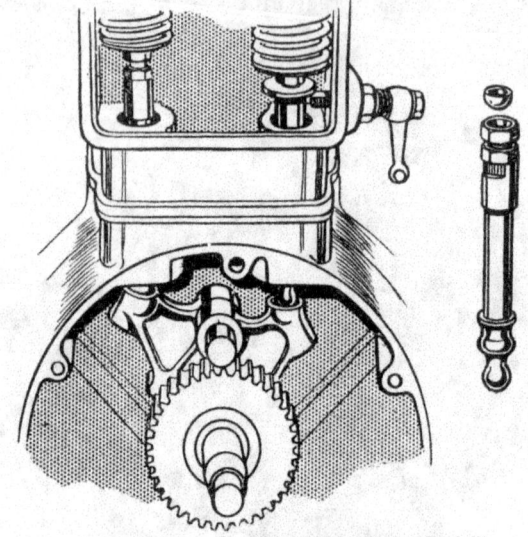

(*From "The Motor Cycle"*)
Fig. 6. Showing Details of the 1935 Side-valve Tappets and the Timing Gear

a valve chest cast integral with the cylinder and provided with a finned cover, operate in detachable cast-iron guides, and have duplex valve springs with split collet anchorages. As may be seen in Fig. 6, the arrangement of the tappets is unusual in that tappet guides are not used. Instead, the adjustable tappets have ball-ended lower ends resting direct in sockets formed in the two cam lever rockers, and have cupped upper ends to receive hardened hemispherical caps which are pushed on to the ends of the valve stems. This arrangement facilitates the entry of oil mist into the valve chest, and the valves and their springs benefit considerably thereby. A simple type of exhaust valve lifter is provided at the side of the valve chest, and there is an adjustment for the lever itself as well as one at the cable stop.

As may also be seen in Fig. 6, the timing gear consists of a single cam wheel meshing with the small engine pinion, and two

THE RANGE OF ARIEL MOTOR-CYCLES

toggles having a common pivot. The magneto driving sprocket is a friction-fit on the camshaft from an extension of which the pump drive is taken. A feature of the timing gear is that the small engine pinion runs submerged in oil, which can only pass into the upper part by way of the gear teeth. This provides a cushioning effect, and also makes for silent running and absence of whine from the gears.

The Dry Sump Lubrication System (All Single-cylinder Models).

Dry sump lubrication has for some years past been adopted by the majority of motor-cycle manufacturers, including the Ariel concern. This is not surprising, for this system possesses many advantages over other types of lubrication systems. First, the system is entirely automatic, and the rider is relieved of all responsibility in regard to lubrication other than regular oil replenishment and periodical draining of the filters; secondly, a large volume of oil is left in constant circulation and, therefore, the oil actually delivered to the engine is cool and reasonably fresh after filtering; thirdly, the engine does not become dirty outside or quickly carbonized inside; fourthly, the plugs do not tend to oil up; fifthly, a very low oil consumption is obtained. On some Ariels it is possible to average 4,000 m.p.g., and the oil is continually circulated at the rate of about a pint every ten minutes.

Briefly, the working of the Ariel dry sump lubrication system is as follows. Oil is gravity-fed from the tank to the double plunger pump, which is eccentrically driven off the camshaft. The larger capacity plunger is for scavenging the oil from the sump and returning it to the tank, and the smaller capacity one is for delivering the oil to the engine. The oil after reaching the pump (which, of course, works at a speed proportional to the engine revolutions per minute) is pressure-fed by the delivery plunger to a pipe projecting into the timing side mainshaft. Before reaching the mainshaft, however, it has to pass a spring-loaded ball valve (see page 90), and the oil pressure at this point is, of course, equal to the spring pressure, which may be adjusted by means of an oil pressure regulator screw. The correct adjustment should give a normal pressure of 10 to 15 lb. per sq. in. This pressure can be verified, for some oil is by-passed at a point between the pump and ball valve to an oil pressure gauge mounted on the instrument panel. The oil under pressure passes right along the mainshaft until it reaches the flywheel centre, when it is diverted through oilways in the flywheel and crankpin to the big-end rollers. A patented centrifugal oil purifier is incorporated in the flywheel to trap impurities which may have accumulated in the oil, and the action of this ingenious device is fully explained on page 93. Sufficient it is to mention here that the trapped impurities can be readily cleared out by removing a plug on the flywheel rim accessible on detaching the sump. Lubrication of the cylinder walls and small-end bearing is by oil thrown off the big-end. The surplus drains into the sump, and is returned by the scavenging pump plunger to the oil tank. It is possible to observe the oil in circulation by removing the oil tank filler cap and noting the ejection of oil from the return pipe orifice which is immediately over the filter. Nothing has so far been said with regard to timing gear and valve lubrication, but lubrication of these parts is simply carried out. Oil spray from the crankcase

FIG. 7. THE 1938-9 600 C.C. SIDE-VALVE DE LUXE MODEL VB

is forced through vent holes into the timing case which it fills till the engine pinion is submerged, the remainder draining back into the crank-case proper. Oil thrown off the half-time pinion assists to lubricate the contents of the valve chest. No adjustment of the lubrication system is necessary. Additional information will be found on pages 55 and 86.

Carburettor (VA3, VA4, VB). This is a two-lever, semi-automatic down-draught, large-bore Amal instrument, and its type number is 76/112. It is flanged-fixed to an exceedingly short induction pipe, and the downward inclination is primarily to provide more room for the air intake, but improved performance is said to have resulted from this inclination. The carburettor has a slow-running air adjuster screw and also a throttle stop to enable a "tick-over" setting independent of the cable adjustment to be obtained. Twist-grip control is provided for the throttle,

THE RANGE OF ARIEL MOTOR-CYCLES

and a handlebar lever controls the air slide. A size 160 main jet is used in conjunction with a 6/5 valve with a ·1065 needle in position 3. This setting gives plenty of speed and acceleration, and also a fuel consumption of 80–85 m.p.g. The operation and tuning of the Amal carburettor are dealt with on pages 76 and 130 respectively.

Ignition (All Models except 4F, VH, NH, LH). The sparking plug fitted as standard and recommended is a two-point, mica-insulated, 18 mm. Lodge H.1. This is a sports type plug with a recommended gap at the electrodes of ·02 in. (i.e. approximately $\frac{1}{2}$ mm. or $\frac{1}{50}$ in.).

The "juice" is generated by a Lucas magneto or M.S. "Magdyno" (see page 2) driven by chain off the inlet camshaft at half engine speed clockwise (viewed from C.B. side). The instrument, which is mounted behind the engine, is protected from dirt and water by means of a neat shield. The spark advance is varied by means of a movable cam ring controlled by a handlebar lever, and the contact-breaker is designed for a "break" of ·012 in.

Frame and Forks (All Models). The same type of frame is used for all the 1935 Ariel machines, and it is, therefore, designed upon particularly robust lines. It is of the cradle type, and from a one-piece steel head lug are arranged the top tube and a front down tube of $1\frac{1}{2}$ in. diameter. All the main tubes are of Aero quality steel and all are straight. The top tube runs to a seat pillar lug, into the rear ends of which are brazed the back forks. The base of the front down tube carries engine plates, and the rear engine plates are bolted to a sturdy seat pillar. This frame gives a saddle height of only $26\frac{1}{2}$ in., a wheel base of $54\frac{1}{2}$ in., and a ground clearance of $4\frac{3}{4}$ in. It possesses exceptional torsional stiffness, and is famous in the trials world for its excellent steering qualities and weight distribution. Special lugs are provided for sidecar attachment.

The forks, which are shown in Fig. 8, although in appearance very like Webb forks, are of Ariel design and manufacture. They are of the single-barrel tension spring type, and their design has recently been much improved. The use of high-grade taper steel tubes and massive bridges ensures great lateral rigidity and general strength for solo and sidecar use. Fork rebound is controlled by large frictional shock-absorbers provided with a hand adjustment on the off-side. A neat disc-type steering damper facilitates sidecar driving, and prevents any tendency for wheel wobble at high speeds. It is anchored to the front down tube. Grease nipples are provided for fork spindle lubrication.

Gearbox and Clutch (VA3, VA4). The three-speed gearbox used on model VA3 is a Burman, type "TP" countershaft gearbox with pivotal mounting, hand control, constant mesh gears, enclosed kick-starter mechanism, layshaft-driven speedometer drive, ball bearing mainshaft, and dog clutches. With 23-tooth and 21-tooth engine sprockets it provides the following solo and sidecar gear ratios—

Solo . . . first, 13·7 to 1; second, 7·7 to 1; third, 4·7 to 1.
Sidecar . . first, 15·0 to 1; second, 8·4 to 1; third, 5·2 to 1.

The clutch used in conjunction with the three-speed gearbox is a four-plate one with alternate fabric inserted and steel plates. The insert plates are kept in contact with the steel plates by four springs arranged radially on the outer cover, and the tension of these springs is adjustable. Clutch release is effected by a floating plunger in the mainshaft pushing against an adjusting screw in the centre of the cover. The driven friction plates have tongues which engage with grooves in the dished plate, and the plate is attached to the chain wheel in such a way that the drive is taken through rubber shock-absorbing buffers. These rubber buffers allow of a radial movement of approximately $\tfrac{3}{16}$ in., with the result that a big cushioning effect is obtained.

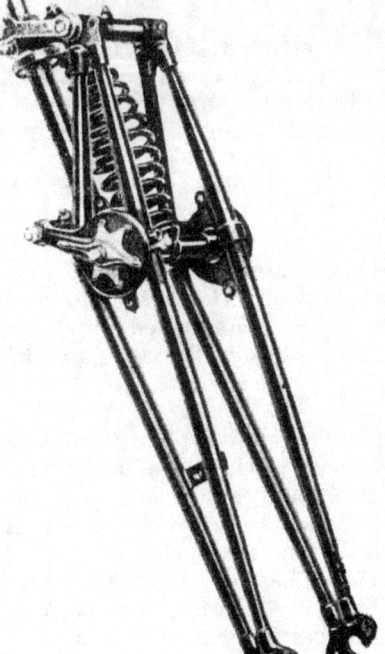

Fig. 8. The Ariel Forks
(Fitted to 1935–9 models.)

The four-speed gearbox fitted on model VA4 is also a pivot-mounted Burman, type "BAP," and in general design is somewhat similar to the three-speed "TP" type, except for the provision of an additional speed and a different system of internal clutches. Instead of the usual dog clutches being used, toothed extensions on either side of the mainshaft and layshaft sliding gears mesh with internally toothed rings formed on the adjacent gears. This system makes for ease of gear changing and absence of wear on the dogs. With 23- and 21-tooth

THE RANGE OF ARIEL MOTOR-CYCLES

engine sprockets the four-speed gearbox provides the following ratios—

    Solo . . . first, 12·6 to 1; second, 8·0 to 1; third, 6·0 to 1; fourth, 4·7 to 1.

    Sidecar . . first, 13·8 to 1; second, 8·8 to 1; third, 6·6 to 1; fourth, 5·2 to 1.

FIG. 9. THE 1936–9 600 C.C. S.V. ENGINE WITH DETACHABLE HEAD REMOVED SHOWING VALVES

As regards the clutch, this is also a four-plate shock-absorber type, but cork instead of fabric inserts are used and oil flingers are provided.

Transmission (All Models except 4F, VH, NH, VG, VB). Coventry "Ultimate" roller chains are used for both the primary and secondary transmission, and the dimensions are $\frac{1}{2}$ in. × ·305 in. and $\frac{5}{8}$ in. × $\frac{3}{8}$ in. respectively. Both chains are automatically lubricated by means which are described on pages 97 and 98, and longevity and silent running are thus assured. The primary chain which has an engine shaft shock-absorber and also a clutch wheel shock-absorber to ensure smoothness and absence of transmission snatch is simply adjusted by means of the pivotal gearbox mounting, and is totally enclosed in a steel chain-case. The secondary chain which has a rear wheel drawbolt adjustment for tension is provided with a steel guard. A polished aluminium oil-bath chain-case is available as an extra on model VA4.

Brakes, Wheels, Tyres (All Models except LF3, LF4, LH). The design of the brakes used on Ariel machines is in accordance with modern motor-car practice. On all models both front and rear brakes are 7 in. in diameter, and operate on the internal-expanding principle. The brake shoes are of aluminium fitted with Fibrax linings. Dual, internal coil springs are used to return the shoes, and quick hand adjustment is provided for both brakes; in addition there is a special fulcrum adjustment in the rear brake. This brake has a detachable chain sprocket. An improvement to the appearance of this year's machines is obtained by the provision on the front brake of a chromium-plated dust cover. The wheels run on taper roller bearings, have well-base rims with heavy butted spokes, and carry 26 in. × 3·25 in. wired-on Dunlop tyres.

Tanks (all except " de luxe " Models, " Red Hunters," 4F). The saddle fuel tank is of welded steel, and has a shock-absorber attachment to the frame. With its large bulbous nose, black enamel finish, and gold lining it is particularly attractive looking, and has a capacity of $2\frac{1}{2}$ gal.—sufficient on the side-valve machines for a mileage of at least 200 at cruising speed. A flush-fitting, black-enamelled instrument panel (see page 3) is let into the top of the tank, and incorporates the quick-release, cam-operated filter cap and the oil-pressure gauge. Provision is also made for a gearbox-driven speedometer and clock, which are available as extras. On electrically equipped models a panel light is also included. The pneumatic knee-grips and the gate-change for the gear lever are attached to the tank sides. If desired, a chromium-plated tank similar to that fitted on the *de luxe* models may be specified.

A separate welded steel oil tank is mounted on the off side of the saddle pillar, and has a capacity of $3\frac{1}{2}$ pints. A large submerged filter removes all impurities which may collect in the engine and be returned to the tank. As in the case of the fuel tank, the finish is in black enamel.

Miscellaneous. The handlebars, which have an overall width of 30 in., are of the new patented "resilient" type (see Fig. 2). This type of semi-flexible bars prevents wrist fatigue, and is an aid to high speed cornering. All handlebar controls are adjustable to suit individual requirements. Rubber footrests having a wide range of adjustment, and also special lugs for pillion footrests, are provided, and the saddle is an "Aero" elastic soft top type

THE RANGE OF ARIEL MOTOR-CYCLES 19

(adjustable). Strong ribbed section steel mudguards are fitted as standard, but valanced mudguards (see Fig. 12) may be specified as an extra. The tail of the rear guard is quickly detachable to facilitate rear wheel removal. A forged steel girder "spring-up" stand is provided at the rear and a tubular one at the front. Included in the equipment of every Ariel which measures 54½ in. from stem to stern are specially shaped number plates, a large steel toolbox between the rear chain stays, a very complete set of tools, and a grease-gun and tyre inflator.

1935 MODEL VB (550 c.c. S.V.)

The de luxe version of the large capacity side-valve model has a specification identical to that of the standard side-valve model VA4, except for the following differences—

Fuel Tank. In place of a standard black-enamelled fuel tank of 2½ gal. capacity, a 3¼ gal. tank is fitted, and this has a chromium finish with black transfer and gold lining. To prevent sun dazzle the instrument panel is finished in black as on the other models.

Transmission. The primary chain, instead of being enclosed in a pressed steel chain-case, runs in a polished aluminium oil-bath chain-case.

Mudguards. These are similar to those used on models VA3, VA4, except that they have deep valances (see Fig. 7).

1935 MODELS VF3, VF4 (500 c.c. O.H.V.)

These two popular standard overhead-valves have specifications similar to those of the standard side-valves (models VA3, VA4) other than the following—

The Standard 500 c.c. Overhead valve Engine. This has a bore and stroke of 86·4 and 85 mm. respectively, giving a capacity of 497 c.c. Below the cylinder the engine shows no appreciable differentiation from the side-valve engine previously described, and many parts are interchangeable. The dry sump lubrication system is of exactly the same type as that used on the side-valve engine, except that some of the oil lubricates the valve guides. Cast-iron flywheels, ball and roller bearing mainshafts, and a double roller bearing big-end are incorporated. The timing gear is also unchanged, it consisting of the engine pinion and a single camwheel. The tappets, however, which rest on the toggles, operate in detachable guides. Above the crankcase the engine displays all that is best and recognized as sound practice in modern high efficiency overhead-valve engine design.

Fig. 10. Close-up View of the 1936-7 Ariel Overhead-valve Engine

Inset is shown one of the snap-on valve spring covers and the O.H. rocker adjustment.

THE RANGE OF ARIEL MOTOR-CYCLES

The three-ring aluminium alloy piston which has a fully-floating gudgeon pin provides a compression ratio of 6 to 1, and works in a closely finned cylinder notable for its unusually thick flange. Bolted to the ground upper face of the cylinder without the interposing of a gasket is a two-port head with vertical finning. As on the side-valve engines, the two exhaust pipe locking nuts are also finned, and the inlet port is downwardly inclined. A hemispherical combustion chamber is used, and the sparking plug is situated slightly to the near side. The two nickel-chrome steel valves which are of the hollow-headed tulip pattern have duplex springs with split collet anchorages for the collars, and reciprocate in detachable cast-iron guides. Both inlet and exhaust valve guides are automatically lubricated by two pipes from the rocker-box. The valves are actuated by means of one-piece alloy steel overhead rockers, with grub-screw and lock-nut adjustment for the valve clearances (Fig. 10). The grub-screws are not in direct contact with the valve stems, but with hardened steel caps slipped over the ends of the valve stems. Plain bearings are used for

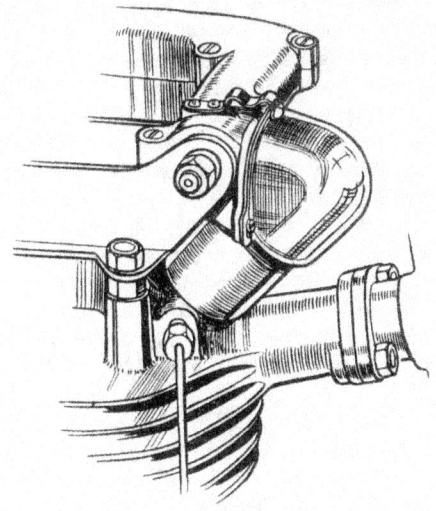

(From "The Motor Cycle")

FIG. 11. SHOWING VALVE SPRING ENCLOSURE (1935-7)

1935-7 models have both valve guides lubricated by pipes from the rocker-box.

the rockers, and each rocker has a small return spring, the method of fitting which can be observed in Fig. 10 (inset). The rockers are completely enclosed in a two-piece, die-cast aluminium rocker-box secured to the cylinder-head by two side plates. The rocker spindles themselves are utilized to attach the rocker-box to the plates, and these spindles are drilled and fitted with grease-gun nipples on the outside of the large side plate to enable the rocker bearings to be periodically greased. A small quantity of oil finds its way up the push rod covers, but this is quite inadequate for proper lubrication. An original and patented feature of the Ariel rocker-box is that the enclosure extends to the valve springs as well as the rockers. How this is accomplished may be gathered from Figs. 10 and 11. Quickly detachable visors held by spring clips entirely enclose the ends of the rockers and the upper part of the springs, while tubular thimbles surround and are held in place by the lower part of the springs. This arrangement, besides giving a particularly neat appearance, keeps the valves and their springs absolutely clean, and enables them to receive a small amount of lubrication in the form of oil mist *via* the push-rod covers and rocker-box.

The exhaust-valve lifter cable is led direct to a lever on the off side of the rocker-box, and there is an adjustment for the lever as well as one at the cable stop. The push-rods actuating the rockers are of steel, with their detachable steel lower ball ends resting in the cupped tappet heads, and their cupped upper ends fitting over the ball ends of the inner rocker-arms. Both push-rods are enclosed in plated oil-tight tubular covers having oil-sealing gland nuts at their bases and fibre washers at the top, where they are in contact with the rocker-box. Owing to the fact that the cylinder head retaining bolts are situated below the rocker-box, it is necessary to remove the rocker-box before the cylinder-head can be dealt with. This is necessary, however, on the majority of overhead-valve singles on account of the lack of space. Dismantling of the Ariel overhead-valve engine for decarbonizing is extraordinarily easy, and can be undertaken by the veriest novice with absolute confidence.

Carburettor (VF3, VF4, VG). This is a flanged-fixed semi-automatic, two-lever, down-draught Amal type 76/024, similar in design and working to the carburettor fitted on the side-valve models, but it has a different setting. A size 170 main jet is used in conjunction with a 6/4 valve and ·1065 needle in position 3. This combination will be found to provide economical running (80 m.p.g. is obtainable at cruising speeds), fierce acceleration, smooth tick-over, and a really good maximum speed.

Exhaust System (All Standard Overhead-valve Models). The two chromium-plated exhaust pipes terminate in tubular Carbjector silencers having spiral-shaped baffles. A high degree of silence is obtained and back-pressure is very small, particularly as with the downswept arrangement no sharp bends in the pipes are used.

Gearbox and Clutch (VF3, VF4). Pivot-mounted three- and four-speed Burman gearboxes with four plate shock-absorber clutches are provided, and they are similar to those fitted to models VA3, VA4, respectively, and have exactly the same gear ratios (page 16). Model VF4 is, of course, exactly similar to model VF3, except for the provision of a four-speed gearbox and cork insert clutch.

THE RANGE OF ARIEL MOTOR-CYCLES

1935 MODEL VG (500 c.c. O.H.V.)

The specification of this four-speed *de luxe* overhead-valve model is exactly the same as that of the standard overhead-valve four-speed model VF4, with the exception that *de luxe* equipment similar to that on the *de luxe* side-valve model VB (page 19) is provided. This includes a $3\frac{1}{4}$ gal. chromium-plated fuel

FIG. 12. THE 1938-9 500 c.c. DE LUXE OVERHEAD-VALVE MODEL VG

tank, an aluminium oil-bath chain-case, and valanced mudguards. The handsome and compact appearance of model VG is well known.

1935 MODELS NF3, NF4 (350 c.c. O.H.V.)

These two fast standard overhead-valve "three-fifties" are in design and construction almost indistinguishable from the standard overhead-valve "five-hundreds," models VF3, VF4. The only appreciable differences in specification are as follows—

The Standard 350 c.c. Overhead-valve Engine. This high efficiency two-port little power unit is built upon exactly similar lines to the larger standard engines, but a smaller cylinder is fitted, and the aluminium alloy piston which has a 6 to 1 compression ratio has a stroke of 85 mm. The bore is 72 mm., and the cubic capacity 348 c.c. As on the other overhead-valve engines, dry sump lubrication is used, and there is an oil feed to the inlet valve guide. A downswept exhaust system with tubular silencers is also used as on the other standard engines.

Carburettor (NF3, NF4). A down-draught, two-lever, semi-automatic, flanged-fixed type 75/014 Amal instrument of similar design to that provided on all the other engines is responsible for carburation, and it has the following setting: main jet size, 110; 5/4 valve; ·1065 needle in position 3. With this setting 95–100 m.p.g. is feasible, and a thoroughly good performance obtainable.

Gearbox and Clutch (NF3, NF4). A three-speed, pivot-mounted Burman gearbox with hand control and four-plate shock-absorber clutch with fabric inserts is used on model NF3. This gearbox is exactly the same as that fitted to the three-speed standard side-valve model VA3 (page 16), and with a 20-tooth engine sprocket provides the following gear ratios—

First, 15·8 to 1; second, 8·9 to 1; third, 5·4 to 1.

In the case of model NF4, a four-speed, pivot-mounted, type "C.P." Burman gearbox with hand control and four-plate shock-absorber clutch with cork inserts is specified, and this is very similar to the box used on model VA4, except that with a 20-tooth engine sprocket the machine has the following gear ratios—

First, 15·3 to 1; second, 10·1 to 1; third, 7·3 to 1; fourth, 5·7 to 1.

1935 MODELS LF3, LF4 (250 c.c. O.H.V.)

As with the standard overhead-valve "three-fifties," so do the Ariel "two-fifty" models follow very closely the specification of the standard "five-hundreds," models VF3, VF4. The two £1 2s. 6d. tax "babies" differ from these models only as follows.

The Standard 250 c.c. Overhead-valve Engine. "Small but good" sums up this neat little small capacity but very efficient engine, built exactly like the larger engines, but provided with a considerably smaller and somewhat differently finned cylinder. The bore and stroke are 61 mm. and 85 mm. respectively, giving a capacity of 249 c.c. In spite of its small size the engine lacks nothing in robustness, and has ball bearings for both mainshafts, a double roller big-end, and an aluminium alloy piston with a compression ratio of 6 to 1. Lubrication is, of course, by dry sump, and the inlet valve guide is positively lubricated by the engine.

Carburettor (LF3, LF4). The carburettor flange-fixed to the inlet port is a down-draught, semi-automatic two-lever Amal, type 74/024, of normal design, and the correct setting is to fit a size 85 main jet in conjunction with a 4/3 valve and ·1065 needle in position 3. With the above setting it should be possible to obtain a very lively performance accompanied by a very

THE RANGE OF ARIEL MOTOR-CYCLES 25

economical fuel consumption. This should lie between 95 and 100 m.p.g.—that is at moderate speeds.

Gearbox and Clutch (LF3, LF4). Model LF3 is fitted with a three-speed, pivot-mounted Burman gearbox and four-plate shock-absorber clutch similar to those on model VA3, and with

Fig. 13. The 1938–9 350 c.c. De Luxe Overhead-valve Model NG

an 18-tooth engine sprocket the following gear ratios are provided—

First, 15·8 to 1; second, 8·9 to 1; third, 5·4 to 1.

Model LF4 has a four-speed, pivot-mounted Burman gearbox and four-plate clutch similar to those on model NF4, and with an 18-tooth sprocket the gear ratios are—

First, 17·0 to 1; second, 11·2 to 1; third, 8·2 to 1; fourth, 6·0 to 1.

Tyres. Dunlop 26 in. × 3 in. tyres are used instead of those measuring 26 in. × 3·25 in.

1935 MODEL VH (500 c.c. O.H.V.)

The specification of the large capacity "Red Hunter," while similar, generally speaking, to that of the large capacity standard overhead-valve model, has many important variations, all of which are designed to render the machine an ideal mount for the serious-minded competition rider, and the sportsman who requires real "pep" and a super performance all round, together with good road-holding qualities. The most important variations from the standard specification are detailed below.

The "Red Hunter" 500 c.c. Overhead-valve Engine. This sports engine, which develops a power output of no less than 27 h.p., has a bore and stroke of 86·4 mm. and 85 mm. respectively, giving a capacity of 497 c.c. Externally, as may be seen by comparing the machines, the engine appears almost identical to the standard engine except for a slight shortening of the pump

Fig. 14. The 1938-9 500 c.c. "Red Hunter" Overhead-valve Model VH

housing, and the provision of a very thick (1 in.) cylinder base to withstand the stresses set up by a high revving engine in racing tune, but internally there are substantial modifications. The crank-case is heavily ribbed and contains a pair of forged steel flywheels hardened and tempered so as to preserve the crank pin tapers. A ball bearing is used for the timing side mainshaft, but a ball and roller bearing for that on the driving side. As on the standard engine, a double roller bearing is used for the big-end of the connecting rod, which is made of a special alloy steel and polished like the flywheels to reduce skin friction.

Attached to the small-end by a fully-floating gudgeon pin and circlips is a standard compression (6 to 1) aluminium alloy piston which is fitted for normal road use, but another high compression piston is also supplied with each engine for racing purposes. Each engine is specially tuned and bench-tested with the high compression (7·5 to 1 compression ratio) piston fitted to deliver a power output equivalent to a road speed of 87 to 90 m.p.h. Inlet and exhaust ports are, of course, highly polished to allow the unburnt and exploded charge to enter and leave the combustion chamber as quickly as possible. To further ensure this, best quality "Aero" valve springs of the duplex type are fitted. The valves themselves are made of the finest steel for the purpose, and

THE RANGE OF ARIEL MOTOR-CYCLES

are actuated by alloy steel rockers controlled by two steel pushrods and steel tappets resting, with toggle levers interposed, on racing type cams of very precisely calculated contour. Lubrication is by the usual dry sump system, with positively lubricated valve guides and oil purifier incorporated in the flywheels. The exhaust system comprises two upswept plated pipes terminating in round spiral baffle silencers. Downswept pipes (Fig. 13) may be specified without extra charge, and these are undoubtedly slightly more efficient.

Carburettor. The carburettor flange fixed to the inlet port is a type 89/014, two-lever, semi-automatic, large bore, down-draught Amal, and the fuel is fed from the tank to the float chamber by a Petroflex pipe. This carburettor has a somewhat smaller air intake than the other models. The recommended setting is to use a size 200 main jet in conjunction with a 6/4 valve, and ·1065 needle in position 3. The above setting gives abundant speed and vicious acceleration, but for special competition work it may be desirable to experiment with different settings.

Ignition (Models VH, NH, LH). The current is generated, except on electrically equipped models where a Lucas M.S. "Magdyno" is specified, by a Lucas racing magneto, which prior to dispatch from the makers is subjected to a test corresponding to a road speed of 200 m.p.h. The insulation is also tested at 40,000 volts, at least three times the maximum operating voltage limited by the safety gap. The magneto, which is thoroughly water-proofed, has a standard timing range of 30 degrees, but for special racing purposes the range may be increased to as much as 40 degrees. The contact-breaker is of normal design, and with the contacts fully open the "break" should be ·012 in. Rubber protecting caps are provided for the fixing of the pick-up, which has 9 mm. instead of the more usual 7 mm. cable. The magneto or "Magdyno" is chain-driven off the inlet camshaft as on the other models.

The sparking plug advised, but not fitted as standard, is a Lodge R.14. This is a special 14 mm. long-reach plug designed to withstand very high combustion temperatures without deterioration of the electrodes. It is also designed to prevent pre-ignition on large throttle openings. It is somewhat more expensive than the H.1 plugs, but gives long and entirely satisfactory service (see page 122). The gap advised is ·020 in.

Gearbox and Clutch. The gearbox is a pivot-mounted, four-speed Burman of the same type and with the same gear ratios as that fitted to the standard side-valve model VA4 (page 17), but a foot gear control with "neutral" indicator (page 5) is used instead of hand control. As on the standard model, the clutch is a four-plate, shock-absorber type of Burman manufacture with cork inserts.

Transmission. The $\frac{1}{2}$ in. × ·305 in. primary chain is enclosed in an aluminium oil-bath chain-case.

Tank. This is a welded steel saddle tank, with built-in instrument panel and knee-grips, similar to that on the standard model, but it has a capacity of $3\frac{1}{4}$ gal., and is beautifully finished in chromium with red panels and gold lining.

Wheels and Tyres (VH, NH). The wheels, which have taper roller bearing hubs, have chromium-plated rims with red centres, and are shod with 26 in. × 3·25 in. studded rear and 26 in. × 3 in. ribbed front Dunlop tyres. This arrangement provides excellent road grip and stability.

Backrest (VH, NH, LH). To enable a rider to "get right down to it" when racing, a backrest is fastened to the rear mudguard just behind the saddle.

1935 MODEL NH (350 c.c. O.H.V.)

This overhead-valve "three-fifty" "Red Hunter" is, but for its smaller capacity engine, practically identical to the larger model VH, the only differences being as follows.

The 350 c.c. Overhead-valve " Red Hunter " Engine. With the exception that a slightly smaller cylinder and two-port head are fitted, and an aluminium alloy piston giving a compression ratio of 7 to 1 is used as standard, the engine is absolutely similar to the 500 c.c. engine. The bore and stroke are 72 mm. and 85 mm. respectively, giving a capacity of 347 c.c. The engine is specially tuned and bench-tested to deliver a road speed of 75 to 78 m.p.h.

Carburettor. This is a type 89/014 two-lever, large bore, semi-automatic, down-draught Amal, and is flanged-fixed to the inclined inlet port. The recommended and standard setting which enables 75 m.p.g. approximately to be obtained and also gives a high general performance is as follows: Main jet, 150; valve, 6/4; ·075 needle in position 3. Petroflex piping is used to avoid damaged joints when racing.

Gearbox and Clutch. The gearbox is a four-speed, type "C.P." Burman with foot control (p. 5), and has a pivotal mounting. It

THE RANGE OF ARIEL MOTOR-CYCLES

is similar in many respects to the "BAP" gearbox used on the larger capacity Ariels, and has a ball-bearing mainshaft, enclosed kick-starter mechanism, and a layshaft speedometer drive. Dog type clutches are scrapped in favour of the new internal gear system. With a 20-tooth engine sprocket the following gear ratios are provided—

First, 15·3 to 1; second, 10·1 to 1; third, 7·3 to 1; fourth, 5·7 to 1.

The clutch is a three-plate type with cork-inserted friction plates. It is of similar design to the "BAP" clutch, and incorporates shock-absorbers in the chain wheel. Hand control is used.

Tank (NH, LH). The tank is identical to that on the 500 c.c. "Red Hunter," except for the fact that it has a slightly smaller fuel capacity. The capacity is 2½ gal.

1935 MODEL LH (250 c.c.)

The last of the single-cylinder models and the smallest of the "Red Hunters" differs from model NH only as follows.

The 250 c.c. Overhead-valve "Red Hunter" Engine. Absolutely the same as the 350 c.c. engine, except that with a 7 to 1 high compression piston it is bench-tested and tuned to give a road speed of 67 to 70 m.p.h. The bore and stroke are 61 mm. and 85 mm. respectively, and the capacity 249 c.c.

Carburettor. A type 75/014 two-lever, semi-automatic, downdraught Amal, with flange fixing and Petroflex supply pipe. Seting: main jet, 110; valve, 5/3; ·075 needle in position 3. Fuel consumption, 95 to 100 m.p.g. at moderate speeds.

Gearbox and Clutch. The same as for model NH, except that with an 18-tooth engine sprocket the ratios are—

First, 17·0 to 1; second, 11·2 to 1; third, 8·2 to 1; fourth, 6·0 to 1.

Transmission. The primary chain has a steel chain-case.

Tyres. Dunlop tyres measuring 26 in. .× 3 in. are fitted to both wheels. The rear tyre has a studded tread and the front tyre a ribbed tread.

1935 MODEL F4 (600 c.c. O.H.C.)

Model F4, alias the "Square Four" or "Squariel," has, except for its unorthodox and in many ways unique four-cylinder, over-head-camshaft engine, a specification similar to that of the *de luxe* side-valve model VB. The differences in specification are as follows—

The 600 c.c. Overhead-camshaft Engine. This has a bore and stroke of 56 mm. and 61 mm. respectively, giving a capacity of 597 c.c. The principal feature of the engine is its exceptional compactness, the engine being little larger externally than a normal 500 c.c. engine. This compactness has been obtained by the adoption of entirely new principles, and the abandoning of design principles usually followed in multi-cylinder engine construction. A detailed partly sectional view of the 1935 power unit will be found on page 31, and a brief description of it here will be given.

The crankcase, which is a particularly massive casting of aluminium, is well ribbed for strength and rigidity, and is divided horizontally instead of vertically as is usually done. Screwed to the upper crankcase half are the rearwardly inclined magneto chain-case and the vertical chain-case for the overhead camshaft drive. The lower half contains the oil pump and also a large sump and dipper lubrication pans from which the big-ends pick up the oil. The crankshaft assembly is, perhaps, the most interesting point about the engine. It comprises twin-parallel crankshafts mounted on ball bearings of large diameter, geared together as shown in Fig. 16 by two large hardened and ground coupling gears of specially developed tooth form. These coupling gears are completely enclosed in a separate oil-fed chamber within the crankcase. Four main flywheels are provided and, as may be seen in Fig. 16, overhung type cranks are used, except in the case of the crank utilized for mounting the connecting rod corresponding to the rear cylinder on the driving side. This crank is of the orthodox built-up flywheel type to enable the drive to be taken through to the engine sprocket, and the mainshaft on which the sprocket is fixed has an extra ball bearing. The use of overhung cranks renders the big-end bearings extremely accessible.

Light nickel-chrome steel connecting rods are used and these have single roller bearings. Attached to the small-end of each connecting rod by a fully-floating gudgeon pin with spring cir clips is a normal type Aero alloy piston giving a compression ratio of 5·8 to 1. Two piston rings are fitted, the lower one being spring loaded. These rings are designed for a side clearance in their grooves of approximately ·003 in., and the recommended gaps (when new) are ·004–·006 in. and ·010–·014 in. in the case of the upper and lower rings respectively.

The cylinders in which the pistons reciprocate are vertical, and are cast *en bloc* (Fig. 16A) in square formation, giving abundant cooling area. Seven large fins entirely surround the cylinder

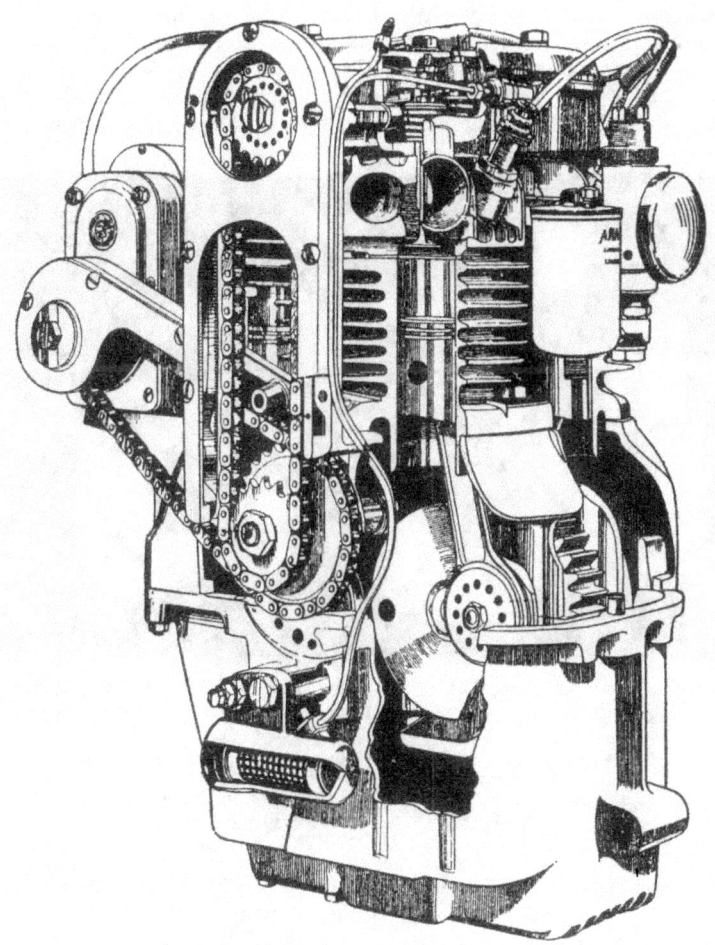

Fig. 15. The 1935–6 600 c.c. Four-cylinder Overhead-camshaft Engine

This engine differs from earlier engines of the same type (see Fig. 54) in that the lubricating oil is carried in the sump, and, as may be seen, a quickly detachable Tecalemit oil filter is fitted under the camshaft chain-case. A single plunger pump is also used instead of a twin gear type pump. Note the external feed to the cambox and the oil restrictor at the end of the pipe. The second of the two pipes shown is for connection to the pressure gauge. The 1937 engine has push-rods.

block, which is bolted direct on to the machined face of the crankcase. Secured by eight bolts to the cylinder block is the detachable head in which are cast integral the exhaust passages, and an ingenious radial induction manifold to which a special carburettor is fixed. The cylinder head also is provided with adequate finning arranged vertically. Eight vertical valves, two

FIGS. 16, 16A. SHOWING (Left) THE TWIN-GEARED CRANKSHAFTS AND (Right) PLAN VIEW OF THE ENGINE WITH CYLINDER HEAD AND ROCKER GEAR REMOVED

Diametrically opposite pistons move in unison, giving superior balance than that of the four-cylinder in line car engine. The square formation of the cylinder—the secret of the power unit's compactness—is well shown in Fig. 16A.

for each cylinder, are responsible for admitting the explosive mixture and passing the products of combustion into the exhaust system. They are actuated by rockers from an overhead camshaft, which is chain-driven from the half-time shaft (Fig. 15). The chain itself is automatically tensioned by a spring steel tensioning device of the type used on other overhead-camshaft engines, such as the A.J.S. "Trophy" engines. The camshaft, which runs in ball bearings, together with the valve rockers (which have grub-screw and lock-nut valve clearance adjustment) and valve springs, are enclosed and automatically lubricated in a large rectangular aluminium cambox spigoted to the chain-case, and provided with a quickly detachable lid giving immediate access to the whole of the overhead-valve gear. The magneto distributor is placed on the near side of the cambox, and the

THE RANGE OF ARIEL MOTOR-CYCLES

distributor arm is fixed to the camshaft. The magneto situated behind the cylinder block on a platform cast integral with the crank-case is, like the camshaft, driven off the half-time shaft by a roller chain with automatic self-tensioning device. The sparking plugs are all situated in inclined accessible positions in the cylinder head, two being at the front and two at the rear.

With regard to the timing gear, the arrangement is very simple and, provided the camshaft and half-time shaft sprockets are kept in mesh with the chain, the valve timing cannot be disturbed. A vernier camshaft timing adjustment is incorporated to enable the rider to make small alterations in the timing should he so desire. Both sprockets, which are of the same size, are keyed to their shafts, and the 2 to 1 reduction is obtained by a small hardened and ground gear on the front crankshaft meshing, with a similar gear of twice the diameter on the half-time shaft which has a plain bearing on the side of the inner gear-case, and a ball bearing in the crankcase wall.

Lubrication. The lubrication system employs a large single-plunger pump driven by an eccentric from the half-time shaft and bolted to the inside of the crank-case, and is removable. Oil is pumped from the reservoir, which is a separate compartment at the rear of the crankcase, and is first forced, after passing through a large external oil filter and purifier, into the chamber enclosing the main crankshaft gears. From thence the oil overflows into troughs, and is picked up by dippers on the big-ends. The remainder of the internal moving parts of the engine are lubricated by oil mist, whilst a separate lead from the supply pump is taken to the overhead camshaft and cambox, when it returns to the sump *via* the camshaft chain-case. The main oil supply also drains back to the reservoir which, incidentally, has a capacity of approximately ½ gal., and has an accessible filter and dipstick level indicator. As on the other Ariel models, some of the oil is led to a pressure gauge mounted on the instrument panel, and an oil pressure regulator is also included.

Carburettor. The carburettor fitted is a type 74/007 semi-automatic, two-lever, large bore Amal specially designed for the "Square Four," and is attached to the inlet manifold between the exhaust ports in such a position that a considerable degree of pre-heating is secured. The best general performance is obtained by using the maker's setting, which is as follows: Main jet, 90; valve, 4/4; ·016 needle in position 3. Throttle control is by twist-grip.

Ignition. The alternatives are a Lucas magneto or an "M.S."

"Magdyno" (extra). A magneto cut-out switch is incorporated on the instrument panel. The standard plug is a Lodge H.1.

Gearbox and Clutch. A four-speed, pivot-mounted Burman gearbox with four-plate, shock-absorber clutch is fitted. It is similar to that on models VA4, VB, but provides with 21- and

FIG. 17. THE 1935-6 600 C.C. OVERHEAD-CAMSHAFT MODEL 4F
(THE "SQUARE FOUR")
On the 1937 version foot-gear control is standard.

19-tooth engine sprockets the following solo and sidecar gear ratios—

    Solo . . . first, 13·8 to 1; second, 8·8 to 1; third, 6·6 to 1; fourth, 5·2 to 1.
    Sidecar . . first, 15·3 to 1; second, 9·7 to 1; third, 7·2 to 1; fourth, 5·7 to 1.

Exhaust System. The two chromium-plated pipes have interconnected round spiral baffle silencers. Fish-tail silencers (Fig. 12) may be specified without extra charge.

Wheels. The wheels which have 26 in. × 3·25 in. tyres have chromium rims and black centres.

SIDECARS

Many riders habitually drive with a passenger, and while a pillion seat offers many attractions, especially to young ladies of a sporting nature, a sidecar undeniably gives a far greater degree of comfort. Added to this, statistics of insurance companies tend to show that passenger-carrying in a sidecar is distinctly safer than carrying a pillion passenger. As a matter of fact, a 20 per cent reduction is now allowed on sidecar outfit premiums. Further, a sidecar outfit is ideal for touring, as accommodation is

THE RANGE OF ARIEL MOTOR-CYCLES 35

available for light luggage and the carrying of miscellaneous articles for picnics, etc. Several excellent Ariel sidecars are available for both touring and sporting purposes. Prices are about £20 upwards.

THE 1936-7 RANGE

With the exception of the introduction of a striking new four-cylinder model of large capacity, no radical alterations have been

FIG. 18. SMART AND COMFORTABLE—A TYPICAL ARIEL SIDECAR

made in Ariel design and most of the 1935 models have been continued for 1936 and 1937 with detail improvements only. Altogether nine machines are available, all of which have Lucas "Magdyno" lighting, electric horn, and four-speed Burman gearboxes fitted as standard.

The Side-valve De Luxe Model. The 1935 Models VA3, VA4 have been dropped, but the de luxe Model VB is retained with some excellent improvements. This machine, which is a real "good looker" with a fine performance, has a four-speed Burman gearbox and full de luxe equipment. It is sold at £58 10s. The capacity of the 1935 S.V. engine has been increased from 550 c.c. to 598 c.c. by lengthening the stroke from 95 mm. to 102 mm. This decidedly improves performance and provides a larger air space between the cylinder head and valve chest. Improvements to the machine comprise foot control for the four-speed gearbox, a more powerful clutch, a new system of clutch enclosure (Fig. 4) which prevents oil getting on the plates and facilitates dismantling, a rear brake pedal having greater leverage with its shaft mounted on a frame lug instead of on the chain case, sturdier cup and cone steering head bearings, more spacious tool-box, etc.

The Overhead-valve De Luxe Models. These consist of three two-port machines, namely Models VG, NG, LG, which are priced at £61 10s., £54 10s., £50 10s. respectively. Model VG is similar to the 1935 model and the 500 c.c. engine now has both valves automatically lubricated and the crankcase has been

FIG. 19. 1937–9 1,000 C.C. DE LUXE "SQUARIEL" (MODEL 4G) CAPABLE OF 10 TO 100 M.P.H. IN TOP

This machine is a development of the earlier 600 c.c. "Squariel" and will do about 45 m.p.g. at a cruising speed of 40 m.p.h.

stiffened. The gearbox, clutch, rear brake, steering head improvements mentioned above are also incorporated. Model NG with de luxe equipment replaces the 1935 Models NF3 and NF4 and is similar to Model VG except that the engine is of 350 c.c. capacity and a new spiral baffle silencer of circular section with integral fish-tail is provided. Model LG with its 250 c.c. engine replaces the 1935 Models LF3 and LF4 and has the same general specification as Models VG, NG.

The Overhead-valve "Red Hunters." The three 1935 "Red Hunters," Models VH, NH, LH (representing the 500 c.c., 350 c.c., 250 c.c. classes) are offered again for 1936–7 with little alteration in specification or prices which are (with lighting and electric horn) £66 10s., £58 10s., £55 10s. respectively. These high performance and outstandingly handsome sports models can be had with competition equipment (undershield, nail catchers, competition tyres, etc.) for a small sum, and electric lighting equipment

THE RANGE OF ARIEL MOTOR-CYCLES 37

is fitted. Lucas " Magdynos " are fitted as standard. The improvements made to the de luxe O.H.V.s have been incorporated and in addition the forged steel flywheels are now machined all over their outer faces so as to reduce "oil drag" to the minimum. The crank assembly has also been stiffened. If preferred, a single-port cylinder head may be specified instead of a two-port head.

The New 1,000 c.c. " Squariel." This most attractive addition to the Ariel range announced on the eve of the 1935 Olympia Show is sure to prove a centre of great interest. It has been designed by Mr. E. Turner to give a speed range in top gear of 10 to 100 m.p.h., lightning acceleration and exceptional reliability with very little attention. The newcomer is conventional, yet unconventional. Space available forbids of a detailed description, but it may be mentioned that the machine (known as Model 4G) is similar to Model 4F except in regard to the engine. This has a similar cylinder arrangement and geared crankshafts are used, but instead of the valves being operated by an overhead camshaft, enclosed push-rods are employed with the actuating camshaft situated between the crankshafts and driven by chain off the rear one. The offside end of the camshaft operates a conventional oil pump and also drives the "Magdyno" by a Weller-tensioned chain. Interesting features of a unique engine are the light alloy connecting-rods, the long skirt non-slap pistons, the split big-ends, white metal bearings, duralumin push-rods, etc. The price is £90.

The 600 c.c. " Squariel." This machine has been entirely redesigned and is now for practical purposes a smaller edition of the 1,000 c.c. model. Model 4F sells at £84.

THE 1938 RANGE

The 1938 Ariel range which is tabulated on page 1 comprises eight striking machines, all of last year's models being retained with one exception—the 600 c.c. "Squariel" (Model 4F). No alterations have been made to the 1,000 c.c. "Squariel" (Model 4G), but a number of detail improvements have been made to the single-cylinder machines.

The Side-valve De Luxe Model. Model VB has undergone little alteration, but a slight improvement to the cam gear gives still more power. Externally the gearbox has been cleaned up and domed nuts secure the cover. To prevent the access of dirt, a moulded rubber sheath now encloses the clutch operation. Another worth-while improvement is the provision of a floating bracket for the front brake cam spindle. Advantages are that load is taken off the brake cable, some servo action is obtained and the shoes become self-centring. The appearance of Model VB is enhanced by a chromium plated instead of enamelled instrument panel, a smarter steering damper and a better shaped tank top panel. The price is £62 10s.*

The Overhead-valve De Luxe Models. Models VG, NG, LG, which are priced at £65 10s., £58 10s., £54 10s. incorporate all the above improvements and in addition the cylinder head and overhead-valve gear have been completely redesigned. Details of the new two-port cylinder head and valve gear are clearly shown in Fig. 20. Two separate rocker-boxes instead of a one-piece box as hitherto are utilized. They are secured to the head by four bolts with gaskets interposed. No distortion can occur. The rocker spindles are drilled and positively lubricated; excess oil drains to the bottom of the wells housing the valve springs and then passes down the push-rod covers to the cams. Screwed caps on the rocker-box sides give access to the rocker arm adjusters, and thick washers prevent any tendency for oil leakage at the push-rod covers.

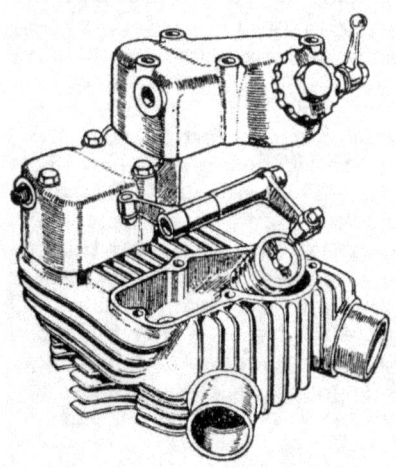

(*From "The Motor Cycle"*)
FIG. 20. THE REDESIGNED CYLINDER HEAD AND OVERHEAD-VALVE GEAR ON THE 1938-9 SINGLES

The Overhead-valve "Red Hunters." The "Red Hunter" range as during 1937 consists of Models VH, NH, LH, and their prices are £70 10s., £62 10s., £59 10s. respectively. The engines are specially bench tested and polished and high compression pistons are obtainable. The whole of the above-mentioned improvements have been incorporated.

The 1,000 c.c. Square Four. The price of the magnificent Square Four (Model 4G) which is identical to the 1937 version is £95.

THE 1939 RANGE

As has been stated on page 1, eleven models are available. A brief outline of the 1939 range will be found on page 168.

* All prices include electric lighting and horn. Automatic voltage control is standard.

CHAPTER II

THE RUNNING COSTS OF AN ARIEL MOTOR-CYCLE

Overheads and Mileage Costs. The actual expenses must be considered under two separate headings—standing costs, or overheads, and actual running costs. The overheads are generally the heavier, unless the motor-cycle is used extensively, and they will therefore be taken first.

Overheads include interest on capital, depreciation, the annual tax, the driving licence, insurance, and garage rent—in fact, all items which vary but little, if at all, whether the machine is driven 1,000 or 20,000 miles during the year. Apart from depreciation, they can be assessed accurately at the beginning of the year. Depreciation, however, cannot be gauged exactly, since it depends partly on the mileage covered and the attention given to the machine, and partly on the owner's ability to find a prospective purchaser.

Depreciation. Some figure must, however, be taken, and for purposes of arriving at the overhead costs depreciation is considered to be at the rate of $33\frac{1}{3}$ per cent per annum, this to include a sum for loss of interest on capital. This means that a 1937 model " VG " Ariel, equipped with a dynamo lighting set, speedometer and electric horn—a total cost of £63 17s. 6d.—is reckoned to be worth £42 11s. 8d. only after twelve months' use, depreciation being £21 5s. 10d. Provided that the machine is carefully kept and is not driven an excessive distance, the allowance may be said to be on the generous side.

What Constitutes Running Costs. The actual running expenses are easy to calculate. They include, in the main, the cost of petrol, oil, grease, tyres, and repairs. An allowance must be made for " bad luck " in respect of the two latter items. A tyre, for instance, may be badly cut early in its life and rendered useless, whilst one rider may be more unfortunate than another as regards the repairs and overhauls which become necessary. This depends largely, apart from luck, on driving ability, and a general average only can be taken. Washing and polishing are not included under running costs, since the majority of motor-cyclists clean their machines themselves. The same applies to decarbonizing.

In the case of the solo machine depreciation has been fixed at

£21 5s. 10d. A comprehensive insurance policy costs something like £6, tax is £3, and driving licence 5s. Garage can be neglected, since a solo machine can be stored in any passage or entry; if, however, the rider has no facilities for this, he will have to add the price charged by the local garage. The total overheads, then, are as follows—

	£	s.	d.
Depreciation	21	5	10
Insurance	6	0	0
Tax	3	0	0
Licence		5	0
	£30	10	10 per annum.

A model "VG" machine fitted with a roomy sidecar, electric lighting set, and an electric horn costs £85 12s. 6d. Depreciation will therefore be £28 10s. 10d. Insurance will also cost approximately 2s. more, since there is a small additional charge if the value of the machine exceeds £50. The sidecar machine will in most cases have to be garaged elsewhere than on the owner's premises, the cost of this being approximately 2s. 6d. per week.

The overhead charges for the sidecar machine are therefore—

	£	s.	d.
Depreciation	28	10	10
Insurance	6	2	0
Tax	4	0	0
Licence		5	0
Garage	6	10	0
	£45	7	10 per annum.

We come now to running costs. These are entirely dependent upon the mileage covered and upon luck. The latter element makes it difficult to forecast the running costs accurately, since new tyres may be badly cut by broken glass, etc., whilst repairs on one machine may be heavier than those on another. The estimates here quoted assume, therefore, average good luck, since allowance for all contingencies would make it impossible to arrive at any standard of running costs whatever.

Petrol and Oil Consumption. Petrol consumption for ordinary mileages is one of the smaller of motor-cycling costs, now that petrol is sold at so low a figure. The price of petrol is constantly fluctuating, but it is assumed to average out at 1s. 4d. a gallon. With careful driving, the solo machine should do 80 miles to the gallon and the sidecar 60 miles. Oil consumption will probably work out at about 4,000 miles per gallon either solo or sidecar, oil being considered to average a cost of 7s. per gallon.

RUNNING COSTS OF AN ARIEL MOTOR-CYCLE 41

The next important item of running costs is the tyre bill. Provided that the tyres are sufficiently inflated, it is fair to estimate the mileages obtainable with a sidecar to be as follows: rear tyre, 5,000 miles ; front tyre 8,000 miles ; sidecar tyre, indefinite, say 20,000 miles. On a solo machine it is probable that the rear tyre will do 6,000 miles and the front tyre 10,000.

In calculating running costs it is essential to estimate some mileage per annum ; the examples given hereafter, therefore, are based on (1) 5,000 miles per annum, and (2) 10,000 miles per annum.

Petrol consumption for the solo machine has been estimated

Fig. 21. Ariel Machines Far from the Beaten Track

at 80 miles per gallon ; so for 5,000 miles, reckoning petrol at 1s. 4d. per gallon, the cost will be approximately £4 3s. 4d. Similarly, the cost for the sidecar machine will be £5 11s. 1d., the 10,000 mile figures being £8 6s. 8d. and £11 2s. 2d. respectively. Oil will cost 8s. 9d. for either type of machine, this being doubled for the 10,000 miles. Five shillings' worth of grease will last an indefinite time ; it is therefore included as a first charge and can be ignored later.

These items complete the running costs, with the exception of repairs and replacements. Tyres, for 5,000, do not enter into the matter, and since the machine is new no replacements or repairs of a major nature should be necessary. It is advisable, however, to set aside a lump sum for minor repairs, and for these £3 should be ample for 5,000 miles ; repairs might be somewhat higher for the 10,000 miles (but not double), and for this purpose £4 10s. is included in the schedule of costs. It is assumed that the rider will decarbonize the engine himself; if he does not intend to do so, the amount charged by the local garage must be ascertained and added.

Running costs for 5,000 miles, therefore, for the solo machine may be estimated to be—

	£	s.	d.
Petrol	4	3	4
Oil		8	9
Grease		5	0
Repairs	3	0	0
	£7	17	1

For the sidecar machines the costs will be—

	£	s.	d.
Petrol	5	11	1
Oil		8	9
Grease		5	0
Repairs	3	0	0
	£9	4	10

The Question of Tyres. On the 10,000 mile basis, tyres also have to be taken into consideration. It has been assumed, in the case of the solo machine, that the lives of the rear and front tyres are 6,000 and 10,000 miles respectively. Therefore a new back tyre will have to be bought during the year, and will be two-thirds worn out at the end of the twelve months' running. The tube should not be worn out but, for safety, its price is included in the total of £1 15s., which at the time of writing is the cost of a 26 in. by 3·25 in. Dunlop wired-on cover and tube.

The calculations for the sidecar tyres are carried out in the same way. There must be a new rear tyre—and this will want replacing at the end of the year; there must also be a new front tyre which will, however, be only a quarter worn.

The running costs for the 10,000 mileage are therefore as follows—

Solo Machine	£	s.	d.	Sidecar Machine	£	s.	d.
Petrol	8	6	8	Petrol	11	2	2
Oil		17	6	Oil		17	6
Grease		5	0	Grease		5	0
Repairs	4	10	0	Repairs	4	10	0
Proportion of tyre cost	1	3	4	Proportion of tyre cost	2	3	9
	£15	2	6		£18	18	5

RUNNING COSTS OF AN ARIEL MOTOR-CYCLE

To discover the total cost of owning an Ariel motor-cycle it is only necessary to add the overheads to the running costs. The figures work out as follows—

Solo Machine

	5,000 Miles £ s. d.	10,000 Miles £ s. d.
Overhead charges	30 10 10	30 10 10
Running costs	7 17 1	15 2 6
Total	£38 7 11	£45 13 4

Sidecar Machine

	5,000 Miles £ s. d.	10,000 Miles £ s. d.
Overhead charges	45 7 10	45 7 10
Running costs	9 4 10	18 18 5
Total	£54 12 8	£64 6 3

Many riders consider that when they have bought a machine the money spent is gone, and they do not think it worth while to take depreciation into account. Without reckoning depreciation, therefore, the total cost comes out as follows—

	5,000 Miles £ s. d	10,000 Miles £ s. d.
Solo	17 2 1	24 7 6
Sidecar	26 1 10	35 15 5

The cost per week, which is what interests most riders, is thus, to nearest pennies, 6s. 6d. and 9s. 4d. respectively for the solo machine, and 10s. and 13s. 9d. respectively for the sidecar.

From the figures given above the intending purchaser of an Ariel machine will be able to see at a glance how much motor-cycling is likely to cost him. Should he decide to buy the machine on the easy payment system, he should write to the Ariel Company for particulars of their extended payments system, and by a simple calculation he can gather the probable amount of his weekly or monthly expenditure. It must be borne in mind that the greater the mileage the less will be the total cost per mile.

CHAPTER III

THE LAW, LICENCES, INSURANCE

BEFORE the owner can take a new motor-cycle on the road there are several formalities which must be completed in accordance with existing laws. The first is that the rider himself must have a driving licence, and the second is that he must obtain a registration licence permitting the use of the *machine* on the road. The driving licence can be obtained either by personal application or by post from the Town Council of the County Borough in which the owner resides, or from the County Council should he live outside a County Borough. The charge is 5s. per annum, from the date on which the licence is taken out.

A driving licence is the same price whether it entitles the owner to drive a motor-cycle alone or a motor-cycle and a car. The earliest age one can obtain a licence is sixteen, and this applies only to motor-cycles, seventeen years being the youngest at which one can obtain a licence to drive a car also. When applying for a licence, therefore, the prospective motor-cyclist should, if he be seventeen years of age or over, apply for one to cover the driving of both a car and a motor-cycle, since this costs no more and may be useful in the future. A declaration of physical fitness must be made at the time of application. New applicants (see page 52) must pass a driving test. Should a licence be lost or destroyed a new one will be supplied on payment of 1s.

Renewing a Driving Licence. Although a driving licence is so easy to obtain and costs so little it is one of the motor-cyclist's most valuable possessions for, should he fall foul of the police, it may be suspended for a period. The licence is non-transferable, and the authorities do not give information when its renewal becomes due. The rider must, therefore, make sure that he does not let the twelve months overrun, since he may at any time be pulled up, and, if the licence has expired, will become liable to certain penalties.

After a conviction of a motoring offence the licence may be endorsed on the back, the endorsement carrying particulars of the offence and the penalty inflicted. A police officer, when examining a rider's licence, is not allowed to take note of the endorsements on the back. This is so that he shall not be influenced by any past offences. In a police court itself, too, no reference must be made to endorsements until the magistrates have decided

THE LAW, LICENCES, INSURANCE

whether the defendant is guilty or otherwise. If they decide the former they may then request the defendant to produce his licence, so that they may consider his past history before inflicting the fine or other penalties.

Registration. Up to 1st January, 1935, motor-cycles were taxed rather unkindly, a tax at the rate of 30s. per annum being imposed on all machines having engines of not over 250 c.c. capacity. All machines of over 250 c.c. capacity were subject to taxation at the rate of £3 per annum, and where a sidecar was attached an additional £1 per annum was required. At last long-clamoured-for concessions have been granted in regard to registration licence fees and these concessions should help to popularize motor-cycling. Under the new scale of taxes, machines of under 150 c.c. capacity are taxed at 12s. per annum, machines of 150 c.c. up to 250 c.c. at £1 2s. 6d., and machines of over 250 c.c. at £2 5s. per annum. In the case of machines registered prior to 1st January, 1933, and weighing not more than 224 lb., the tax is £1 2s. 6d. per annum. Where a side-car is fitted the additional tax is 15s. per annum instead of the old tax of £1.

In connection with the tax paid for a motor-cycle, a registration licence is issued, a circular disc that the law requires to be mounted on the near-side of the machine in certain definite places, such as the front number plate or forks. Unless this disc, which is in effect a receipt for the tax, be fixed on the machine, it is unlawful to use it. A licence application form (R.F. 1A) may be obtained from any head post office, from which renewals for the same type and period may be obtained. It should be very carefully filled in and posted to the licences department of the county council in whose area the machine is normally kept, together with the cost of the licence and a certificate of insurance, without which a licence cannot be obtained. They will send along the necessary licence and also a registration book, in which all particulars of the machine, such as engine number,* frame number, horse-power, etc., and its history are entered. Application for annual licence renewal should be made between the 1st and 15th of January each year. An annual licence expires, of course, on 31st December; but in addition to the annual licence there are the quarterly licences expiring on 24th March, 30th June, 30th September, and 31st December. The cost of a quarterly licence is 12s. 5d. for machines over 250 c.c. and 6s. 3d. for machines up to 250 c.c. Part-year licences, expiring 31st December, are available for any period from four to twelve months. 5 per cent

---

* On every 1939 Ariel machine the engine number is stamped on the driving side of the crankcase just below the cylinder flange, while the frame number is on the right side of the saddle lug.

extra is charged. A rebate can be obtained for the unexpired portion of a licence if surrendered, conditional upon the unexpired portion being not less than one month.

The Registration Book. The registration book must be kept in a safe place by the owner, except in the following four cases, when it must immediately be returned to the authorities for amendment—
- (a) On change of address.
- (b) On change of ownership or on sale.
- (c) When substantial alterations are made (s/c attachment).
- (d) On the machine being destroyed, broken up, or exported.

The Motor-cyclist and the Police. A few words here may well be said concerning the rider's dealings with the police. The average British policeman is an excellent fellow, polite, and courteous. He is, however, only human, and many riders cause themselves a lot of unnecessary trouble by being rude to him when he stops them. There are very few policemen who want to cause trouble on their own account, but if they are abused it is only natural that they should become annoyed and should exercise their powers to the fullest extent—an extent which may be unpleasant for the rider.

Never try to bribe a policeman. This is a most serious offence, and will probably be met by a very much larger fine than would the original alleged offence for which the rider was stopped.

NEW MOTOR LAWS

The following data has been extracted from the Road Traffic Act, 1930, and it is hoped that this information will be of value to readers of this book.

Accidents (What to do). Stop immediately. Give name and address and registration number of vehicle, if requested. Failing this, the accident must be reported within 24 hours at a police station or to a police constable.

The Minister of Transport may direct an inquiry to be made into the cause of any accident involving a motor vehicle. A person authorized by the Minister may inspect the vehicle, and at a reasonable time enter premises where the vehicle is situated. Obstruction of that person is an offence. The report of an inquiry shall not be used in legal proceedings instituted in consequence of the accident.

THE LAW, LICENCES, INSURANCE 47

Address. If a motorist is alleged to have driven recklessly, dangerously, or carelessly, he must give his name and address to any person having reasonable ground for requiring the information. If he refuses, or gives a false name and address, he is guilty of an offence.

Careless Driving. A person shall not drive without due care and attention or without reasonable consideration for other road users. A first or second conviction for this offence does not entail disqualification for holding or obtaining a licence.

Dangerous Driving. A person shall not drive recklessly, or at a speed or in a manner dangerous to the public.

Penalties—

Not exceeding £50, or up to four months' imprisonment for the first offence.

Not exceeding £100, or up to four months' imprisonment, or to both such fine and imprisonment for the second or subsequent offence.

Six months' imprisonment or a fine (amount unlimited), or to both such imprisonment and fine on conviction or indictment. All convictions to be endorsed on the driving licence, with power to disqualify for holding or obtaining a licence.

Drunkenness. Any person convicted of driving, or attempting to drive, or in charge of a motor vehicle on a road or other public place, when under the influence of drink or drugs to such an extent as to be incapable of having proper control of the vehicle, shall be liable—

(a) On summary conviction, to a fine not exceeding £50 or imprisonment up to four months. For a second or subsequent conviction, to a fine not exceeding £100 or up to four months' imprisonment, or to both such fine and imprisonment.

(b) On conviction on indictment, to imprisonment up to six months, or to a fine (unlimited) or to both imprisonment and fine.

A police constable may arrest, without warrant, any person committing this offence.

Unless, for special reasons, the Court thinks otherwise, disqualification for a period of twelve months shall follow a conviction. Particulars of conviction and disqualification shall be endorsed on the driving licence.

Eyesight Test. Are you able to read at a distance of 25 yd. in good daylight (with glasses, if worn) a motor-car number plate containing six letters and figures. Applicants who answer " No " to this question are debarred from obtaining a licence.

Horn. A motor vehicle must be fitted with a suitable instrument for giving audible warning of approach. When a vehicle is stationary on the highway, no person shall use or permit the

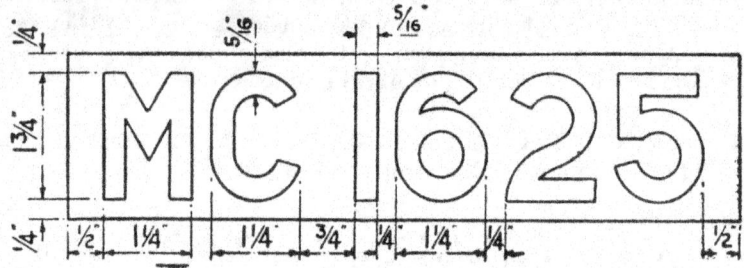

Fig. 22. Front Number Plate Dimensions

horn to be used, except when such use is necessary on the grounds of safety. The silence hours are between 11.30 p.m. and 7 a.m.

Lights. Motor-cycles with sidecars attached must show two white lights forward (indicating total width), and a red light showing to the rear.

Solo machines must carry one white light in front and a red light at the rear, together with proper illumination of the rear number plate (Fig. 23).

Number Plates. Both in the registration book and on the licence card will be found the index letters and number which have been allotted to the machine, and these must be affixed to the number plates, the lettering being of the dimensions shown in Figs. 22 and 23.

Insurance. A person may not use or permit any other person to use a motor vehicle on the road unless such use is covered by insurance against third party claims. This does not require the owner to cover a person in his employ against death or bodily injury arising out of and in the course of his employment—a liability which is covered by other statutes.

Where compensation is paid under the provision of compulsory insurance, and where to the knowledge of the insurer a third party has received hospital treatment, the insurer shall also pay to the hospital a sum not exceeding £25 for each person so treated.

THE LAW, LICENCES, INSURANCE   49

This obligation does not apply where a charge has already been made by the hospital.

In addition to the usual policy, or cover note, the insurance company shall hand to the owner a " certificate of insurance " in the prescribed form, and when applying for his motor-cycle licence, the applicant must—by production of the insurance cer-

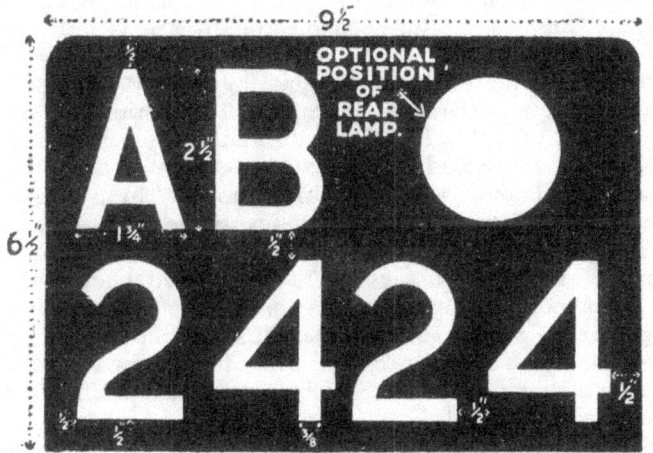

Fig. 23. Rear Number Plate Dimensions

tificate or otherwise—satisfy the Licensing Authority that the necessary cover against third party risks will be in force at the time the motor-cycle licence becomes operative.

The driver of a motor vehicle shall, when requested by a police constable, give his name and address, and produce the insurance certificate. If he cannot produce it immediately, he must produce it *in person* within five days at any police station he may specify.

Where an accident occurs involving personal injury to another person, if the driver is unable to produce his certificate at the time, he shall report the accident to a police station as soon as possible, *and in any case within* 24 *hours of the accident*, and shall there produce his certificate. If the certificate is not available for immediate production, the driver may produce it *in person* within five days at any police station he may specify.

Proceedings for offences may be brought (*a*) within six months of the commission of the alleged offence, or (*b*) within a period which does not exceed three months from the date on which the offence came to the knowledge of the prosecutor, or one year from the date of the commission of the alleged offence, whichever period is the longer.

Penalties—

Up to £50 or imprisonment up to three months, or both such fine and imprisonment. A person convicted under this section is automatically disqualified from holding or obtaining a driving licence for twelve months, but without prejudice to the power of the Court where there are special reasons to order otherwise.

The rider is well advised to insure with a company of good standing. Some small insurance companies may offer policies which show a slight reduction in cost, but as often as not this reduction is far more than outweighed by the difficulty of obtaining satisfactory settlement of claims. The details given below are quoted from the R.A.C. unlimited motor-cycle insurance policy, which is reserved for the exclusive benefit of members and associate members of the Royal Automobile Club. The benefits obtained in the R.A.C. unlimited policy are as follows—

1. CLAIMS BY THE PUBLIC. A full, complete, and unlimited indemnity (excluding passengers) to the insured against all claims made for personal injuries or damage to property or animals by, through, or in connection with the insured motor-cycle or any motor-cycle not belonging to him, provided his own is not in use. Law costs incurred with the Society's consent paid in addition to compensation awarded.

2. FIRE. Loss of or damage to motor-cycle, including sidecar whilst attached thereto, and accessories and spare parts in, on, or about the motor-cycle (whether cycle damaged at the same time or not) by fire, lightning, explosion, or self-ignition.

3. BURGLARY. Loss of or damage to motor-cycle, including sidecar whilst attached thereto, and accessories and spare parts in, on, or about the motor-cycle (if cycle stolen at the same time) by burglary, house-breaking, larceny, or theft, or any attempt thereat.

4. TRANSIT. Loss of or damage to motor-cycle, and sidecar whilst attached thereto, and accessories and spare parts on the cycle during transit by road, rail, or inland waterway in the United Kingdom, and during sea transit between any ports in the United Kingdom or by short sea routes between the United Kingdom, and continent of Europe. A special policy is needed to cover long overseas journeys.

5. ACCIDENTAL OR MALICIOUS DAMAGE to motor-cycle including sidecar whilst attached thereto and accessories and spare parts (whether machine damaged at the same time or not), and the reasonable cost of removing the cycle from the scene of the accident to the nearest competent repairers and their fair charge for re-delivery to the assured. Tyres are also covered if the machine is damaged at the same time.

If no claim is made or arises during any year of insurance, a

THE LAW, LICENCES, INSURANCE 51

bonus of 10 per cent of the premium is allowed, provided that the policy is renewed in full. There are also a number of discounts of which the rider may take advantage, just as there are several special charges for exceptional risks.

The discounts are offered if the insured bears various amounts of each claim. If, for instance, he bears the first 50s. there is a 15 per cent reduction, if the first £5, a 20 per cent reduction, if the first £10, a 33⅓ per cent reduction. These are very substantial, and if the rider feels that he can risk a certain amount of money, he may well take advantage of one or other of them.

You Must Insure for Pillion Riding. Amongst the additional regulations which have been introduced, the most important is that which applies to pillion riding on a solo machine. Insurance is now obligatory. It must be remembered that, even with the full premiums payable, the machine is only insured for one driver, and the following charges are made for other drivers: one named driver in addition to the insured, 33⅓ per cent extra; any additional driver, 50 per cent extra. A premium of 30s. is charged to cover personal accidents on a certain set basis.

There is a number of special features which are attached to the R.A.C. policy, these being clearly detailed on the proposal form. This policy, or that issued by any first-class company, is recommended to motor-cyclists, and from the details given below it will be seen that third party claims, at any rate, can be covered for a trivial sum.

Garaging. If circumstances permit, it is the best plan to erect a small shed, which would cost £4 or £5, and overhauling and adjustments can then be carried out comfortably and in seclusion. If no suitable site is available, there will be no option but to garage the machine at a public garage. Usually a satisfactory lock-up for a solo mount can be found for 2s. 6d., with an extra shilling a week for a sidecar, although many proprietors endeavour to induce motor-cyclists to pay more. Many excellent ready-made sheds which are built in sections and only require fitting together are now available, and the author has seen some really fine examples at very moderate prices.

FURTHER MOTORING LEGISLATION

In spite of widespread "Safety First" propaganda among all classes of road users during the past few years, road casualties appear to have increased rather than diminished, and the annual figures make really appalling reading. There are about 220,000 accidents involving 7,000 deaths. Think of it—twenty people killed every day! The author would ask every reader of this book to do his utmost to see that under no circumstances shall he help to add to this unnecessary mass slaughter and maiming. Accidents *could* be reduced to negligible quantities if every road user would (*a*) cultivate road sense, (*b*) use his imagination, (*c*) drive at a speed reasonable having regard to all the circumstances, (*d*) not be damned selfish. Only by reducing the number of accidents can motorists hope to avoid further legislation.

A 30 m.p.h. Speed Limit. While for private cars and motor-cycles there is now no general speed limit, a speed limit of 30 m.p.h. is enforced in "built-up" areas, officially defined as roads where the street lamps are not more than 200 yds. apart. In the case of unpopulated areas and other doubtful places a road or stretch of road may be classified as "built-up," or not "built-up," after consultation between the local authorities and the police. In any case, a suitable notice (Fig. 26) is erected to indicate that a road, concerning which road users might have reasonable doubt, is subject or not subject to a speed limit of 30 m.p.h.

Tests for Driving Licences. New applicants for driving licences (not having held a licence prior to 1st April, 1934) are required to pass a driving test, the fee for both the licence and test not to exceed 12s. 6d. Applicants are required to provide a vehicle for the purpose of the test. Provisional licences are issued to those learning to drive prior to a test. Learners must carry "L" plates.

Short-term Disqualifications. Courts of Summary Jurisdiction may disqualify for short periods drivers convicted of "careless driving" for the first or second time, the disqualification being for not more than one month for a first offence, and not more than three months for a second offence. Disqualified drivers may subsequently be called upon to pass a driving test before a licence is returned.

Insurance. No longer can an insurance company back out of a claim for third-party risks on the grounds that the rider's machine has not been properly maintained. This is a sound point, for the author has unhappy recollections of once breaking an old man's leg in a fog, and the poor fellow after six months in hospital got nothing from the insurance company because the front brake of the motor-cycle concerned (a 1912 Humber!) had insufficient stopping power—at least that is what the company relied upon to evade payment.

Pedestrian Crossings. In certain places pedestrians have absolute right of way, such places to be indicated by road markings

THE LAW, LICENCES, INSURANCE 53

and also by special "cross here" signs taking the form of an orange coloured globe or "Belisha beacon." The regulations stipulate that: (a) pedestrians must not loiter; (b) vehicle traffic must give way to pedestrians using the marked crossings. Penalties for pedestrians and motorists misusing the crossings are enforceable.

Driving Off the Highway. It should be noted that it is now illegal to *drive* off the public highway on to commons, etc., for more than a distance of 15 yd. for parking purposes. The only exception to this law is in case of an emergency when preventing an offence, extinguishing fire, saving life, etc.

Keep the Brakes Perfect. Every Ariel owner should frequently give his brakes the "once over." Quite apart from the question of personal safety and the safety of others, it may be mentioned that the police are now empowered to test brakes either on the road or in the garage (subject to the owner's permission).

Smooth Tyres Illegal. It is now illegal to continue to run tyres after the tread has worn away and it may thus be far from economical to extract the last mile from a tyre. In any case smooth tyres invite skidding.

Sign Your Driving Licence. A driving licence must as soon as issued be signed by the owner. Presenting an unsigned licence to the police may now incur a "blue paper"!

Speedometer. Every motor cycle other than an invalid carriage or a motor cycle of 100 c.c. or under must be fitted with an instrument to indicate to the driver (within a 10 per cent margin) when the speed limit is being exceeded.

Concerning Mascots. An immense variety of attractive mascots are now available, but it is well to remember when fixing a mascot to the front mudguard that it must be in such a position or of such a kind that in the event of a collision with a pedestrian there is no risk of a protuding point causing injury.

CHAPTER IV

RUNNING-IN AND DRIVING HINTS

BEFORE setting out on a new machine the first thing to do, obviously, is to fill the oil and petrol tanks. The oil advised by the manufacturers is Patent Castrolaero or Mobiloil D (see also notes on page 168). For racing purposes Patent Castrol "R" may be used. The fuel recommended is No. 1 petrol for the standard models, and 60/40 benzole mixture for high compression "Red Hunter" machines. The oil tank should not be filled above the level of the return pipe on 1932 lightweights, or above 1 in. below the return pipe on the 1933-9 singles, and the level should not be allowed to drop below about two-thirds. This leaves a minimum quantity of one pint in circulation. The more oil there is in the tank, the better. See also page 63.

Any Ariel model is quite easy to start by means of the kick-starter, provided that the rider sets the levers, etc., in a suitable position and acquires the knack of using the kick-starter efficiently.

When starting for the first time on a solo motor-cycle it will usually be advisable to place the machine on the stand. The petrol should be turned on and the carburettor flooded by two or three sharp depressions of the tickler. The throttle control should only be opened about one-eighth of its movement, the air lever closed, and the spark lever one-third advanced (ignition "on," 4F, 4G, 4H).

Kick-starting. Having carried out these operations, see that the gear lever is in neutral position, and push down the kick-starter pedal until the compression of the engine is felt. Then allow the starter pedal to return to its original position. Push the exhaust valve lifter trigger forward (omitted on 4F, 4G, 4H) and with the instep of the foot (use the right foot) on the kick-starter pedal, push down the starter as far as it will go, releasing the exhaust valve lifter just before the starter pedal is half way down; the engine should then fire.

It may, however, back-fire. This shows that everything is in order except that the ignition lever is advanced slightly too far. Retard the ignition lever a little and repeat the operation. As soon as the engine fires, advance the ignition fully and open the air. The speed of the engine should then be adjusted by means of the twist-grip throttle control.

On 1932 "Sloper" models a decompressor is fitted to facilitate starting. As soon as the engine fires cut it out.

RUNNING-IN AND DRIVING HINTS 55

The Oil Supply. On old type Ariels it was then necessary to adjust the regulating screw to the sight feed lubricator, but on 1932–9 models there is no adjustment. The oil return at the tank should be checked, however, and an eye kept on the pressure gauge. This should register 10–15 lb. per sq. in. (60 lb., model 4G, 4H).

Is Gear Lever in Neutral? Make sure that a gear is not engaged. When the machine is on the stand, it will, of course, start almost

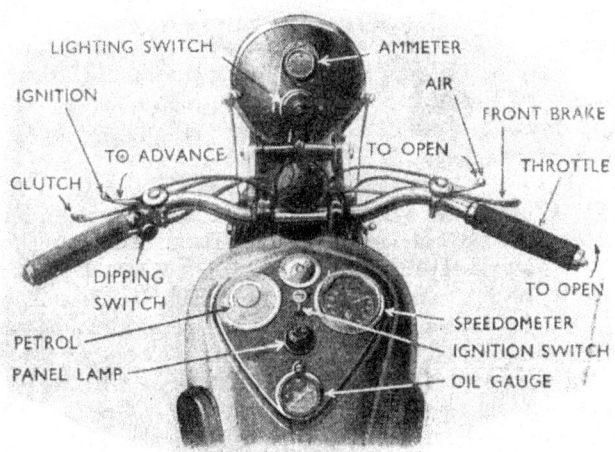

FIG. 24. SHOWING THE CONTROLS OF THE ARIEL "SQUARE FOUR."
The singles have an exhaust lifter, but no ignition switch, and the ignition lever is advanced by outward movement.

as easily with a gear engaged as with it in the neutral position, and when the engine fires the back wheel will revolve. To make certain, therefore, that the lever has not inadvertently been put in the wrong place, apply the back brake and see that the wheel comes to a stop before pushing the machine off the stand, which will spring up out of the way. Then straddle the machine, keeping both feet on the ground. If the machine is equipped with a steering damper, make sure that this is slacked right off.

Moving Off. Depress the clutch lever fully and engage first gear. Open the throttle gradually, at the same time letting the clutch in steadily. The machine will then move forward until, at a speed of about 4 miles per hour, the clutch can be fully engaged. It is not advisable for the novice to take his first run on either an uphill or downhill gradient. On the former he may tend to stop his engine by engaging the clutch too rapidly or not giving sufficient throttle opening, and on the latter the machine may tend to run away with him. When a speed of about 10 miles per hour has been obtained, second gear should be engaged. To do this close the throttle slightly, lift the clutch, and move the gear smartly into the second position; then re-engage the clutch and open the throttle. Pause in neutral when changing up.

When the machine has reached a speed of about 20 miles per hour the rider may change into third gear, following this by changing into fourth or top gear. When it comes to changing down the method is similar, except that it is not necessary to close the throttle whilst moving the gear lever, although the clutch must, of course, be disengaged. It is not advisable to run on top gear up any gradient at under 20 miles per hour, nor is it wise to change down into second gear at speeds of over 25 miles per hour, and bottom gear at over 10 m.p.h.

Use of the Clutch and Front Brake. It must be remembered that if the clutch is of the cork insert type (although extremely smooth and in every way satisfactory), it should not be slipped unduly. It must not, for instance, be slipped in order to assist the engine up hills. The gearbox is made to be used, and in the learning stages gears should be changed frequently, as this will assist the rider in the manipulation of his machine and will also save the engine and transmission.

It should also be borne in mind that the front brake is extremely powerful. It is perfectly smooth and safe in action, but should not be applied harshly. It is advisable, indeed, for the novice to get thoroughly conversant with its action first, so that it can be correctly used when the occasion arises. As a general rule it should be applied gently and slightly after the rear brake. A little practice in this respect will soon give the rider confidence, and once he has obtained this confidence he will find the powerful front brake extremely useful.

The Use of the Steering Damper. When 700 miles have been covered the rider may give his machine full throttle and see how it behaves at speed. Ariel motor-cycles are noted for their excellent steering qualities, but even so the roughness of most roads makes it advisable to use the steering dampers which are fitted to all the present Ariel models. The rider should work up to the feel of speed gradually. As he reaches high speeds, so he should tighten the steering damper slightly, remembering, before slowing down to a single figure speed, to release the damper; otherwise steering will be stiff at these low speeds and he may have considerable

RUNNING-IN AND DRIVING HINTS

difficulty in negotiating sharp corners, etc. On a sidecar machine, incidentally, since the element of balance does not enter into the matter, the steering damper may be kept reasonably tight for all speeds. A little practice in the use of this device will soon make its operation apparent. On exceptionally bad roads, tightening up the hand adjustment for the fork dampers will give increased riding comfort.

Hand Signals. One of the most common causes of accidents is the failure of one or all parties concerned to give the proper hand signals, or to give them at the proper time. Last-minute hand wagging is futile and most dangerous. All signals which are intended to convey anything should be clear, and should be given at a time when the following driver is in a position to heed the warning without having to resort to heavy braking. The signals that should be used are those shown in Fig. 25, and are the ones officially recognized. Implicit reliance should not be placed on the other man paying regard to the signal; the eyes and ears should be used also. It should be noted that the hand signal shown at *D*, Fig. 25, is not the official signal, although quite clear. The official signal is to extend the right arm and rotate it slowly from the shoulder anti-clockwise.

Skidding. Skidding is one of the greatest mishaps that the motor cyclist has to guard against, particularly in unfavourable weather. Below are given a few hints on how to avoid a skid—

(*a*) Interchange the rear with the front cover, or fit a new tyre when the tread wears off the back tyre.

(*b*) Cross tramlines at a wide angle.

(*c*) Apply the brakes gently, the rear one first, and do not declutch.

(*d*) Stop at home if you feel " nervy."

The correction of a front wheel skid is a matter which cannot be fully explained in print, for it is an art which only practice teaches. It is not intended, of course, that readers should deliberately practise front wheel skids, but circumstances so much affect this type of mishap that it is impossible to lay down hard and fast rules concerning it.

To correct a rear wheel skid, steer into the skid and bring the machine under control again if there is room. The important thing is to remain quite calm and to avoid sudden braking.

Subsidiary Roads. Quite a number of accidents occur through a driver entering a main road from a subsidiary road without being aware of the fact, and it is not reasonable to expect main-road traffic to give way, although at present the law concedes no

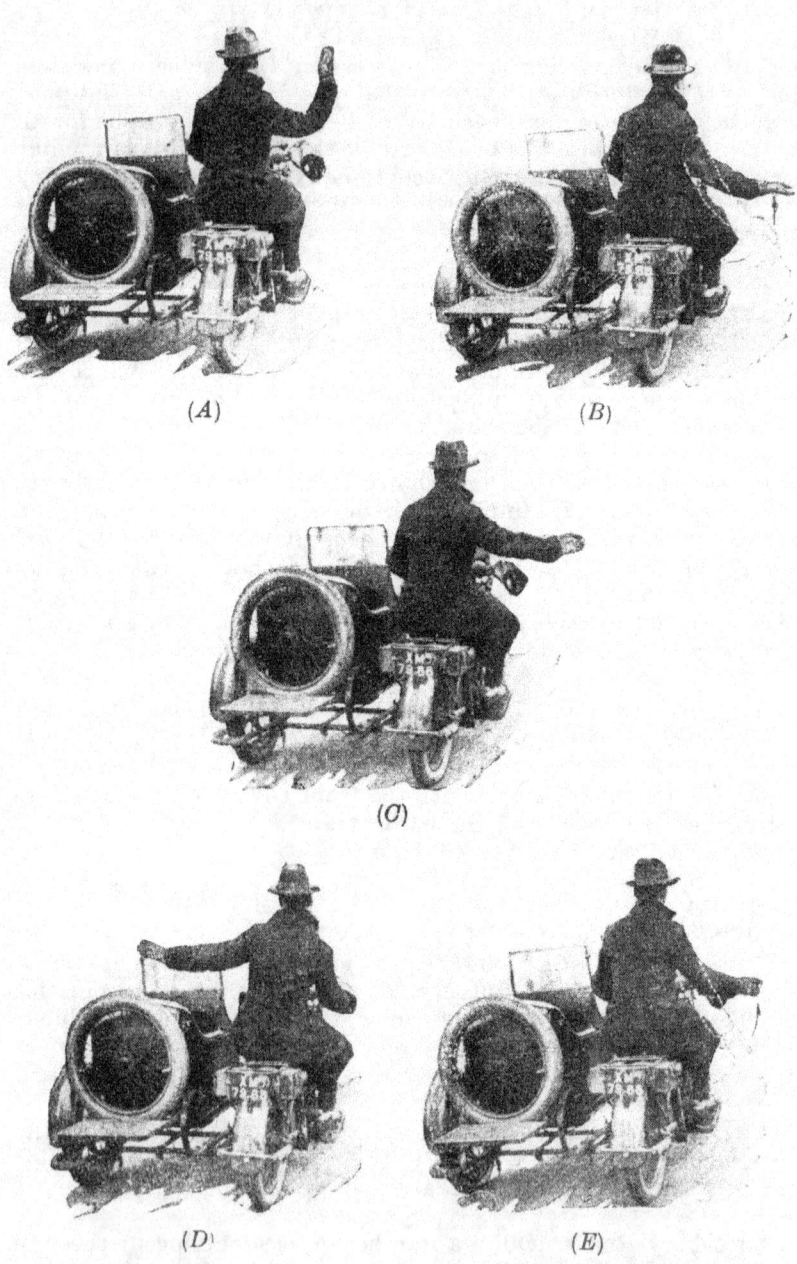

(From "The Motor-Cycle")

FIG. 25. RECOGNIZED SIGNALS TO BE USED BY DRIVERS
A = Signal to stop   C = Turning to right   E = You may over-take me
B = Slowing down   D = Turning to left
(see page 57)

RUNNING-IN AND DRIVING HINTS 59

priority to main-road traffic. To prevent this type of accident, one of two signs is often erected at dangerous crossings where subsidiary roads are entering the main roads, so that drivers need be under no illusion as to the nature of the road upon which they are travelling. Both signs comprise a triangle within a circle and in one case the sign has the words "SLOW MAJOR ROAD AHEAD" and in the other "HALT AT MAJOR ROAD AHEAD." It is wise to observe such signs carefully and in the case of the second sign its disregard is an offence.

Danger Signs. Apart from the recently-introduced subsidiary road sign, there are numerous others scattered at various points

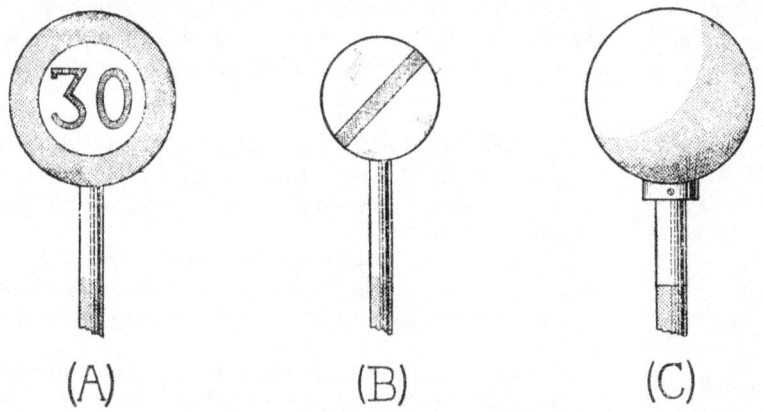

FIG. 26. SOME IMPORTANT ROAD SIGNS

throughout the country. The more important types are shown at A, B, C (Fig. 26). The signs illustrated at A and B are, respectively, the 30 m.p.h. speed limit sign, and one indicating that the end of a "built-up" area has been reached, with no speed limit in force. At C is shown a "Belisha beacon" or pedestrian crossing sign.

White Lines. Always faithfully observe the white lines at road intersections and corners. They have already done a vast amount of good and have given a certain sense of security to careful drivers. Traffic "lanes" are now replacing some of the white lines.

Automatic Traffic Indicators. By the end of 1937 automatic traffic control signals, almost entirely of the three-light pattern (see Fig. 26A), were employed at some thousands of centres, and they have now come into general use.

Red by itself means "Stop" before reaching the line.

Amber following the red, or simultaneously, means " Prepare to start."

Amber following the green means " Stop before reaching the line," unless, when the amber first appears, a vehicle is so close to the line that it cannot be safely pulled up, in which case it should proceed and get clear of the crossing.

Green means " Go ahead."

At night the showing of the red and green lights is sometimes discontinued, and the amber light only shown, either steady or flashing.

A standard preliminary warning sign has been recommended by the Ministry of Transport to notify drivers that they are approaching such signals, but in most cases no warning whatever is given. The standard warning sign is also shown at Fig. 26A.

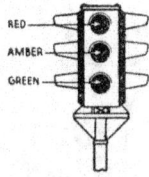

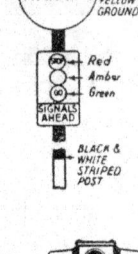

Fig. 26A
Automatic Signal (below) and Warning (above)

General Hints. In the following paragraphs a number of hints and tips are given, under the heading of what constitutes bad riding, which are worthy of mention—

1. Racing the engine unnecessarily and letting the clutch in so quickly that the wheel skids or jerks the machine forward. *Take a pride in a neat getaway.*

2. Jambing on the brakes at the last minute instead of slowing down steadily. *Drive on the throttle and not the brakes.*

3. Racing the engine or grinding the gears when changing gear. *A good driver is a neat driver.*

4. Applying the brakes when rounding corners instead of slowing down before reaching them. *Brake early and be neater, safer, and faster.*

5. Remaining in top gear when the engine is obviously labouring, instead of dropping down into a lower gear. *Never force an unwilling engine.*

6. Opening the throttle quickly when the machine is travelling slowly, thus causing the engine to " pink." *Change down for a quick " getaway."*

7. Running with the ignition too far retarded, causing overheating and loss of power. *Advance the ignition as far as the engine will allow.*

8. Using the exhaust lifter lever to slow down instead of shutting the throttle. *The exhaust lifter is for starting only.*

9. Holding the clutch " out " too long instead of dropping into neutral. *Excessive slipping soon heats up the clutch.*

RUNNING-IN AND DRIVING HINTS

10. Interfering with the silencing system to obtain a heavy bark. *Silence is fine, but noise brings a fine.*
11. Using the machine when out of adjustment. *Check everything over at frequent intervals.*
12. "Blipping" on the ignition switch (four-cylinder models). *This switch is for stopping the engine.*
13. Taking unnecessary risks. *Obey the rules of the road scrupulously.*
14. Cutting-in. *This is relegated to suicides and murderers.*

The instructions applying to the novice's first ride have been given briefly only, but it is hoped that they are sufficient to indicate the method of procedure. The finer points in driving can be gradually acquired after learning how to master the machine.

Pillion Riding. In spite of much criticism levelled against this form of passenger carrying, pillion riding *can* be absolutely safe—perhaps safer than solo riding, owing to the better grip of the rear tyre on the road. The law now requires a proper pillion seat to be *fixed* to the machine, and, of course, the pillion rider must be insured. The author suggests the following tips for those carrying, or about to carry, pillion passengers—

1. See that the passenger is as close to the driver as possible.
2. Ensure that suitable footrests are provided.
3. Avoid swerving as you do when riding solo.
4. Do not travel excessive distances two-up at night.
5. If the roads are slippery, keep the speed down.
6. Instruct the passenger to lean with the machine, and not try to balance it.
7. Avoid lack of concentration due to conversation.

Cornering with a Sidecar. When first attaching a sidecar to an Ariel, caution should be observed with regard to cornering until experience is gained, otherwise you may "come a cropper," due to disregarding the action of centrifugal force. Left-hand corners should be approached at a moderate speed, and the engine throttled up gradually as the sidecar rounds the bend; this causes the sidecar to pivot on the near-side wheel. When rounding a right-hand bend, throttle down and gently apply the rear brake as the sidecar negotiates the bend; this causes the sidecar to pivot on the off-side wheel.

Running-in. Every Ariel machine is fitted with an aluminium piston. Now for the best results to be obtained from an aluminium piston, as well as from the engine generally, it is essential that the first few hundred miles should be run at a moderate speed, and the engine handled with exceptional care.

Some manufacturers instruct riders of their machines that a speed of 20 to 25 miles per hour should not be exceeded during the first 500 miles. Actually the makers of the Ariel say that 30 miles per hour should not be exceeded for the first 700 or 800 miles. This is as much as can be said in any brief warning, but it is far more important that the engine should not be allowed to labour than it is that it should be kept below definite speeds. For the engine to give good results later in its life, it is important that throughout the running-in period of, say, 500 miles, the throttle opening should never be very great, and that the actual internal heat should be kept as low as possible. Descending a slight hill on half throttle at, say, 40 miles per hour, will do far less harm than climbing the same hill on full throttle at 25 miles per hour. Similarly, the ascent of a steep hill on a sidecar machine using second gear may be very injurious to a new engine if a wide throttle opening be needed, even if the speed of the machine be only 10 to 15 miles per hour. *Light running*, therefore, is what must be aimed at during the first 700 miles. Towards the end of this distance it will do no harm to open the throttle for occasional short spells, but it must not be kept open for any length of time until about 1,000 miles have been covered; violent acceleration should be avoided.

It is extremely difficult, especially for the accomplished rider, to refrain from opening out during the earlier periods, but abstinence in this respect is well worth while. He can console himself, moreover, with the knowledge that expert track and road-racing motor-cyclists pay particular attention to this matter unless, of course, they know that the engine has already been run-in for many hours on the bench. This is possible in the case of specially made racing engines, but would make the price of production models prohibitive.

The reasons why running-in is so important are that (*a*) only by gentle friction can the crystalline metal-bearing surfaces become hardened and of uniform consistency; (*b*) insufficient working clearances will at high speeds result in excessive friction accompanied probably by overheating and, perhaps, distortion; (*c*) small working clearances are apt to prevent thorough distribution of the lubricating oil.

Always Run on Main Fuel Supply. Do not run on the reserve supply till the main supply is exhausted. To open the reserve supply pull out knob "Pull reserve" and also leave open the knob "Pull on." It is wise to ascertain how far the machine will travel on the reserve supply, so that in future there is no risk of being stranded by running completely out of fuel. Normally, keep the reserve tap closed, but open it when replenishing. To

RUNNING-IN AND DRIVING HINTS 63

shut off the fuel supply, push in both knobs of the Ewart's two-level cork-seated tap, and to lock the tap open give the plunger a quarter turn after pulling out.

Concerning Replenishment. Those who have come into possession of new models should make a note of the proper method of removing and replacing the petrol tank filler cap. To remove the cap slacken the centre screw, rotate the cap one-quarter of a turn anti-clockwise, and lift up. To replace the cap drop it into position, rotate the cap clockwise as far as possible, and tighten the centre screw.

Suitable Engine Oils. Patent Castrolaero and Mobiloil D are recommended on page 54, but it should be mentioned that Messrs. Ariel Motors, Ltd., also recommend various other brands and grades, details of which will be found on pages 168, 169. These oils will mix with Colloidal Graphite.

Colloidal Graphite for Running-in. The mixing of Colloidal Graphite with engine oil in the proportion of one pint to a gallon of oil is strongly advocated during the running-in period. It protects the bearing faces from metal pick-up and makes for cooler running; it also is beneficial to the valves. The compound is obtainable from most garages and it is a good plan to continue to use it even when the running-in period has been completed. In this case the quantity used can be reduced by one-half.

CHAPTER V

WHEELS AND TYRES

EVERY motor-cyclist naturally wants to get as many miles out of his tyres as is possible with safety. The tyres on an Ariel are of large section, and should therefore last for a very considerable time. It has been mentioned in Chapter II that the life of a rear and front tyre on a solo machine should be 6,000 and 10,000 miles

FIG. 27. PROVISION FOR REAR WHEEL
ALIGNMENT AND CHAIN ADJUSTMENT

K—Adjusting screw
F—Lock nut
G—Cone adjusting nut
H—Cone adjusting lock nut
E—Spindle nut

respectively, those of a sidecar machine being as follows: rear 5,000, front 8,000, sidecar indefinite, say 20,000.

If the tyres and the machine itself receive proper attention the former should last these distances without difficulty, and in some cases very much greater mileages may be obtained. If the tyres, however, are misused or the machine is run with the wheels out of line, excessive wear will take place.

The greatest thief of tyre life is misalignment of wheels, and the rider would be well advised to check this alignment from time to time. This can easily be done on a solo machine with the aid

WHEELS AND TYRES

of a straight piece of wood and on a sidecar machine with two similar pieces of wood.

It is, of course, absolutely essential that the edge of the board should be dead straight and square, and that it should be at least as long as the machine itself. Let us take the case of the solo motor-cycle first. Put the machine on the stand and place the straight edge of the board alongside the two wheels, as high up as possible. Then turn the front wheel until the board touches both sides of the front tyre and at least one side of the rear tyre. If

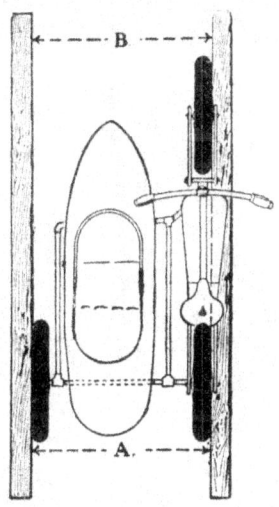

FIG. 28. CHECKING WHEEL AND SIDECAR ALIGNMENT

the wheels are in line the board should also touch both sides of the rear wheel tyre; if it does not do so the alignment of the rear wheel must be altered by means of the chain adjusters. If the front and rear tyre sizes are different the board will not touch the front tyre and the distance between the tyre and board should be measured on both sides.

Alignment of a Sidecar Machine. When lining up a sidecar the two wheels of the machine itself must first be checked in the manner described above. The board must then be set along the offside of the tyres and a similar board placed across the sidecar tyre as shown in Fig. 28. The distances between the boards at A and B must then be measured. In theory these distances should be equal, but, in practice, it is found that better steering is obtained if B is about $\frac{1}{4}$ in. less than A. Wheel alignment is obtained by sliding the drop arm from the rear ball joint along the sidecar frame tube.

It is next necessary to make sure that the machine itself is dead vertical. For this purpose the outfit must be wheeled on to a level surface and measurements must be taken from the front forks as shown in Fig. 29. In the sketch a piece of board is shown, but a walking stick or anything similar may well be used. The stick, or whatever is employed, should be rested against a given point on the front fork, and the distance between its lower extremity and the centre of the front tyre should then be measured. This distance is shown as C in Fig. 29.

A similar operation should then be carried out on the other side of the machine, and the two distances C should be equal. If

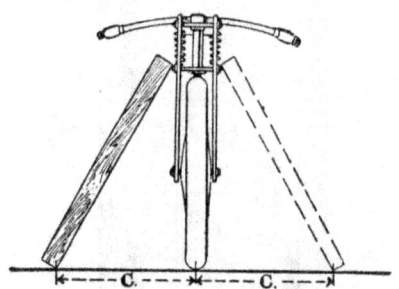

Fig. 29. If a Sidecar Machine is Vertical the Distances "C," shown Above, should be Equal

it is found that the right-hand distance C is greater than the left-hand, it proves that the machine is leaning towards the sidecar, and adjustments to the chassis must therefore be carried out in order that a true vertical setting may be obtained. Some sidecar drivers prefer, however, to adjust the sidecar connections so that the motor-cycle leans outwards very slightly, but on no account should it lean inwards. Vertical alignment of the motor-cycle is obtained by means of the screwed yoke end at the top of the seat pillar connection tube. A further adjustment can be made by sliding the chassis clamp lug, to which the tube is attached, along the frame. When the required adjustment has been made, the sidecar connections must be screwed up dead tight. Whether or not any alteration to the alignment is made it is advisable to check the sidecar connections from time to time.

The Matter of Tyre Pressure. As regards the tyres themselves, it is of primary importance that they should be inflated to the correct pressure. With the old type of tyre valve it was impossible to measure the pressure accurately, although expert riders could gauge it very nearly by appearance and feel.

WHEELS AND TYRES

All Dunlop tyres, however, are now fitted with Schrader valves and, with the aid of a pressure gauge, measurements can be taken accurately. The author recommends the Dunlop Pencil Type No. 1 gauge, illustrated in Fig. 30A. This gauge is extremely convenient as it has a clip to fit the waistcoat pocket. To use this gauge, the valve dust cap (Fig. 30) is taken off, and the end of the pressure gauge is pressed on to the open end of the valve. It depresses the pin and allows air to enter the gauge and push up the piston calibrated in pounds per square inch. It is always wise to keep the dust caps screwed on, though some riders throw them

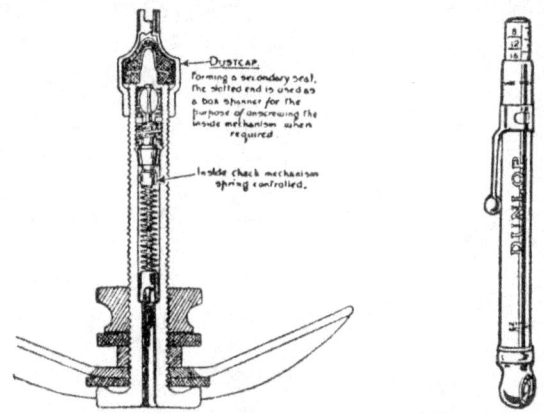

FIGS. 30, 30A. SHOWING (Left) DUNLOP VALVE AND (Right) CONVENIENT PRESSURE GAUGE

away! Dust or grit getting into the valve stem is liable to interfere with the valve action of the little spring-controlled plunger (Fig. 30) and cause leakage. About once a year valve "insides" should be replaced. They can be removed by taking off the valve cap and using the slotted end as a screwdriver.

A chart of the minimum inflation pressures recommended for Dunlop Cord tyres fitted to Ariels is given on page 68.

It must be borne in mind that under-inflation causes severe strain to be set up in the casing of the tyre. If run at too low a pressure the casings will crack and the tyres will be rendered useless when there are still many miles of wear left in the tread. The pressures recommended are, incidentally, for machines which are fully equipped, and if the driver and passenger are very heavy, or if a pillion passenger is habitually carried, higher pressure in the rear tyre, at any rate, is advisable. For a pillion passenger at least an extra 5 lb. per sq. in. should be allowed for the rear tyre.

It is, again, inevitable that the tyres will become cut by the glass and sharp flints which are to be found on all our roads. A superficial cut in the rubber is of little account, but it may spread, and it should therefore be filled with a suitable tyre stopping. If, however, this cut extends to the fabric of the tyre, wet will penetrate into the latter and, in due course, will rot it. Any cut of this nature should therefore be repaired efficiently. The only way to get this done is to vulcanize the tyre.

RECOMMENDED 1935-9 INFLATION PRESSURES (DUNLOP)

Ariel Model	26 in. × 3·25 in. Lb. per sq. in.			26 in. × 3 in. Lb. per sq. in.	
	Front	Rear	Sidecar	Front	Rear
LF3, LF4—Solo	—	22	—	20	—
LH, LG, OH, OG,—Solo	18	22	—	20	—
NH, NG—Solo	18	22	—	20	—
—Sidecar	20	28	16	26	—
VH—Solo	18	22	—	20	—
—Sidecar	20	28	16	26	—
NF3, NF4, VA3, VA4, VF3, VF4—					
Solo	18	22	—	—	—
Sidecar	20	28	16	—	—
VB, VG, VA.—Solo	18	22	—	—	—
—Sidecar	20	28	16	—	—
4F—Solo	18	23	—	—	—
—Sidecar	20	28	16	—	—
4G, 4H, 1937-9 4F—Solo	20	28	—	—	—
—Sidecar	20	28	16	—	—

Obviously, if long tyre life is sought, freak hills and extremely rough surfaces should be avoided. Wheel spin in particular is extremely detrimental to the rear tyre. The majority of riders never subject their tyres to these exceptional conditions, but many of them do not appreciate the strain which they impose on their tyres by bad driving. Fierce braking, rapid acceleration and fast cornering (particularly on a sidecar machine) should be avoided as far as possible, the same applying to quick engagement of the clutch with a wide throttle opening. This latter procedure, incidentally, is also detrimental to the transmission system. Two important points not yet mentioned are: (*a*) avoid crossing upraised tram lines or running in the lines; (*b*) do not allow the tyres to stand in patches of oil or paraffin.

Worn Tyres and Their Danger. There is one point which solo riders in particular should remember. When a tyre is worn right through to the casing it should be treated with great care. A solo machine should never be driven at high speeds when either of its tyres is in this condition. The Dunlop tyres fitted to

WHEELS AND TYRES

Ariels are of the wired-on type, and upon rapid deflation they do not leave the rim as was possible with the old pattern beaded-edge tyres. If a machine is driven at high speeds, however, and the front tyre suddenly bursts, a crash is almost inevitable. This is extremely likely if a rear tyre bursts at a speed of over 50 to 60 miles per hour, but the expert rider may be able to hold his machine and escape injury, provided that he has a clear road. A burst tyre on a sidecar machine is by no means so dangerous, but should it occur on a bend at high speed, it may cause the outfit to leave the road. If tyres, therefore, are in this badly worn condition they should be thrown away and replaced. Should the rider feel that he cannot afford this, he should drive with extreme caution and never exceed 35 to 40 miles per hour until new tyres are fitted. See page 53.

For tyres to give best results they should be checked for pressure every week or fortnight, and if found to be below the recommended pressure should be inflated accordingly. At the same time they should be examined carefully throughout their circumference; any tiny flints found embedded in the rubber should be removed, and any cuts should be repaired in the manner already described.

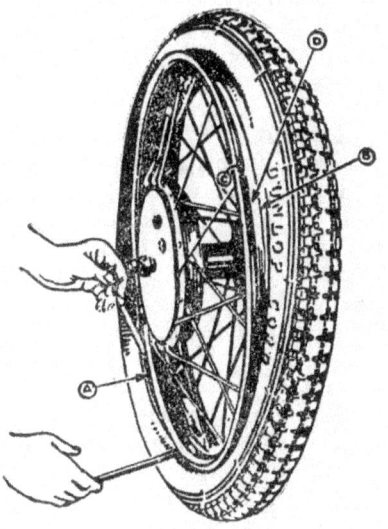

FIG. 31. HOW TO REMOVE A FRONT COVER

The tyre edges at *A* cannot be levered off until the edges at *B* are first pushed down into the well-base rim *D* off the rim *C*.

Tyre Removal. A few words on the subject of removing and refitting tyres may not be out of place, and those new to motorcycling would do well to acquaint themselves with the correct procedure, so that when the unexpected puncture does occur a minimum amount of time and patience is required to effect a repair. It is by no means an uncommon sight to witness a motorcyclist *struggling* to remove a tyre, and through faulty refitting the tube is sometimes pinched and a second repair becomes necessary. Tyre removal and replacement need offer no difficulty whatever if a few simple precautions are taken. All Ariel motorcycles are now fitted with Dunlop cord tyres which have inextensible wired edges fitting into well-base rims. To remove this type of tyre, first completely deflate it by removing all the valve parts, including the check mechanism (Fig. 30). Then, at a point opposite the valve, push the edges of the cover into the wellbase rim. Proceed to remove the tyre edge as shown in Fig. 31, by inserting two small levers, one each side of the valve about 4 in. apart. No force should be necessary *as long as the edges of the tyre opposite the valve are right down in the rim*. Gradually work round until the whole of the tyre edge comes off the rim, enabling the tube to be withdrawn. Do not employ large tyre levers.

Refitting a Tyre. Assuming one edge of the tyre is already in position, slightly inflate the inner tube, insert it inside the cover, and push the valve stem through the hole in the rim. Do not tighten up the lock-nut securing the valve to the rim, and also see that the tube is not twisted. Then start to fit the second edge of the cover at a point diametrically opposite the valve, by placing it over the rim and pushing it down into the rim base. Push on the rest of the cover and, with a pair of small tyre levers, work round each side in such a way that the part near the valve is refitted last. On no account use excessive force, and while inflating see that the edges of the cover bed down evenly on the rim. Finally, replace the valve lock-nut and pump up the tyre to the recommended pressure. After a puncture has been repaired do not immediately pump up to full pressure, but give the patch a chance to stick on hard. In connection with punctures, the following two points are important: (*a*) See that the solution is "tacky" before applying the patch, (*b*) don't be stingy with the french chalk.

Rim Sizes and Oversize Tyres. The rims used for the 3·25 in. × 19 in. wired-on tyres measure 2½ in. × 19 in., and suitable oversize tyres for these rims are 3·5 in. × 19 in. and 4·0 in. × 19 in., but the last mentioned is best fitted to a 3 in. × 19 in. rim. The 3·5 in. × 19 in. cover runs with ample clearance, but the 4·0 in. × 19 in. cover runs rather close to the rear chain guards, and this size of cover can only be fitted if the mudguard is not valanced, the lower chain guard is removed and the top guard cut away near the tyre. In connexion with tyre sizes it may be mentioned that the descriptions of different wired-on tyres have been altered and standardized. The 26 in. × 3 in. cover is now referred to as the 3·00—20; the 26 in. × 3·25 in. is equivalent to the 3·25—19, and the 26 in. × 3·5 in. cover is called the 3·50—19. Oversize 4·00—19 covers were previously described as 27 in. × 4·00 in.

CHAPTER VI

THE ENGINE AND GEARBOX

SINCE it is probable that over 90 per cent of the readers of this book are fully familiar with the working of the internal combustion engine, the briefest details of it only will be given in these pages. For those who are entirely ignorant of the principles on which the I.C. engine operates, the following elementary notes should serve as a guide.

Motor-cycle engines are of two types—two-stroke and four-stroke. All Ariel engines are of the latter type, which is so known since the piston makes four distinct movements, or strokes, for each power impulse. The main components of a single-cylinder, four-stroke, motor-cycle engine are: cylinder, valves, piston, connecting rod, flywheels, little- and big-ends, main shafts, crank-pin, cam gear, crank-case, carburettor, and magneto.

The cylinder is comparable to a "pot," by which name, incidentally, it is often known, and in it the piston moves up and down. A gudgeon pin passes through the walls of the piston (strengthened by bosses) and the little-end of the connecting rod. The big-end of the connecting rod is attached to the flywheels by a crank pin, and from the centre of each flywheel protrudes a short, stiff main shaft; these shafts are free to revolve in bearings in the crankcase. The near-side shaft extends through the crankcase and has a driving sprocket attached to it; the offside shaft drives the camshaft and magneto at *half engine speed*.

The Working Operations. A reference to Figs. 32-35 makes it clear that as the flywheels revolve so the piston must move up and down; the amount of its movement is known as the engine's "stroke." At the top of the cylinder are two valves—an inlet and an exhaust. Fresh gas from the carburettor is drawn into the cylinder via the inlet valve and expelled, when burnt, through the exhaust valve. In order that the valves should open and close when desired, cams are fitted in the crankcase. These cams are driven by the cam shaft and lift each valve once every alternate revolution. Springs are attached to the valves in order to return them to the seatings, and to make the upper part of the cylinder—the combustion chamber—gas tight. The piston has slots cut in it to receive spring rings, known as piston rings. These prevent gas from blowing past the walls of the piston and yet allow the latter to have a sufficient working clearance.

Imagine the piston at its uppermost position—at the top of its "stroke." The four "strokes" are then as follows—

INLET. The inlet valve opens and the piston descends. A partial

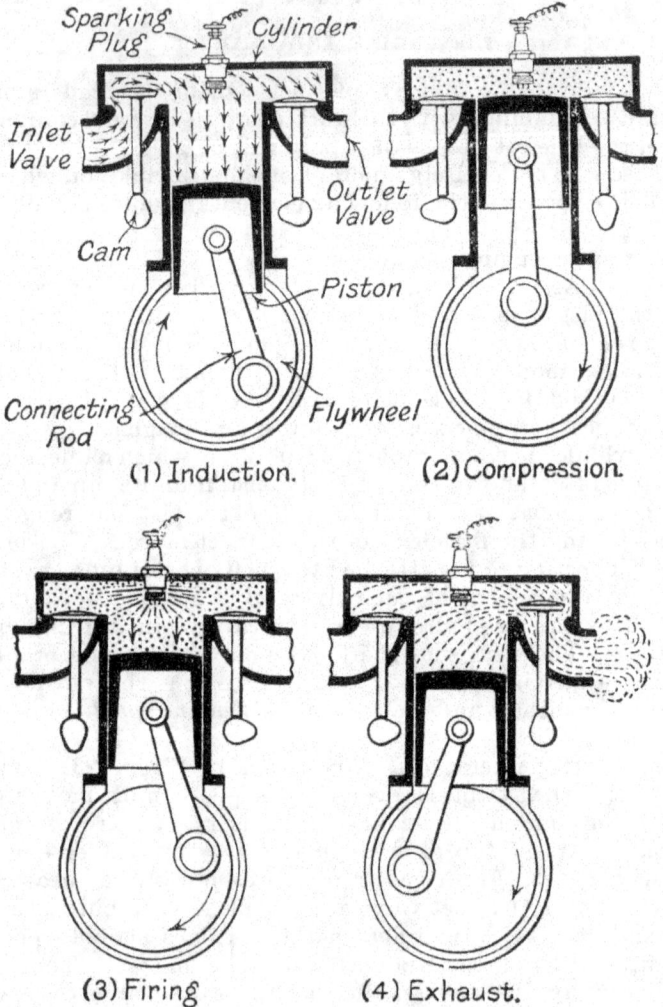

FIGS. 32-35. THE PRINCIPLE OF THE FOUR-STROKE ENGINE

vacuum draws gas from the carburettor into the combustion chamber. The piston reaches the bottom of its stroke and reverses.

COMPRESSION. The inlet valve closes as the piston rises. Nothing else opens at the top, so the gas becomes compressed.

THE ENGINE AND GEARBOX

COMBUSTION. When the piston has reached the top of its stroke and has thus finished compressing the gases, a spark appears at the points of the sparking plug and ignites the gases. This combustion, which is the only power impulse of the four strokes, drives the piston downwards.

EXHAUST. Just before the piston reaches the bottom of its combustion stroke the exhaust valve opens and the piston, rising, pushes the burnt gases out of the cylinder. At approximately the top of the stroke the exhaust valve closes, the inlet valve opens, and the cycle of operations is repeated.

That, briefly, is the action of the four-stroke engine. It must also be mentioned that the carburettor is a device for mixing liquid petrol with air and allowing controlled amounts of the mixture to enter the combustion chamber; the electric current for the sparks is also supplied by an instrument known as a magneto, which is driven from an extension of the cam shaft.

On Ariel engines the various parts are made of the following materials: cylinder, cast iron; valves, steel; piston, aluminium; connecting-rod, steel; flywheels, cast iron*; big-end, main shafts, and cam gear, steel; crankcase, aluminium.

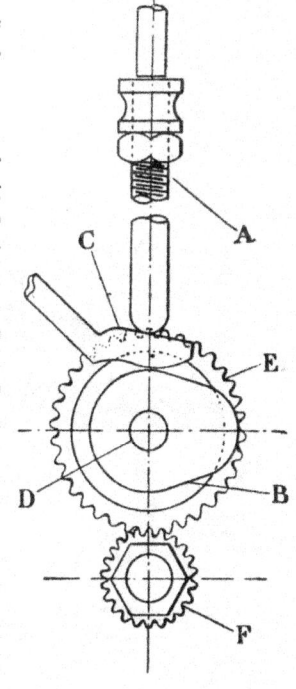

FIG. 36. CAM VALVE ACTION

Location of Valve Gear. The valves are disposed in two ways. On the VA3, VA4, and VB *de luxe* models they are set side by side, with their heads in the side of the combustion chamber and their stems pointing downwards; an engine with this valve disposition is known as a side-valve engine. On the LG, VG, NG, LF, VH, NH, LH models the valve heads are in the top of the cylinder and their stems point upwards, these engines being therefore called overhead-valve engines. The orifice through which the gas enters is called the inlet port; that through which it is expelled is called the exhaust port.

Side-valve Ariel engines have one of each ports, and some of the single-cylinder overhead-valve engines have one inlet and two exhaust ports.

* The highly-tuned "Red Hunter" engines have polished forged steel flywheels.

THE PRINCIPLE OF THE CARBURETTOR

It has been found by experiment that the most satisfactory way of encouraging petrol to evaporate is to drive it under pressure through a very tiny hole, called a jet, and the process is assisted by heating the spraying device. Owing to the proximity of the carburettor to the combustion chamber, ample heat is, of course, conducted to it *via* the induction pipe, once the engine has warmed

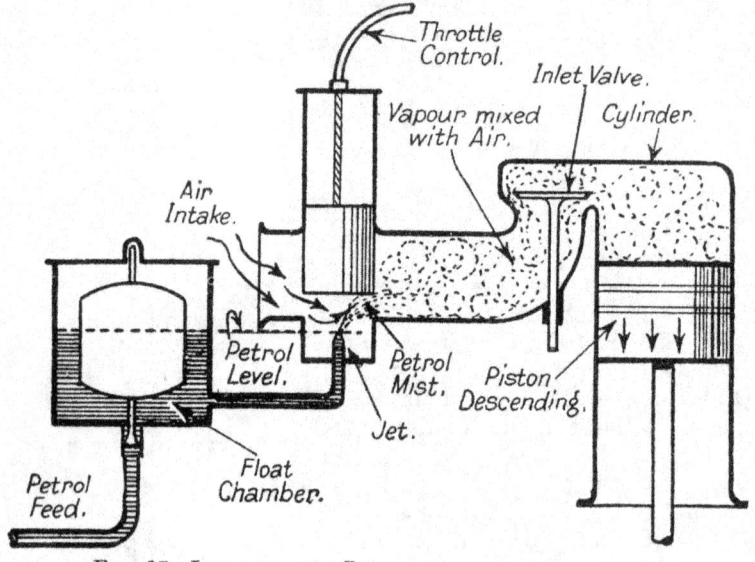

FIG. 37. ILLUSTRATING PRINCIPLE OF THE CARBURETTOR

up. The powerful suction through the inlet pipe on the inlet stroke can be relied upon to atomize the fuel completely. Let us refer to Fig. 37, which shows the salient features of a carburettor in action. It will be observed that the petrol level in the jet must be below the orifice at the top; otherwise the petrol will overflow and cause *flooding* of the carburettor. The level is automatically regulated by the action of a *float* attached to a spindle, which operates a needle valve, thereby cutting off the petrol supply immediately the level in the chamber reaches the height of the jet orifice. On the downward stroke of the piston, air is sucked in through the air intake; past the partially open throttle, which is a closely fitting hand-controlled slide, operating up and down in a barrel; past the jet; past the inlet valve, and thence into the cylinder. The extremely high velocity air current that must obviously sweep over the jet causes the fuel to issue in a small fountain, and simultaneously causes the spirit to be atomized and

THE ENGINE AND GEARBOX

diffused with the air rushing in towards the combustion chamber. This, briefly, is the principle of the carburettor.

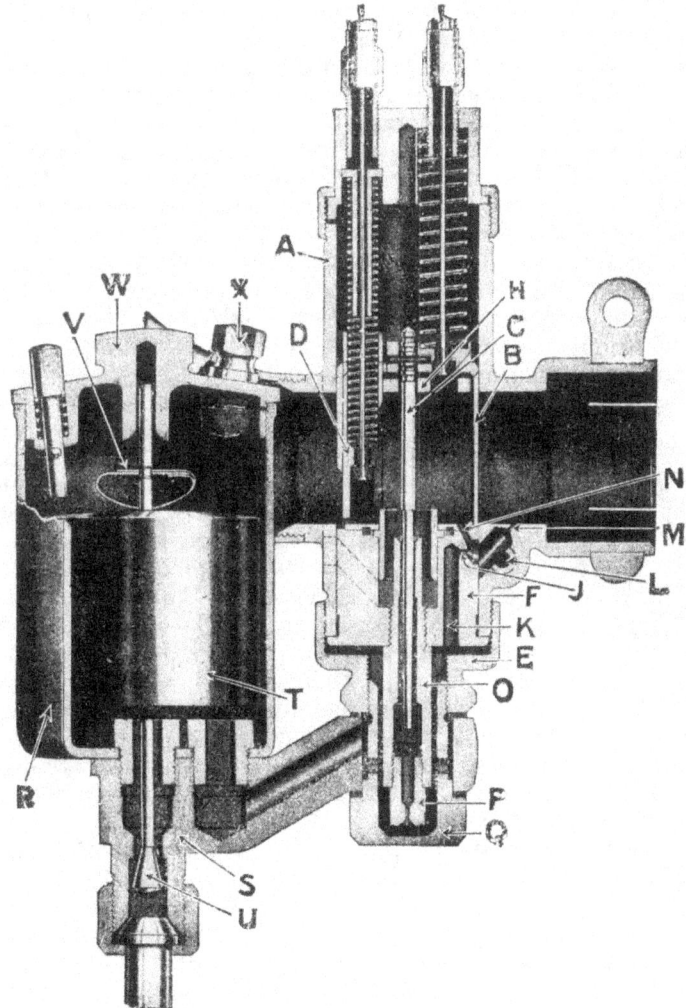

Fig. 38. Sectional View of Two-lever Needle Jet Amal Carburettor

The various refinements and complications that are incorporated in the Amal carburettor are designed to (1) make the mixture as homogeneous as possible; (2) simplify the control; (3) enable automatic slow running to be obtained; (4) enable settings for special purposes to be made.

THE AMAL CARBURETTOR (ALL MODELS)

This carburettor incorporates all the best features of old B. & B., Binks, Amac types. The following description will enable the reader to comprehend its working.

Referring to Fig. 38, showing a sectional view of the instrument, A is the carburettor body or mixing chamber, the upper part of which has a throttle valve B, with taper needle C attached by the needle clip. The throttle valve regulates the quantity of mixture supplied to the engine. Passing through the throttle valve is the air valve D, independently operated, and serving the purpose of obstructing the main air passage for starting and mixture regulation. Fixed to the underside of the mixing chamber by the union nut E is the jet block F, and interposed between them is a fibre washer to ensure a petrol-tight joint. On the upper part of the jet block is the adaptor body H, forming a clean through-way. Integral with the jet block is the pilot jet J, supplied through the passage K. The adjustable pilot air intake L communicates with a chamber, from which issues the pilot outlet M and the by-pass N. An adjusting screw (TS, Fig. 39) is provided at the mixing chamber, by which the position of the throttle valve for tick-over is regulated independently of the cable adjustment. The needle jet O is screwed in the underside of the jet block and carries at its bottom end the main jet P. Both these jets are removable when the jet plug Q, which bolts the mixing chamber and the float chamber together, is removed.

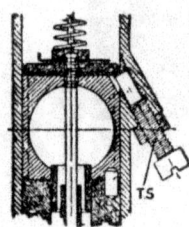

FIG. 39. AMAL THROTTLE STOP

The float chamber, which has bottom feed, consists of a cup R suitably mounted on a platform S containing a float T, and the needle valve U attached by the clip V. The float chamber cover has a lock screw X for security.

The petrol tap having been turned on, petrol will flow past the needle valve U until the quantity of petrol in the chamber R is sufficient to raise the float T, when the needle valve U will prevent a further supply entering the float chamber until some in the chamber has already been used up by the engine. The float chamber having been filled to its correct level, the fuel passes along the passages through diagonal holes in the jet plug Q, when it will be in communication with the main jet P and the pilot feed hole K; the level in these jets being, obviously, the same as that maintained in the float chamber.

Imagine the throttle valve B very slightly open. As the piston descends, a partial vacuum is created in the carburettor, causing a rush of air through the pilot air hole L, and drawing fuel from the pilot jet J. The mixture of air and fuel is admitted to the

THE ENGINE AND GEARBOX

engine, through the pilot outlet M. The quantity of mixture capable of being passed by the pilot outlet M is insufficient to run the engine. This mixture also carries excess of fuel. Consequently, before a combustible mixture is admitted, throttle valve B must be slightly raised, admitting a further supply of air from the main air intake. The farther the throttle valve is opened the less will be the depression on the outlet M, but, in turn, a higher depression will be created on the by-pass N, and the pilot mixture will flow from this passage as well as from the outlet M.

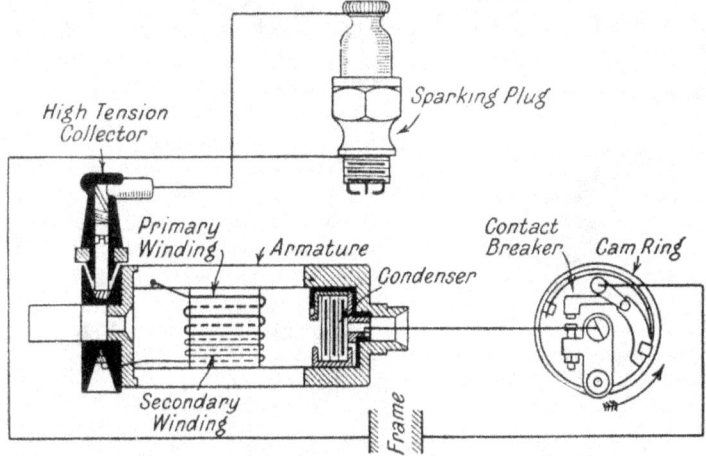

Fig. 40. Magneto Ignition Wiring Diagram

As the throttle valve is farther opened the fuel passes the main jet P, which governs the mixture strength from seven-eighths to full throttle. For intermediate throttle positions the taper needle C, working in the needle jet O, is the governing factor. The farther the throttle valve is lifted the greater the quantity of air admitted to the engine, and a suitable graduation of fuel supply is maintained by means of the taper needle. The air valve D, which is cable operated on the two-lever carburettor, has the effect of obstructing the main through-way, and, in consequence, increasing the on depression the main jet, enriching the mixture.

THE PRINCIPLE OF THE MAGNETO

The magneto primarily consists of three parts: (1) the *armature* ; (2) a *U-shaped magnet* ; (3) the *contact breaker*.

The armature comprises an iron core or bobbin of " H " section, on which are two windings; firstly, a short winding of fairly heavy gauge wire; and, secondly, on top of the former, a very big winding of fine wire. The first winding is known as the *primary* and the second as the *secondary* (see Fig. 40). The armature, which can rotate on ball bearings, is placed such that on rotation it periodically cuts across the *magnetic field* of the magnet, and creates a current in the primary winding. Incidentally, the contact breaker forms part of the primary circuit. This current, however, is at a very low voltage—far and away too small to produce anything in the nature of a spark. But if a *break* is suddenly caused in the primary by separating the platinum contacts when the current is at its maximum flow, a high voltage or tension current will be instantly *induced* in the secondary winding —sufficient to jump a small space, if the circuit be incomplete. In this circuit the sparking plug is included, and things are so arranged that, in order for the secondary circuit to be complete, the current must jump across the electrodes of the plug, or, in other words, a spark must occur. Now in the case of a single-cylinder engine, the points in the rotating contact breaker separate once in every armature revolution (there being one cam only), and the armature to which the contact breaker is fitted being driven off the exhaust camshaft by sprockets and chain runs at half-engine speed; that is to say, a " break " takes place once every two engine revolutions, i.e. four strokes of the piston. Hence, if the initial " break " be timed to occur when the piston is at the top of the compression stroke, all the other " breaks " (and therefore sparks) will occur at this point also, and thus the engine will go on firing correctly. Besides the " break " being timed to take place when the piston is in a certain position (which we call " timing the magneto," see page 155), it must also be timed to occur at the moment when the bobbin is having the greatest effect on the magnetic field (see Fig. 41). This, of course, is allowed for in the design of the magneto, and does not really concern the reader. Also, it is essential that the primary circuit should be complete (i.e. the contacts must be properly closed) both before and after the " break," which should be of very short duration.

FIG. 41. POSITION OF MAGNETO ARMATURE WHEN CONTACTS SHOULD OPEN

The *cam ring*, against which the cam of the contact breaker works, can be rotated by handlebar control through about 25°, thereby giving means of advancing and retarding the spark.

The *condenser* is a device for the purpose of eliminating "arcing," and the *pick-up* is a small carbon brush kept in continual contact with the *slip-ring*, in order to collect or pick up the H.T. current for the sparking plug lead.

THE ENGINE AND GEARBOX

The *cut-out* switch (provided only in the case of the Ariel Square Four) is a small panel-mounted switch for earthing the primary current and thereby preventing a secondary current being induced. It is necessary where no exhaust valve lifter is fitted for stopping the engine. The current is led to the switch from a spring-loaded carbon button (which is fitted on the inside of the contact-breaker cover and bears against the contact-breaker fixing screw).

The *distributor* is a kind of rotary switch responsible for distributing the H.T. current picked up from the slip-ring to the correct

FIG. 42. LUCAS RACING MAGNETO, PARTLY SECTIONED TO SHOW CONSTRUCTION

sparking plugs on a multi-cylinder engine. Usually it constitutes part of the magneto and is driven from the armature, but in the case of the Ariel Square Four the distributor is an entirely separate unit (see Fig. 60). An extension of the camshaft on the near side constitutes the distributor shaft or *rotor*, and to this is fixed the *distributor arm*, insulated from the rotor and carrying a metal electrode which is supplied with the H.T. current from the pick-up through the agency of a carbon brush mounted in the centre of the distributor moulding. As the distributor arm rotates at half engine speed, the electrode passes four metal *segments* arranged radially at 90° to each other inside the distributor moulding and connected to the sparking plugs. Each time a segment is passed a "break" occurs at the contact-breaker and a H.T. current flashes across the *jump-spark gap*, provided to ensure a good voltage and so reaches the plug of the cylinder whose turn it is to fire. It should be observed that in the case of the four-cylinder engine there are four times as many power strokes as with a single-cylinder engine. In other words, a power stroke occurs twice for every engine revolution, or once every half revolution. Hence on the Square Four the magneto is driven at *engine* speed and *two* cams are provided on the cam ring.

The foregoing paragraphs should convey a fairly clear idea as to how the magneto works. A magneto is a fascinating little piece of apparatus and to understand thoroughly its working some knowledge of magnetism and induction is necessary. Present-day magnetos are 100 per cent reliable and will run year after year with little or no attention. This is rather marvellous when one considers that cruising at 2,000 r.p.m. on a Square Four for four hours, no less than 960,000 sparks have to be produced—just on a million! The principal features of a modern magneto can be noted in Fig. 42, where a Lucas racing magneto similar to those fitted on some Ariel "Red Hunters" is shown partly sectioned. An illustration of the Lucas "Magdyno" fitted as standard equipment will be found on page 101.

THE PRINCIPLE OF THE GEARBOX

Those having little knowledge of the petrol engine and general mechanical principles may perhaps wonder why a gearbox is necessary and how it works. It is proposed to give a few elementary facts and then to describe the working of the Burman four-speed gearbox fitted to most Ariel models.

The power output of an engine is, roughly speaking, proportional to the engine revolutions up to a certain point. In technical language one would say that the power curve (r.p.m. plotted against b.h.p.) is a straight line. This means that in order for a motor-cycle to travel fast along the level in top gear (i.e. with the rear wheel rotating about one revolution for every five engine revolutions), or with a direct drive, the engine revolutions must be steadily increased by opening the throttle to overcome the opposing forces. In this case frictional and tractive forces are small and air resistance which increases as the square of the velocity is the only serious factor to prevent the r.p.m. rising to a phenomenal degree. Actually the engine will go on increasing its speed of rotation until at, say, 5,000 r.p.m. the power output is equal to the air resistance plus the small frictional and tractive forces. When, however, the machine comes to a steep gradient, the tractive forces due to gravity tending to pull the machine backwards suddenly make themselves felt and these forces are so great that even with the throttle wide open the engine revolutions immediately decline and the power output quickly drops. It needs little

THE ENGINE AND GEARBOX 81

imagination to appreciate that to lift a motor-cycle and rider several hundred feet in a few minutes requires an enormous expenditure of energy. It can only be done *slowly* and on a large throttle opening. In other words, the speed of the engine must be kept high and the speed of the machine kept low. It is the purpose of the gearbox to enable the ratio of the engine speed to the rear-wheel speed to be varied while riding, and it accomplishes this in a simple manner. The mechanical principle on which it depends is the fact that the speed of rotation of any point on the circumference of a disc or wheel is proportional to the radius or diameter of the wheel. Hence, if two discs, one having twice the diameter of the other, are rotating with their circumferences in contact, one disc will rotate twice as fast as the other. A gearbox is simply an arrangement of toothed wheels mounted on a *mainshaft* and *layshaft* to secure gear reductions other than those obtained by the external sprockets for the primary and secondary drives. Sliding clutches, or gears having clutches, are used to bring about the variation in gear ratio and these sliding members are coupled up to the hand or foot control lever. With top gear engaged no gear reduction occurs in the gearbox, and the gear ratio is thus a ratio of the effective differences in diameters of the sprockets. The circumference, however, bears a constant ratio to the diameter and therefore the top gear ratio can be obtained by the following formula—

$$\text{Top gear ratio} = \frac{\text{No. of teeth on clutch sprocket} \times \text{No. on rear wheel sprocket}}{\text{No. of teeth on engine sprocket} \times \text{No. on gearbox sprocket}}$$

To find a gear ratio approximately, place the machine on the stand and engage the gear concerned. Take a note of the position of the valve in the rear wheel and rotate the wheel one complete revolution. Observe how many turns the engine sprocket makes till the valve returns to its original position. This is the gear ratio.

THE BURMAN FOUR-SPEED GEARBOX (Fitted to Most 1935–9 Ariel Models)

A general description of the Burman four-speed countershaft gearbox and four-plate shock-absorber clutch has already been given on page 16, and here we will consider how the various gear changes are obtained. A sectional elevation of the gearbox is shown in Fig. 43 and the references in the following paragraphs refer to this illustration.

Clutch Operation. Immediately before a gear change is made the engine has to be disconnected from the gearbox. When the clutch

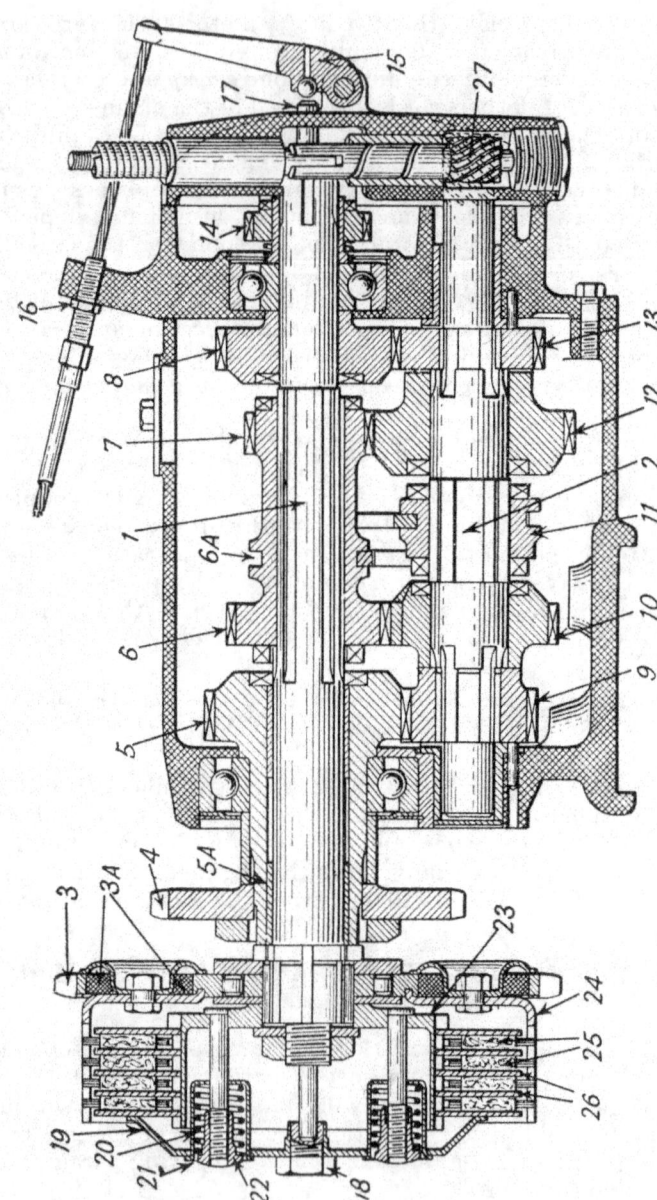

Fig. 43. Sectional View of Burman Four-speed Gearbox and Four-plate Shock-absorber Clutch
The key to the numbered parts is given opposite. For an illustration of the clutch parts dismantled, see page 164.

THE ENGINE AND GEARBOX

KEY TO FIG. 43

1 = Mainshaft (splined)
2 = Layshaft (splined)
3 = Clutch sprocket
3A = Clutch shock-absorber
4 = Gearbox sprocket
5 = Mainshaft fourth gear
5A = Mainshaft sleeve
6 = Mainshaft second (sliding) gear
6A = Groove for striking fork
7 = Mainshaft first (sliding) gear
8 = Mainshaft third gear
9 = Layshaft driving pinion (keyed)
10 = Layshaft second gear
11 = Layshaft clutch
12 = Layshaft first gear
13 = Layshaft third gear (keyed)
14 = Mainshaft K.S. pinion
15 = Clutch actuating lever
16 = Clutch cable adjustment
17 = Clutch operating plunger
18 = Clutch adjuster screw and locknut
19 = Clutch spring plate
20 = Clutch springs
21 = Clutch spring cup
22 = Clutch spring adjuster
23 = Clutch centre
24 = Clutch disked back-plate
25 = Clutch friction insert plates
26 = Clutch-driven steel plates
27 = Worm speedometer drive

handlebar lever is pulled back, the cable pulls forward the actuating lever (15) and the ball near its fulcrum pushes forward the steel plunger (17) floating in the hollow mainshaft (1). This plunger abuts against the adjuster screw (18) situated in the centre of the outer spring plate (19) and therefore the latter is also pushed outwards, taking with it the four radially arranged spring cups (21) and compressing the springs. The effect of this obviously is that the friction insert plates (25) are no longer gripped between the five steel plates (26), and although the clutch sprocket rotates together with the four friction plates which have tongues fitting into the disked backplate (24), the clutch centre (23), secured to the mainshaft and carrying the steel plates, does not rotate and no motion is imparted to the mainshaft *by the engine*. It is completely disconnected from the gearbox although the clutch sprocket is driven by the primary chain. But as soon as the clutch is released the clutch sprocket and mainshaft rotate together.

The Gearbox. The layshaft (2) always rotates while *the machine* is in motion, for the secondary chain drives the gearbox sprocket (4) which is attached to the mainshaft fourth gear (5), the two being able to revolve about the mainshaft on a common sleeve (5A). The layshaft revolves because the layshaft driving gear is fixed to the layshaft and in constant mesh with the mainshaft fourth gear (5). The speedometer drive (27) is thus taken off an extension of the layshaft and the gear trains are arranged so that the speedometer accurately records the speed of the machine on any gear. Adjacent to the layshaft driving gear (9) is the second layshaft gear (10) free to rotate on the layshaft and in constant mesh with the mainshaft second gear (6) which is integral with the mainshaft first gear (7). The gears 6 and 7 constitute the sliding mainshaft gears and can be moved left or right along the splined mainshaft by a striking fork situated at 6A. The mainshaft first gear (7) is in constant mesh with the layshaft first gear (12) which is quite free on the layshaft. On the extreme right are the mainshaft and layshaft third gears shown at 8 and 13 respectively. These are in constant mesh, but the mainshaft gear is free and the layshaft gear is fixed. Between the layshaft second and first gears is the layshaft clutch (11) which has toothed projections for engaging internal toothed rings on these gears and can be slid by a striker along the short layshaft splines left or right. Similar gear clutches are provided on the mainshaft sliding gears. The kick-starter pinion, it will be noticed, is mounted on the mainshaft and therefore rotates the clutch sprocket directly. With regard to the clutch, it will be readily apparent that its main function is to provide a means of synchronizing the speeds of layshaft and mainshaft driven gears to enable the gear clutches to be brought into action readily without noise or damage. This synchronizing is effected by skilled use of the throttle and clutch.

" **Neutral.**" The position of the mainshaft sliding gears and the layshaft clutch for "neutral" is shown in Fig. 43. The drive is passed from the clutch sprocket to the mainshaft and sliding gears, but nothing happens except that the layshaft second and first gears (12, 10) idle on the layshaft. The drive is not passed on to the gearbox sprocket because the layshaft is not set in motion.

First Gear. The layshaft clutch (11) is moved until its right-hand teeth engage the internally cut teeth on the layshaft first gear (12). This locks the gear to the layshaft and the drive is taken *via* the clutch sprocket and mainshaft to the layshaft through the meshing mainshaft and layshaft first gears (7, 12). It is then transmitted to the mainshaft sleeve and gearbox sprocket by means of the layshaft driving pinion (9) and the mainshaft first gear (5). Two large gear reductions are obtained on account of the differences in diameters of the four gears concerned.

Second Gear. In this case the layshaft clutch (11) is moved to the left until the layshaft second gear (10) is locked to the layshaft. The drive from the clutch sprocket is then transmitted from the mainshaft to the layshaft through the mainshaft and layshaft second gears (6, 10) and is then passed to the gearbox sprocket *via* the layshaft driving pinion (9) and the mainshaft first gear (5). Here again two gear reductions occur, but owing to the small difference in diameters of the first set of gears the total gear reduction is not so large as in the former case.

Third Gear. The layshaft clutch is retained in the "neutral" position but the mainshaft sliding gears are moved across to the right until the clutch teeth of the mainshaft third gear (7) engage

THE ENGINE AND GEARBOX 85

the internally cut teeth on the mainshaft third gear (8), so locking this gear to the mainshaft. The drive is passed from the clutch sprocket and mainshaft to the layshaft through the mainshaft and layshaft third gears (8, 13) and finally is transmitted to the gearbox sprocket in the usual way *via* the layshaft driving pinion (9) and the mainshaft fourth gear (5). Two pairs of gears are concerned but a reduction occurs only in the case of the second pair and the total gear reduction is not very great. The third gears neutralize to a small extent (the mainshaft gear being larger than the layshaft gear) the reduction effect of the second pair of gears.

Fourth Gear. With the layshaft clutch in the "neutral" position, the mainshaft sliding gears are moved across to the left until the second gear clutch (6) engages the internal gear of the fourth gear (5). This locks the fourth gear to the mainshaft and the clutch sprocket, gearbox sprocket, and mainshaft rotate together as one. No gear reduction at all occurs within the gearbox and the layshaft only idles, none of its gears being brought into use except the driving pinion (9). We thus have top gear or direct drive.

Do not Forget the Gearbox is Intended for Use. Many riders do not make full use of the gearbox, and it is a common occurrence to see machines being driven slowly on large throttle openings with top gear engaged. The author would point out, particularly to novices, that this is an extremely harmful habit, as it not only subjects the engine bearings to severe stresses but also causes transmission "snatch" which quickly wears the tyres, chains, and sprockets. *Never allow an engine* to continue knocking. At the first indication of the engine labouring, change to a lower gear. Driving conditions vary greatly and it is not possible to lay down hard and fast rules as to the road speeds at which gear changes should be made, but the following may be regarded as a rough guide. Do not travel at less than 18–20 m.p.h. in top gear or 12–15 m.p.h. in middle gear. On a hill, change down into middle gear if the speed drops below about 24–25 m.p.h., and into bottom gear if the speed drops below about 12–15 m.p.h.

CHAPTER VII

LUBRICATION

A SEPARATE chapter has been allotted to the subject of lubrication because this is one of the most vital aspects of motor-cycle maintenance. Failure to provide the right kind and right amount of lubrication speedily destroys mechanical efficiency and ultimately renders necessary the replacement of worn or damaged parts far sooner than would be ordinarily be required. Serious neglect may result in a completely ruined engine. It should always be borne in mind that lubricating oil is virtually the "life-blood" of an engine. So long as a microscopically thin film of oil is maintained between all moving parts the engine will run smoothly and efficiently, but the moment that film deteriorates or is absent, the engine becomes "rough" due to friction and heat and may quickly seize up. When an engine seizes the cylinder and piston are usually scored and perhaps distorted, and no subsequent care will restore them to their original condition. In the case of the engine the lubricating oil not only prevents friction between sliding surfaces such as the piston and cylinder (the former incidentally reciprocates at an average speed of about 25 m.p.h.), but also acts as a shock-absorbing medium at the big- and small-ends and assists in the dissipation of heat from the piston. Since engine lubrication is more important than the lubrication of the cycle-parts we will consider this first.

ENGINE LUBRICATION

The Dry Sump Lubrication System. The dry sump lubrication systems used on the single-cylinder models and the 1932–6 4F have already been described on pages 13 and 33 respectively. To make it more clear to the reader exactly how the oil is circulated on all the singles, a *diagram* of the entire circulation is shown in Fig. 44, and details of the Ariel pump arrangement and feed are illustrated in Fig. 44A. The oil is gravity-fed from the tank to the delivery side of the double plunger pump, which is driven by an eccentric off the camshaft, and is then pressure-fed *via* a pipe projecting into the hollow mainshaft to the big-end bearing, from which it is splashed on to the piston and cylinder, the surplus draining to the sump to be returned to the tank by

LUBRICATION

the return side of the pump. One filter, it will be observed, is incorporated in the tank and one in the sump. The diagram shows the auxiliary oil-feed taken off the main feed for the two valve guides (in the case of the O.H.V. engines). On the side-valve engines oil mist from the timing gear enters the valve chest and lubricates the valves. The auxiliary feed is shown dotted to distinguish it from the main feed, which is shown as a continuous line. The arrows indicate clearly how the oil circulates.

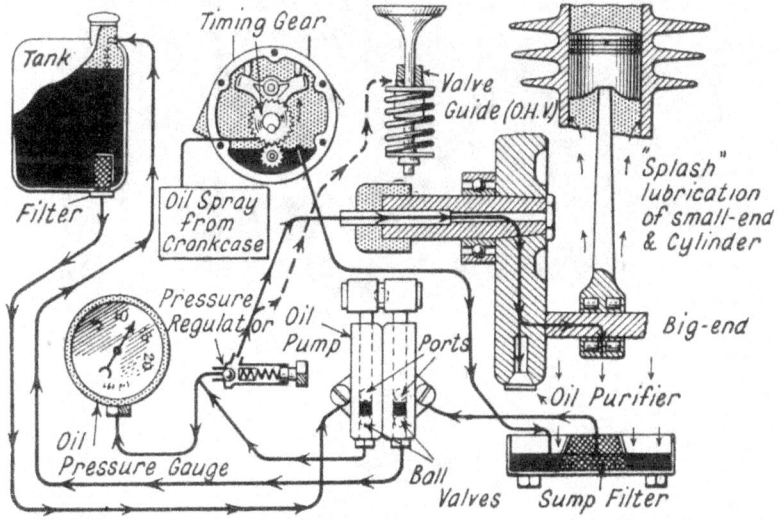

FIG. 44. SHOWING DIAGRAMMATICALLY HOW THE OIL CIRCULATES ON THE SINGLE-CYLINDER MODELS

Points to note are the pressure gauge with a pressure regulator (see page 89) ingeniously incorporated, and the oil purifier (see page 93) embodied in one of the flywheels. On 1938-9 O.H.V. engines oil is fed to the drilled O.H. rocker spindles and lubricates the rockers, push-rod ends, and valve guides.

The Double Plunger Pump. The double plunger pump used on the singles and shown dismantled in Fig. 45 is of very simple design, and it is easy to understand its method of working. The phosphor-bronze pump body, which is screwed to the timing case cover by two fixing screws, comprises in effect two cylinders, one having a bore about twice as big as the other. The cylinder with the larger bore forms the return side of the pump and the other one the delivery side. The return side of the pump is of larger capacity than the delivery side because its duty is to scavenge all oil collected in the sump and return it to the tank. Closely

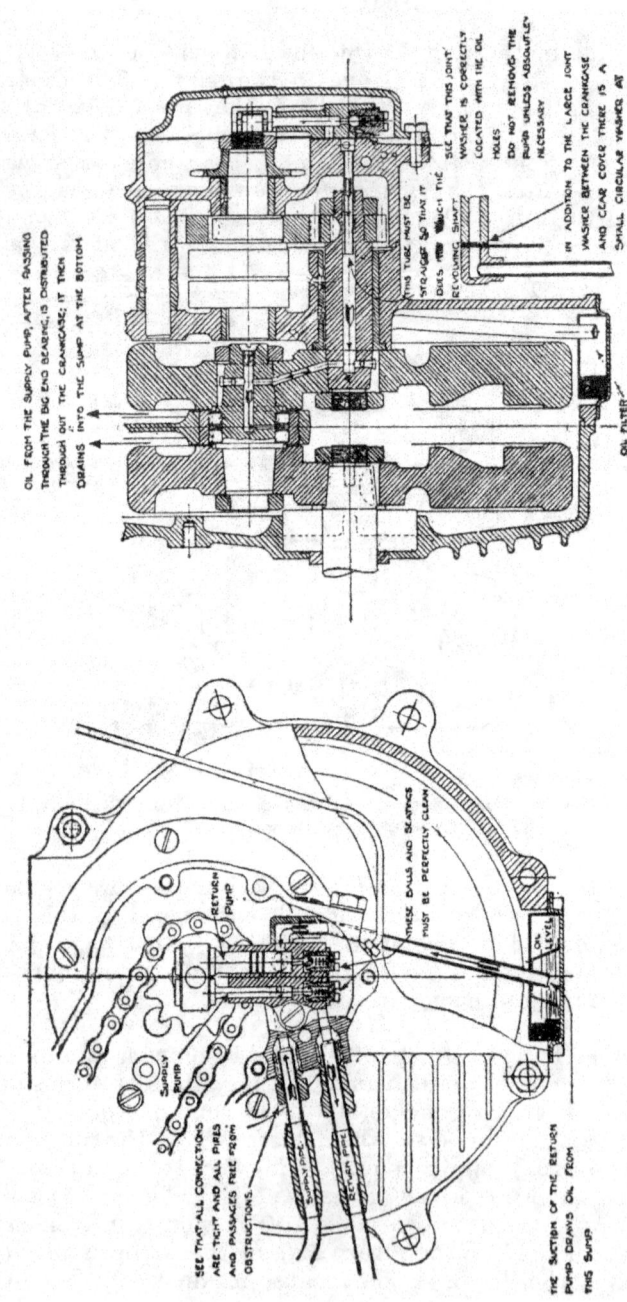

Fig. 44a. The Arrangement of the Ariel Pump on the Single-cylinder Models and Details of the Oil Feed to the Big-end Bearing

LUBRICATION

fitting the two cylinders are the delivery and return plungers which, as may be seen in Fig. 45, are provided at their upper ends with rectangular-shaped bearings to take a duralumin sliding block. This block has a large hole in its centre to engage the eccentric boss (which is really a crank) on the end of the camshaft (see Fig. 71). Thus, as the camshaft revolves, the block slides to and fro in the plunger bearings and at the same time moves up and down. Consequently the delivery and return plungers are caused to reciprocate in the cylinders at a speed

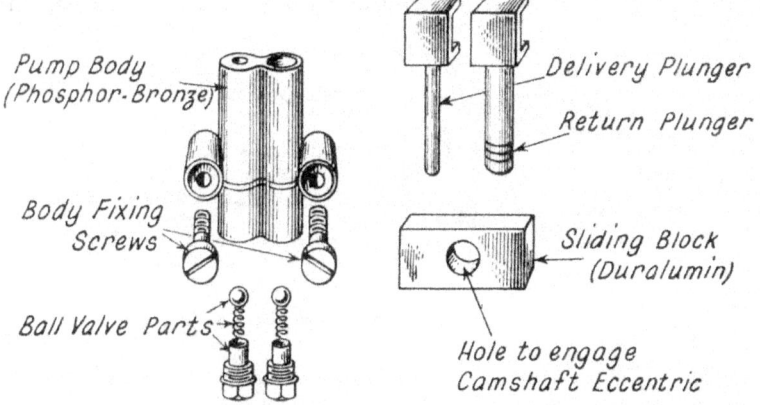

FIG. 45. THE ECCENTRIC DRIVEN DOUBLE PLUNGER OIL PUMP DISMANTLED

proportional to the engine speed. During the upward strokes of the delivery and return plungers oil is drawn into the cylinders from the tank and sump respectively through ports unmasked by the plungers, and as the plungers begin their down strokes these inlet ports are again masked and the oil at the bottom of the strokes is forced past spring-loaded ball valves, formerly kept closed, back into the tank *via* the return pipe and into the engine *via* a pipe projecting into the hollow mainshaft spindle. This can be understood by reference to Fig. 44.

The Oil Pressure Gauge and Regulator. As soon as the oil pump starts working, the oil pressure on the delivery side of the lubrication system (see Fig. 44) is registered by the oil pressure gauge housed at the rear of the tank-mounted instrument panel (Fig. 1). This instrument should give a normal reading of 10–15 lb. per sq. in. To enable the gauge to be set to give this pressure an oil pressure regulator is incorporated between the pump and the feed to the engine. Details of the regulator are shown in Fig. 46. The regulator body is screwed into the right-hand side of the pump housing below the pump, and contains at its inner end a ball valve operated by a coil compression spring partly enclosed in a brass ferrule able to slide in the regulator body. At the other end is an external adjuster screw with locknut. By screwing up or unscrewing the adjuster screw the pressure required to lift the ball off its seat can be varied. Oil from the pump passing along the passage A cannot enter the passage B leading to the engine until it has first lifted the ball off its seat; and since the oil in the passage A is in direct communication with the oil pressure

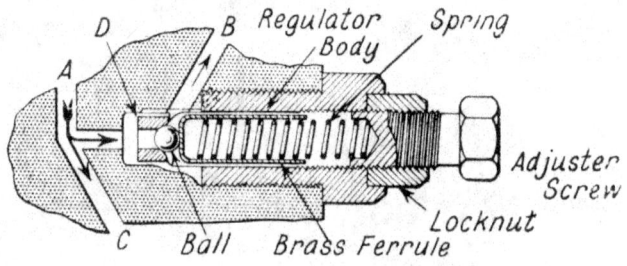

FIG. 46. THE OIL PRESSURE REGULATOR

gauge *via* the passage C, the pressure registered by the oil gauge is equal to the pressure needed to pass the ball valve. To enable the gauge needle to return to zero when the engine stops, the inner end of the regulator body is made slightly smaller than the hole into which it fits, so that oil leaks back from the gauge between them at the point D. Once the pressure regulator has been adjusted to give the correct gauge reading it should not subsequently be interfered with.

It should be noted that on the early 4F models the oil supply to the camshaft can be increased by increasing the oil pressure. By removing the cam box lid the flow can be checked. It should be 35–40 drops per minute with a hot engine.

To increase the oil supply to the camshaft rotate the regulator screw clockwise. It should be noted that increasing the oil pressure does not affect the oil supply to the lower engine parts.

On the single-cylinder models increasing the oil pressure has no effect whatever, and the regulator is only provided to enable a normal reading of 10–15 lb. per sq. in. to be obtained. The quantity of oil passed into the engine is governed solely by the efficiency of the pump and the speed of the engine. On the 1937 4F model and the 1936 4G models the oil pressure regulator is on the timing cover and should be set to give an oil pressure of 60 lb. per sq. in. On the 1937–9 Model 4G set to 40–45 lb. per sq. in.

LUBRICATION

The flow of oil can be tested by removing the plug above the regulator when, with the engine running, oil will be pumped out at this point instead of passing along the oilways to the mainshaft and big-end bearings.

The oil supply can also be checked by removing the oil filler cap on the tank and seeing that the oil is returned *via* the return pipe. The oil will come through in a continuous stream for a few seconds when the engine is first started, but the flow will rapidly decrease until the oil is returning in a series of bubbles. This is the normal condition of the returning oil. See also page 99.

Attention to the D.S. Lubrication System. No adjustment whatever is provided for the pump used on the Ariels. Lubrication is therefore entirely automatic and the rider is relieved of all responsibility other than the regular replenishment of the oil tank and occasional cleaning of the filters in the tank and crank-case. Accumulated deposits in the oil purifier must also be cleaned out from time to time, and on the 1932-7 overhead-valve engines the grease gun must periodically be used to lubricate the overhead rocker bearings.

Oil Replenishment. This has already been dealt with on page 54 and the author would stress the vital importance of using only a good oil and the correct *grade* of oil. Patent Castrol and Mobiloil have been recommended on page 54, but it should be mentioned that other oils (page 63) are also suitable. Never buy "loose" oil, as its lubricating qualities may be poor, and it may cause untold damage. Castrol R is recommended for racing purposes on the O.H.V. and O.H.C. models, but this vegetable oil must never be mixed with a mineral oil, such as Patent Castrol XL or XXL, or Mobiloil D. It should be remembered that when changing over from R to a mineral oil, or *vice versa*, in a four-cylinder engine, it is not sufficient merely to drain the crank-case. The whole engine must be dismantled and thoroughly cleaned. The reason for this is that the oiling system of the four-cylinder engine incorporates a number of troughs and oil ducts from which it is impossible for lubricating oil to escape by itself, even though the sump may be drained.

Inspect the level of oil in the tank every 250 miles and top up if necessary. Do not fill the tank above 1 in. below the return pipe and do not let the level drop below about two-thirds.

On the 1932-6 4F check the level of oil in the sump regularly with the dip stick. Keep the level within the limits of the flat. On the 1937 4F and 1937-9 4G keep the oil tank as full as possible and do not let the level fall below the mark on the tank.

The use of an upper cylinder lubricant, a practice followed by many motor-cyclists, is quite sound (page 63), but on the S.V. and O.H.C. models inlet and exhaust valves are lubricated automatically, and on the O.H.V. models there is a positive feed to the inlet and exhaust valve guides.

Keep a Watchful Eye on the Pressure Gauge. This is advisable because as long as a pressure of 10–15 lb. per sq. in. is maintained it shows that the oil is circulating correctly. Should the pressure gauge fail, or should the rider feel in any way dubious about the oil circulation, it is easily checked on the single-cylinder models by removing the oil filler cap (with the engine running), and seeing that oil is being returned from the engine to the tank *via* the oil pipe just beneath the filler cap (see Fig. 44). On 1932–6 overhead-camshaft models oil circulation can be verified by removing the lid of the cam box. When starting from cold the oil pressure may vary considerably from the normal reading, but as the oil warms up the pressure should not exceed 15 lb. per sq. in. and not be less than 10 lb. per sq. in. on the singles.

If the Pressure Fluctuates. Undue fluctuation in oil pressure should immediately divert the rider's attention to the oil level in the tank or sump in the case of the single- and four-cylinder models (type 4F). If the level is found to be correct (see page 91) obviously a shortage of oil is not causing the trouble, and the most likely alternative is that some dirt in the pressure regulator is causing the ball valve to behave irregularly. In this case the regulator (Fig. 46) should be dismantled and cleaned. When refitting, see that the closed end of the brass ferrule is next to the ball. The order of reassembly is: ball valve, ferrule, spring, adjuster screw, and locknut.

Other possible causes of an erratic or insufficient oil supply are: (*a*) slack pipe connections; (*b*) dirty filters; (*c*) dirty pump ball valves; (*d*) choked oil pipes; (*e*) damaged delivery pipe into mainshaft; (*f*) bad joint between pump face and timing case. In the case of the single-cylinder models it is necessary to remove the magneto chain-case cover (integral with the pump housing) in order to gain access to the ball valves, but on the 1932–6 Model 4F access to the ball valve is obtained *via* the plug at the top end of the groove running up the side of the crank-case just below the timing chain covers.

Rocker-box Lubrication (1934–7 O.H.V.). Although some oil mist penetrates to the rocker-box between the push-rods and covers, this is totally inadequate for lubrication purposes, and to prevent wear of the large size bearings used for the overhead rockers a grease-gun should be applied to the two rocker-box grease nipples about once every 300–400 miles.

LUBRICATION

Grease is forced through the hollow spindles to a central recess and is forced along holes drilled through the rocker arms to the ball-ends which bear in cups at the top ends of the push-rods. Lubricate with Castrolease G (which contains graphite) or Castrolease Medium once every 300–400 miles. See also page 99.

The Ariel Oil Purifier. The centrifugal oil purifier, which is incorporated in the flywheel on all single-cylinder Ariels, is an absolutely automatic and mechanical device for separating dust, grit, dirt, etc., from the oil. No matter how clean an oil is used,

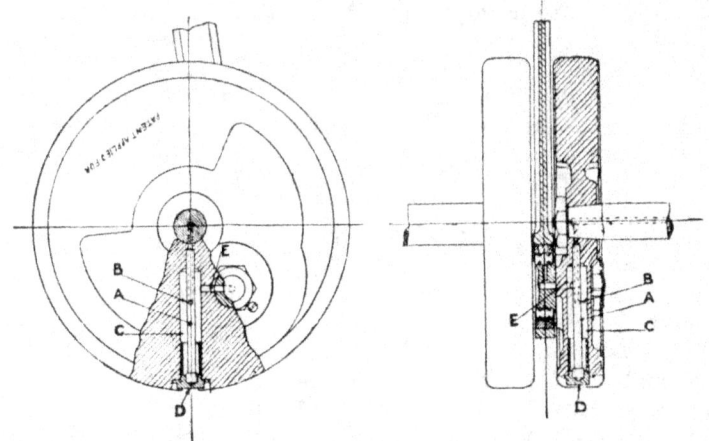

FIG. 47. THE CENTRIFUGAL OIL PURIFIER
Provided on all Ariel Models except the Square Four.

dirt and grit will get drawn into the engine *via* the carburettor, and unless this grit is removed immediately it will help to wear away the bearings. The Ariel oil purifier removes this grit. On "Red Hunters" oil from the hollow mainshaft spindle passes straight into the flywheel reservoir. On other models as follows—

The oil leaves the hollow timing side mainshaft and passes half way along the steel tube A (Fig. 47), emerging at the hole B; this tube is solid at the end away from the centre of the flywheel. As the oil passes from the tube into the reservoir C, the dirt and grit, etc., is thrown by centrifugal force into the cupped cleaning plug D, whilst the purified oil travels back towards the centre of the fly-wheel and enters the crankpin *via* the passage E.

To get at the purifier, remove the crank-case sump by undoing the four set bolts, and drop the sump complete with filter. Rotate the engine until the plug D is immediately above the sump and then undo the plug; this is locked in position by means of a tab washer. When the plug is removed, the dirt (if present in any quantity) will be found packed quite hard inside the cup formed in the plug, and must be removed with the blade of a penknife. See that the tube A is not damaged, and if it drops out replace with the large end in the plug. The plug locates the tube and keeps it in position.

The dirt which has collected in the cupped plug D should be cleared away about every 5,000 to 8,000 miles under normal conditions of use. Where the motor-cycle is used in particularly dusty conditions, so that there is a proportionately greater chance of grit being drawn in through the carburettor, the plug can be removed for cleaning at shorter intervals. It is not a bad plan to remove the plug whenever the filters are being attended to.

When replacing the plug, see that it is screwed up dead tight *and do not forget the tab washer*; one end must be turned up by the side of a flat on the plug. Use a new tab washer every second or third time the plug is removed, as repeated bending of the metal will cause the end tab to break off the washer.

Oil Filters (S.V. and O.H.V.). The sump should be detached and the gauze filter cleaned about once every 1,500 miles. When replacing, see that the suction pipe is located in the hole in the top of the gauze, and do not forget the joint washer. Wire up the set bolts to prevent loss.

Although the Ariel oil purifier will remove all dirt, etc., from the oil, it cannot turn old oil into new, and it therefore becomes necessary to throw away the used oil as it loses its lubricating properties. This is recommended about every 1,000 miles. A suitable drain plug is provided at the bottom of the oil tank.

When draining the oil tank it is desirable to clean the gauze filter in the oil tank. Unscrew the hexagon plug at the base of the tank, clean the gauze in petrol, and replace. See that the delivery oil pipe, which projects right into the tank in line with the filter, is located inside the gauze and screw up the plug securely.

Oil Filters (O.H.C.). The gauze filter in the 1932–6 crankcase sump should be removed and cleaned every 1,000–1,500 miles and at the same time the old oil should be discarded and the crank-case swilled out and refilled with clean oil. Be sure when replacing the sump filter that the internal return pipe is located in the hole through the gauze and support.

On the 1935–6 4F, the felt pad filter housed in the tubular aluminium casing below the camshaft chain-case should be cleaned every 500–750 miles, but if this filter keeps fairly free of impurities the period of cleaning may be extended. To clean this filter undo the end plug and take out the felt filter. Then remove the two locknuts on the centre rod and take off the pair of end plates. Now thoroughly wash the filter in petrol and replace it, being careful to screw up the locknuts to their former positions. This is very important because they control the spring tension of the relief valve which allows the lubricant to by-pass the filter in the event of it getting choked with dirty oil. Be careful not to omit the fixing spring inside the end cap and holding the filter against the shoulder in the casing.

On the 1937 4F and 1937-9 4G it is recommended that the tank and sump should be drained about every 1,000-1,500 miles, when the gauze filter on the inner end of the delivery pipe connection in the oil tank together with the filter in the sump should be withdrawn and cleaned in petrol.

Swill out the tank with petrol to remove all traces of sludge and dirt and refill with fresh oil.

Magneto and Dynamo Lubrication. The bearings of all Lucas magnetos and "Magdynos" are packed with grease by the manufacturers, and no further lubrication is required until a mileage of over 20,000 has been covered. The rider can therefore practically disregard these components as far as lubrication is concerned. In order, however, to minimize wear of the fibre heel of the contact-breaker provision is made for the oiling of the cam rings. A pocket in the contact-breaker housing contains a length of felt soaked in oil, and in the cam ring there is a hole filled with a wick to enable the oil to find its way on to the cam ring surface. It is advisable every 5,000 miles to withdraw the cam ring and place a few drops of *thin* oil on the felt. If this is done it will be found that the magneto will run for long periods without it being necessary to adjust the gap between the contacts. See also notes on page 116.

On 1932 models with a "Maglita" fitted, some oil should be placed in the bearing hole (see Fig. 50A) every 1,000 miles, and at the same time a spot of oil should be applied to the cam surface of the contact-breaker on which the tappet runs, as this will reduce wear and rusting. Excessive oiling, however, will tend to cause misfiring.

THE CYCLE PARTS

Gearbox Lubrication. Never fill the Burman gearbox with a thick and heavy grease, as this not only interferes with easy gear changing but also renders it very likely that some of the gears will run dry. It is particularly important in the case of the four-speed gearboxes having gear type clutches. All Burman gearboxes are sent out filled with grease and they should be

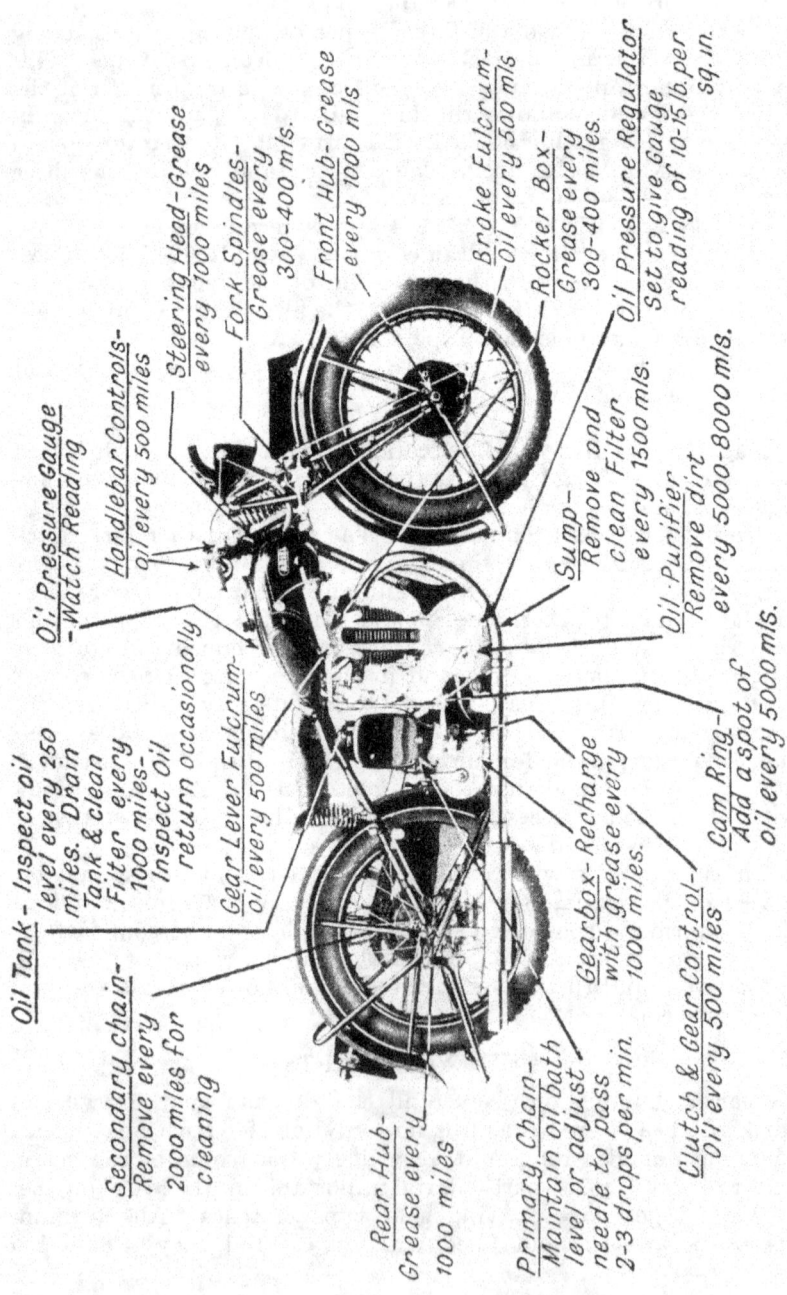

Fig. 48. Lubrication Chart Showing When and Where to Lubricate (See Page 99)

LUBRICATION

replenished every 1,000 miles with approximately 2–3 oz. of either Wakefield's "Castrolease Medium," Gargoyle "Mobilgrease No. 2," or Price's Belmoline C. A gearbox should not be completely filled or grease will be forced out of the bearings. To obtain the best results it should be filled about *one-third* full. When replenishing, rotation of the kick-starter will assist matters. The various gear-change mechanism joints should be oiled about every 500 miles. Do not overlook the fulcrum of the gear lever itself and the various joints and pivots. These should be oiled about every 500 miles. On the four-speed gearboxes when topping up, also grease the enclosed foot-change mechanism, the kick-starter lever bearing, and the spiral gears for the speedometer drive *via* the grease nipples provided. See page 169.

Clutch Lubrication. About every 500 miles the external clutch operation should be oiled, and occasionally the clutch operating plunger should be removed from the hollow mainshaft and greased. It is particularly important that this plunger should be able to slide backwards and forwards with absolute freedom, otherwise it is impossible to maintain an "easy" clutch action. Do not forget to keep the small actuating lever well lubricated, particularly at the point where the ball is in contact with the plunger.

About once a year the roller bearing of the clutch sprocket should be removed and packed with grease.

The Engine Shaft Shock Absorber. In the case of machines provided with oil-bath chain-cases the shock absorber is automatically lubricated by the oil in the chain-case, but on other models the grease-gun should occasionally be applied to the nipple on the end of the mainshaft.

The Primary Chain. The primary chain runs at a high speed, and it is therefore important to keep it well lubricated. On oil-bath chain-case models the chain lower run dips into the oil, and provided the oil level is maintained correct the chain will continue to be properly lubricated. The oilbath (Fig. 4) should be replenished with engine oil whenever necessary. Keep the level up to the "oil level plug," but do not put excessive oil in or it will penetrate into the clutch and set up clutch drag. It should be noted that on some pre-1934 Ariels the position of the "oil level plug" is located a trifle too high up in the case, and should oil exude from the back of the case, or should a tendency for clutch drag be manifested, the oil-bath chain-case should be filled up to about $\frac{3}{8}$ in. *below* the plug.

On ordinary chain-case models the primary chain is automatically lubricated by an oil feed by-passed from the return oil supply and directed through a pipe on to the lower chain run. The oil supply is adjustable by means of a needle valve situated within the chain-case. Access to the adjuster screw can be obtained through a hole in the chain cover just to the rear of the engine sprocket. To obtain the best results adjust the needle valve to pass two to three drops of oil per minute.

The Secondary Chain. Automatic lubrication of the secondary chain is effected on the oil-bath models by an overflow from the oil-bath primary chain-case. This overflow only works when the engine is running, and is controllable by means of a needle valve in the primary chain-case just behind the clutch dome. In order to obtain the best setting observe the condition of the chain during a run, and if it is at all dry increase the overflow by turning the needle adjuster head anti-clockwise.

On the chain-case models the secondary chain is lubricated automatically by means of oil mist led to the chain by a pipe from the ball type engine breather situated underneath the magneto chain cover.

From time to time (say about once every 2,000 miles) it is a good plan to remove the secondary chain and immerse it in a bath of paraffin. The chain should be allowed to soak well to ensure all the dirt from the rollers being removed and afterwards hung up to dry. When the chain has been cleaned it is wise to lubricate it before refitting it to the sprockets. The best method of doing this is to soak the chain in a receptacle containing a mixture of hot graphite grease and engine oil which will permeate all the chain roller bearings. Heat the grease over hot water.

The Steering Head. Two grease nipples are provided for the ball bearings in the steering head, and the grease-gun should be applied to them about once every 1,000 miles. A medium bodied grease, such as that used for the gearbox, is suitable for the steering head and the other cycle parts.

Front Forks. The fork link spindles require periodic lubrication, and the grease gun should be applied to the grease nipples every 300–400 miles.

Wheel Hubs. Both the front and rear hubs should be charged with a medium-bodied grease roughly once every 1,000 miles. When a sidecar is fitted do not neglect to lubricate the sidecar hub. It is very important to keep the bearings of all wheels thoroughly greased, as they are called upon to carry very heavy stresses. Care should be taken not to overcharge the hubs or grease may be forced into the brake drums, with the result that

LUBRICATION

the brakes lose much of their efficiency. As soon as grease begins to leak past the dirt-excluding washers it indicates that the hubs are full and no more grease should be inserted.

Brakes. About every 500 miles each brake cam and fulcrum adjustment should be lightly greased or oiled, also the brake cam spindle, joints, and pedal shaft.

Sidecar Chassis. To prevent a tendency for squeaking it is wise to occasionally grease with graphite the front and rear ball-jointed connections. Also grease periodically the sliding joint at the base of the seat pillar connection tube.

Control Levers. It is possible to postpone the time when Bowden cable breakages occur by occasionally oiling or greasing the cables at places where they are apt to bind on the control mechanism on the handlebars. It is advisable when fitting new cables to charge the casings with grease.

Lubrication Chart. Although Fig. 48 shows a standard O.H.V. model, it applies in general to the whole range, but is intended as a guide rather than to be scrupulously complied with. In the case of 1938-9 models, there is, of course, no rocker-box to lubricate; while on 1932-6 overhead camshaft machines there is a rocker-box or cam-box, but it is automatically lubricated and the feed is adjustable by means of the oil pressure regulator. On this machine the oil is not carried in a separate tank but in the engine sump, and two filters are incorporated on the engine. The sump filter should be cleaned every 1,000-1,500 miles (see page 94).

Rocker-box Lubrication (1938-9). No grease nipples are provided on the 1938-9 models, the overhead valve gear being lubricated automatically. Oil is fed under pressure to the rockers and escaping oil lubricates the valve stems, valve guides, and the cup and ball joints between the push-rods and rockers. An important point to note is that if the valve clearances are excessive, oil leakage occurs at these joints causing a reduction in oil pressure. Therefore keep the clearances correct (see page 119). When the engine is just ticking over the pressure may fall to about 5 lb. per sq. in., but it should revert to 10 to 15 lb. per sq. in. when driving

Draining Oil-bath Chain Case. After a considerable mileage it is a good plan to drain the case and flush it out with paraffin. This may be done by removing the cheese-headed screw immediately below the footrest support.

CHAPTER VIII

CARE OF THE ELECTRICAL EQUIPMENT

It is the object of the present chapter to provide sufficient information concerning the Lucas electrical equipment, now fitted as standard on all Ariel models (see page 2), to enable the rider to maintain it in efficient condition. Not much attention is required, but in order to ensure a continuous powerful beam from the lamp of unvarying intensity when driving at night, a regular amount of care *must* be devoted to the electrical equipment, that is to say the battery and dynamo. Neglect of these two items is liable to cause a lot of unnecessary bother and expense, and perhaps result in the rider now and again becoming stranded in some remote spot. It is safe to say, however, that if the rider will faithfully observe the instructions given in this chapter he will travel thousands of miles without any serious trouble. Always remember "prevention is better than cure." This particularly applies in the case of the lighting equipment, because it is very difficult to cure things in the dark!

The generator used on all 1933-9 models is the Lucas 6-V "Magdyno," but as there are still many 1932 lightweight Ariels having the Lucas "Maglita" in use, this will be dealt with as well as the "Magdyno." The ignition part of the generator is dealt with in the next chapter. Lead-acid batteries of 12 amp.-hr. capacity are standardized on all present models, and the current is fed to an 8 in. diameter Lucas headlamp.

GENERATORS

The M.S. "Magdyno" (all 1933-7 Models). The "Magdyno," as its name implies, consists of two units: the magneto for ignition and the 6-volt dynamo for charging the battery. For the sake of compactness both units are housed together, as shown in Fig. 49, but the dynamo unit is detachable, so that riders who desire to enter their machines for racing and trials riding can easily strip off the whole of their lighting equipment. A suitable fitment is obtainable for protecting the gears when the dynamo unit is taken off. The complete generator weighs approximately 12 lb., and has a 30 watt dynamo (i.e. the output is 5 amp. at 6 volts).

A special feature of the "Magdyno" is the method of output control. The dynamo is fitted with two main brushes, and the positive is insulated and the negative earthed. A third brush

CARE OF THE ELECTRICAL EQUIPMENT 101

is provided on the underside of the commutator bracket which regulates the output at high speeds, thereby keeping it within safe limits. The dynamo is arranged to give an ample output

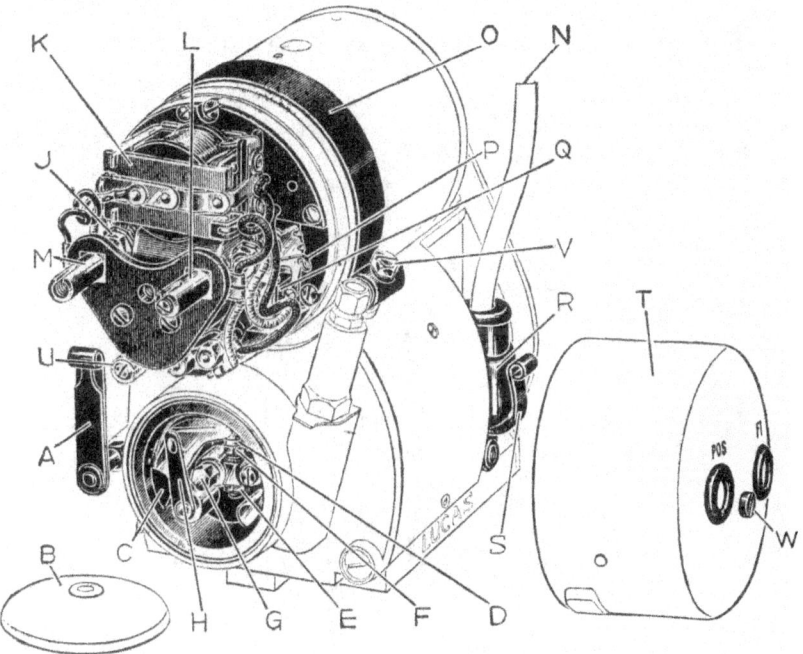

FIG. 49. THE LUCAS "MAGDYNO" FITTED TO 1933-7 MODELS

A = Securing spring for contact breaker cover
B = Contact breaker cover
C = Fibre heel
D = Contact points
E = Locking nut
F = Adjustable contact point
G = Contact breaker fixing screw
H = Locating spring
J = Nut securing brush eyelet
K = Cut-out
L = Terminal marked "F1"
M = Terminal marked "POS"
N = Cable to sparking plug
O = Dynamo securing strap
P = Spring lever holding brush in position
Q = Carbon brush
R = Pick-up
S = Securing spring for pick-up
T = Cover
U = Earthing terminal
V = Screw securing dynamo strap
W = Cover fixing screw

with the switch in the position for daylight running, and this ensures the battery being kept well charged. When the lamps are switched on the dynamo automatically gives an increased output which compensates for the lamp load and electric horn when fitted. This system of control is obtained by inserting in the dynamo field circuit a resistance which is automatically cut out whenever the lamps are switched on. The A.C. current is transformed into

D.C. by a two-brush commutator, above which is an electromagnetic cut-out mounted on the dynamo end bracket. This cut-out is an automatic switch, which prevents discharge of the battery when the dynamo is stationary. Its contacts close when the dynamo voltage rises above that of the battery as the engine is accelerated, and the contacts open when the speed drops and the voltage falls below that of the battery. It does not, however, prevent overcharging. The magneto portion of the "Magdyno" is similar in general design to the plain magneto used on non-electrically equipped models. See also page 116.

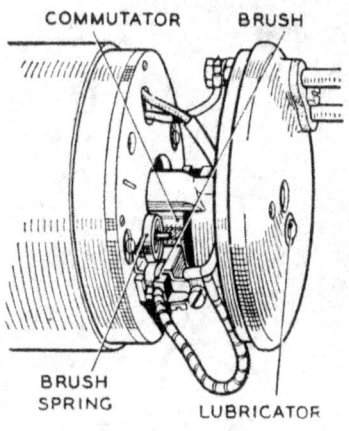

Fig. 50. Commutator End of Lucas "Magdyno" (Dynamo Portion) Fitted to the 1938-9 Models with Automatic Voltage Control

The F.D. "Maglita" (1932 Lightweight Models). This generator works on quite a different principle to the "Magdyno." Only one armature is provided, and this serves the dual purpose of supplying H.T. current for ignition and L.T. current for lighting. A view of the "Maglita" is shown in Fig. 50A, and the essential features of maintenance are well shown. It has an output of approximately 16 watts at 6 volts at 2,000 r.p.m., with a maximum output of 20 watts. The armature has an L.T. primary winding only, and revolves between laminated pole pieces, the upper pole being split and bridged by the ignition core. The magnetic flux is provided by two straight cobalt steel magnets, and as the armature revolves the direction of the lines of force in the bridge portion is alternately reversed. It is this reversal of the magnetic flux which is responsible for the ignition spark, an H.T. current being

CARE OF THE ELECTRICAL EQUIPMENT 103

generated in the stationary ignition coil (by induction) immediately the L.T. primary circuit is interrupted by the contact breaker. The contact breaker is of special design (see Fig. 50A), and quite different to that on the Lucas "Magdynos" or magnetos. A face cam causes movement of a tappet to separate the tungsten contacts and the correct "break" is ·010 in. The end of the ignition coil or secondary winding is connected to an insulated terminal on one of the end plates. A commutator is provided on the armature for rectification, and the usual type of carbon brush is used.

An automatic cut-out is enclosed in a case and carried on the end of the armature. It comprises two contacts, one connected to the end of the armature winding, and the other to the commutator, one brush of which is earthed and the other connected to the battery. With the engine running the contacts are closed by a pivoted rocker arm actuated by centrifugal force. A sliding locking weight is used to prevent the contacts closing when the "Maglita" is revolved in the reverse direction due to the engine back-firing. Both the lighting and ignition circuits are independent of each other, and a resistance in the dynamo-field circuit prevents overcharging of the battery with the switch in the "charge" position. A "Maglita" wiring diagram will be found on page 113.

DYNAMO MAINTENANCE (1932-7)

Before removing the cover for any reason, it is advisable to disconnect the positive lead of the battery to avoid the danger of reversing the polarity of the dynamo or short-circuiting the battery, either of which might cause serious damage.

If at any time a " Magdyno" equipped motor-cycle must be ridden with the battery disconnected, or in any way out of service, it is essential to run with the switch in the "OFF" position.

With the "Maglita" the lamps, in case of emergency, can be run direct off the generator, by disconnecting the battery and turning the control switch to the full "on" position. Under these circumstances the engine speed should be kept down below about 2,500 r.p.m., as otherwise the lamps may burn out. Never run the generator direct with the switch in the "dim" position, as this is likely to burn out both the pilot and tail bulbs. If direct running is necessary, put the control switch to full "on" either before starting up or while the engine is turning over very slowly. Always turn the control switch to the "off" position after stopping the engine, as this prevents the possible discharging of the battery in the event of the cut-out sticking.

Brushes. It is very important to make sure that the brushes work freely in their holders. This can be easily ascertained by holding back the spring lever and gently pulling each flexible lead, when the brush should move without the slightest suggestion of sluggishness. It should also return to its original position directly the lead is let go. When testing the brush in this way,

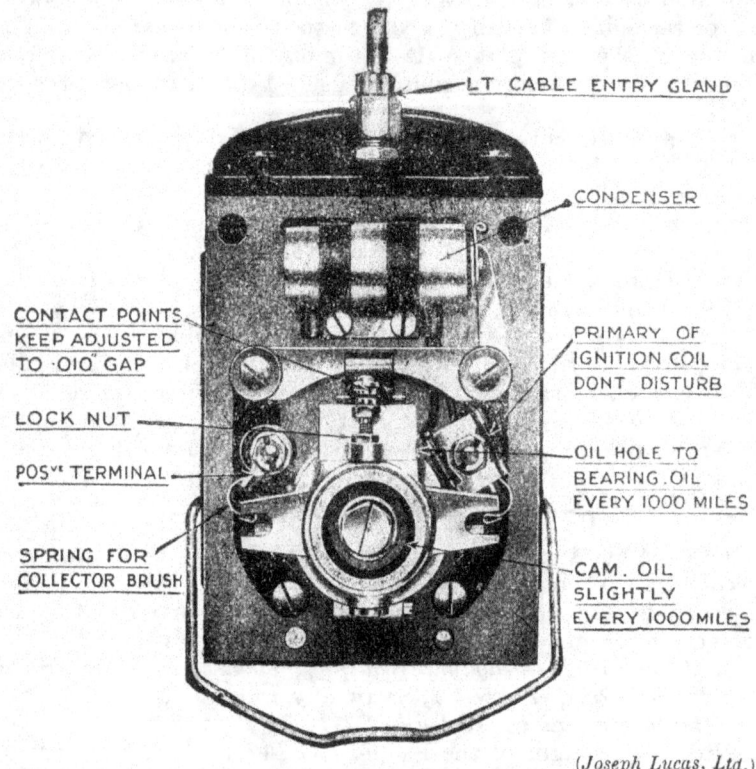

(*Joseph Lucas, Ltd.*)

Fig. 50a. Contact-breaker Side of F.D. "Maglita," Showing Some Points Requiring Attention

release it gently, otherwise it may get chipped. The brushes should be clean and "bed" over the whole surface; that is, the face in contact with the commutator segments should appear uniformly polished. Dirty brushes may be cleaned with a cloth moistened with petrol.

The brush springs should be inspected occasionally to see that they have sufficient tension to keep the brushes firmly pressed against the commutator when the machine is running. It is particularly necessary to keep this in mind when the brushes have

CARE OF THE ELECTRICAL EQUIPMENT 105

been in use a long time and are very much worn down. Do not insert brushes of a grade other than that supplied with the machine, and do not change the tension springs. It is advisable to inspect the brushes about every 3,000 miles in the case of both the "Magdyno" and the "Maglita."

Commutator. The surface of the commutator should be kept clean and free from oil or brush dust, etc. Should any grease or oil work its way on to the commutator through over-lubrication, it will not only cause sparking, but, in addition, carbon and copper dust will be collected in the grooves between the commutator segments. The best way to clean the commutator is, without disconnecting any leads, to remove from its box one of the main brushes and, inserting a fine duster in the box, hold it, by means of a suitably-shaped piece of wood, against the commutator surface, causing the armature to be rotated at the same time.

Cut-out. The cut-out on the "Magdyno" automatically closes, by means of solenoids, the charging circuit as soon as the dynamo voltage rises above that of the battery. When the dynamo voltage falls below that of the battery the reverse action takes place; that is, the cut-out opens and thereby prevents the battery from discharging itself through the dynamo. In the case of the "Maglita" the cut-out has a centrifugal control as already described on page 103.

The cut-out is accurately set before leaving the works, and should not be tampered with or adjusted. Should the cut-out fail to close the circuit on accelerating the engine, the cause of the damage is likely to be found elsewhere. There is no such relation between the operation of the cut-out and the state of charge of the battery.

Should the ammeter at any time show a heavy discharge, the volume of which is sufficient to push the needle right off the dial, then switch off immediately, or serious damage to the ammeter will result. If, when the switch has been put in the "off" position, the discharge still occurs, disconnect the battery positive lead as quickly as possible. Should the ammeter show a discharge of approximately 4 amp. when the switch is in the "off" position, engine still stationary and no lamps are observed to be lit, then the fault is in the dynamo cut-out. This is probably due to the cut-out points being in contact with each other; they might possibly have fused together. The remedy is to disconnect the battery positive immediately, and then clean and readjust the points. The points should be adjusted so that they cut in when the engine is travelling at such a speed as to provide a road speed of 18 m.p.h. on top gear. Connect up to battery positive before testing.

Absence of Fuses. In order to simplify the system as far as possible, no fuse is provided. If all the connections are kept clean and tight, there is no possibility of any excess current causing damage to the apparatus.

Lubrication. The armature bearings are packed with grease by the manufacturers and require no attention until a big mileage has been covered, when it is desirable to return a "Magdyno" or "Maglita" to a Lucas Service Department for cleaning and re-lubricating. Lubricate the magneto portion of the "Maglita" as indicated in Fig. 50A. See also page 116.

A Warning. On no account attempt to remove the dynamo armature unless this is done by a person having sound electrical knowledge, as de-magnetization of the magnets will probably be caused. Also do not adjust the cut-out.

LAMPS AND BATTERIES (1932-8)

The H.52 Headlamp (1932 Heavyweights). This lamp, used in connection with the "Magdyno," is fitted with a double filament main bulb, the one filament providing the normal driving light, while the second one gives an anti-dazzle dipped beam. A handle-bar switch controls the change-over from the normal driving light to the dipped beam. For parking purposes, or driving in well illuminated "built-up" areas, a small pilot bulb is provided.

A centre-zero ammeter is incorporated in the lamp itself, and gives the driver an indication of the amount of current in amperes by which the battery is being charged or discharged, according to the position of the lamp switch. When the lamp is switched on the ammeter is indirectly illuminated. A rotary switch mounted at the back of the lamp has the following positions—

"*Off*"—Lamps off, and dynamo not charging.
C—Lamps off and dynamo charging at half its normal output (i.e. at about 2½ amp.).
H—Headlamp (driving light), tail lamp, and sidecar lamp (when fitted) on; dynamo charging at its maximum output (4–5 amp.).
L—Pilot light, tail light, sidecar light; dynamo on full charge.

All cables are taken to the switch at the back of the headlamp, and this switch is readily removed by undoing two screws, when it can be withdrawn complete with the cables.

The lamp front can be easily detached, as it has a bayonet fixing. The parabolic reflector can also be quickly removed from its three supports. To ensure proper replacement, one of the slots in the reflector rim is marked "top." A special main bulb adjustment is provided for focusing. To move the bulb towards or away from the reflector, the bulb is rotated clockwise or anti-clockwise respectively. Each bulb rotation is indicated by the

CARE OF THE ELECTRICAL EQUIPMENT 107

clink action of a spring stop. The correct main bulb is a 24 watt Lucas No. 70, while the pilot bulb is a 3 watt No. 200.

The DU.142 Headlamp (all 1935–8 Models). This is an improved pattern of the H.52 headlamp, and incorporates a double filament main bulb for normal driving and anti-dazzle purposes, and a pilot bulb for parking and riding in well-lighted areas. As on the H.52 lamp, a centre-zero ammeter is fitted on top of the lamp, and the rotary switch is mounted at the back. The switch positions are the same as for the H.52 lamp on 1935–7 models.

The lamp front and reflector can be withdrawn for bulb replacement when the fixing clip is pressed back. When refitting, locate

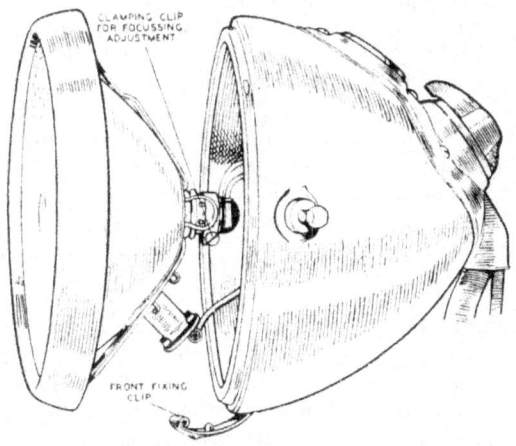

Fig. 51. The Lucas DU.142 Headlamp with Reflector and Front Removed

the top of the rim first. To remove the bulb-holder, press back the two securing springs. The main bulb can be focused by removing the lamp front and reflector and slackening the clamping screw which secures the bulb-holder. Move the holder and bulb until the most satisfactory results are obtained and finally tighten the clamping screw. With regard to bulb replacements, fit a 24 watt Lucas No. 70 main double filament bulb and a 3 watt No. 200 pilot bulb.

The M.40 Headlamp (1932 Lightweights). This headlamp used on the lightweights in conjunction with the Lucas M.L. "Maglita" houses the ammeter and rotary control switch. It has a double filament main bulb, giving anti-dazzle control by a handlebar switch, and a pilot bulb. The control switch has the following four positions.

"*Off*"—Lamps off, and "Maglita" not charging.
C—Lamps off, and "Maglita" charging. (1½–2 amp.)
H—Headlamp (driving light), tail lamp, and sidecar lamp (when fitted) on; "Maglita" charging.
L—Headlamp (pilot light), tail lamp, and sidecar lamp (when fitted) on; "Maglita" charging. (3½ amp.)

Focusing is carried out by adjusting the position of the main bulb-holder after the clamping lever is slackened. The lamp front is secured by a screw and can be removed together with the reflector. The main bulb is a Lucas 12 watt No. 68, and the pilot bulb is a 3 watt No. 200.

Tail Lamps. On the 1932 lightweights with "Maglita" equipment Lucas tail lights type MT110 are fitted, and all other 1932–8 models have type MT110 tail lights. These lamps are of very robust design. The front portion of the MT110 lamp is let into a circular hole in the rear number plate. The bulb-holder is mounted on a rubber diaphragm which prevents vibration damaging the sensitive filament. The MT110 lamp also has a patent rubber cushioning device for protecting the bulb. The MT110 lamp takes 3 watt bulbs, No. 200 of the same wattage as the Watsonian lamps provided on Ariel sidecars. The rear portion of the MT110 lamp is removed for a bulb replacement by giving it a half turn to the left.

Sidecar Lamp. On all sidecars a Watsonian lamp is built into the sidecar mudguard. This lamp, which has a large diameter front and a silvered reflector has no internal wiring, contact being made by springs of special design. For focusing there are several alternative positions for the bulb-holder which takes a 3 watt bulb type 200. To remove the lamp front and reflector it is only necessary to slacken the fixing screw when the bulb-holder can be withdrawn.

Panel Light. This takes a 3 watt No. 200 centre-contact bulb.

Batteries. Batteries on the 1932 "Maglita" lightweights are of the PUW5E type with a capacity of 8 amp. hr. On all other 1932–8 models a PUW7E battery of 12 amp. hr. capacity is fitted. The new "Milam" moulding material entirely prevents leakage. Special separators ensure free diffusion of the electrolyte and a low internal resistance, while the vent design allows the free escape of gas at reduced pressure without leakages of acid and does not allow the ingress of dirt or dust.

CARE OF LAMPS

Cleaning Reflectors. The reflectors are protected by a transparent and colourless covering, which enables any accidental

CARE OF THE ELECTRICAL EQUIPMENT 109

finger marks to be removed with a soft cloth or chamois leather without affecting the surface of the reflectors. On no account should a metal polish be used on Lucas reflectors, as this is liable to ruin the surfaces. If the ebony black of the outer body becomes dull in service, the original lustre can be restored by the application of a little good furniture or car polish.

Focusing Headlamp. The best method of focusing is to take the motor-cycle to a straight, level road, find the correct bulb adjustment, and then move the lamp in its adjustable mounting until the best road position is obtained. The driving light should be switched on when focusing is carried out. Special care should be taken to see that the filament is in its correct position relative to the reflector.

Replacement of Bulbs. Always use Lucas bulbs with Lucas reflectors. When it is found necessary to replace the main headlamp bulb, turn it gently in the socket in an anti-clockwise direction. This will release the pressure on the bulb contacts and enable the bulb to be withdrawn easily. Care should be taken that the bulb is fitted the correct way round, i.e. with the dipped beam filament above the centre filament. Spare bulbs are best carried in a Lucas bulb case.

CARE OF THE BATTERY (1932-7)

It is of the utmost importance that the battery should receive regular attention to keep it in good condition.

The following are the most important maintenance hints—
1. Keep the acid level $\frac{1}{4}$ in. above the top of the plates.
2. Add only distilled water, never tap water.
3. Test the condition of the battery by taking readings of the specific gravity of the acid with a hydrometer.
4. The battery must never be left in a discharged condition.

Topping-up. At least once a month the vent plugs in the top of the battery should be removed and the level of the acid solution examined. If necessary, distilled water, which can be obtained at all chemists and most garages, should be added to bring the level above the tops of the plates, but well short of the bottom of the vent plugs. If, however, acid solution has been spilled, it should be replaced by a diluted sulphuric acid solution of specific gravity, 1·285. It is important when examining the cells that naked lights should not be held near the vents, on account of the possible danger of igniting the gas coming from the plates.

Storage. If the equipment is laid by for several months, the battery must be given a small charge from a separate source of electrical energy about once a fortnight, in order to obviate any permanent sulphation of the plates. In no circumstances must the electrolyte be removed from the battery and the plates allowed to dry, as certain chemical changes take place which result in permanent loss of capacity.

Testing the Condition of the Battery. It is advisable to complete the inspection by measuring the specific gravity of the acid, as this gives a very good indication of the state of charge of the battery.

An instrument known as a "hydrometer" is employed for this purpose. These can be bought at any Lucas Service Depot. Voltmeter readings of each cell do not provide a reliable indication of the condition of the battery, unless special precautions are taken.

How to Use the Hydrometer. First see that the acid is at the correct level and that the electrolyte is thoroughly mixed. To ensure the latter condition, hydrometer readings should be taken after a run on the motor-cycle. To use the Lucas hydrometer, the instrument should be held vertically over the battery cell and after compressing the bulb the red rubber tube should be dipped as far as possible into the electrolyte. Then gradually release the bulb until the acid solution rises in the body and lifts the hydrometer float about one inch. Now remove the hydrometer and note the scale reading at the surface of the electrolyte. This reading shows the density or specific gravity. When taking the reading avoid letting the float touch the bulb.

After taking the S.G. return the solution to the cell, take the S.G. of the other cells. If one cell reading differs greatly from the remainder possibly some of the acid has escaped or there may be a short between the plates. In such a case expert attention is required. The correct S.G. readings for the Lucas 12 amp. hr. battery are as follows: fully charged, 1·250–1·300; half discharged, 1·150–1·250; fully discharged, below 1·150.

Battery-charging Period. It is difficult to lay down rigid instructions on this subject, as the conditions under which motor-cycles are used vary considerably; and, obviously, the amount of charging a battery will require is directly dependent on the extent to which the lamps are used. The following suggestions will serve as a rough guide.

On a solo machine used normally, and not left standing for long periods at night with the lights on, daylight charging with the switch in the C position should be not less than about 50 per cent of the night running with the switch in the H position. With a sidecar outfit the period of daylight charging may be equal to the night running, and when an electric horn is fitted generous daylight charging is recommended. As a rule, little or no harm follows overcharging so long as gassing and waste

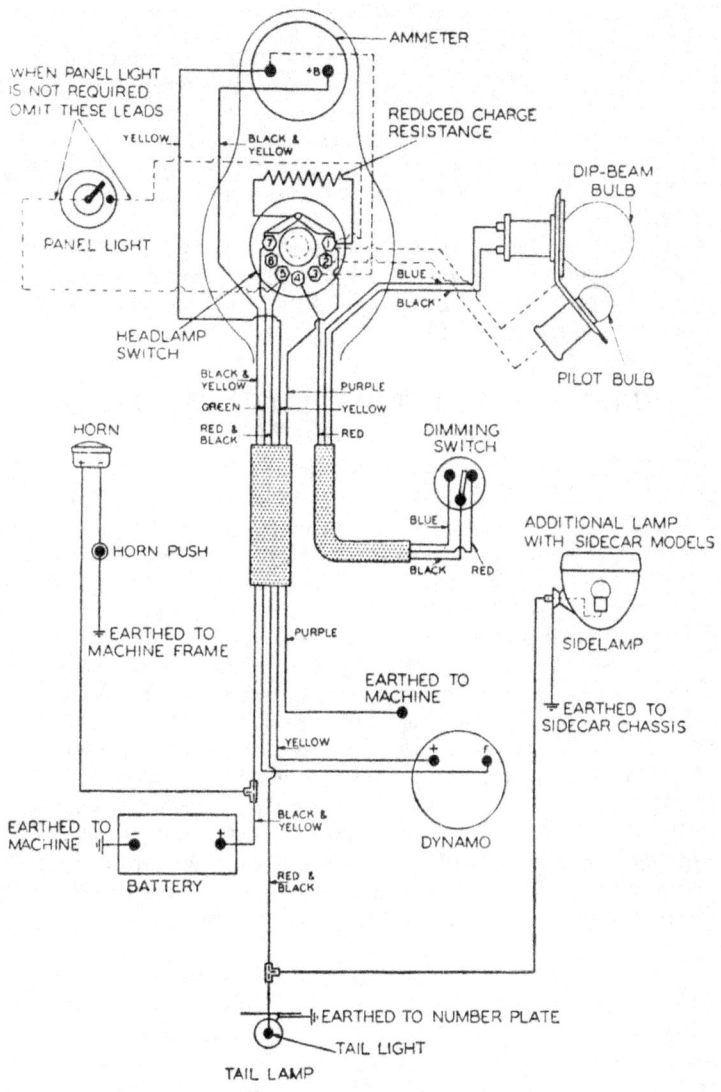

(*Joseph Lucas, Ltd.*)

Fig. 52. Wiring Diagram for Lucas M.S. "Magdyno" Lighting Equipment without Automatic Voltage Control (Applicable to all 1935–1937 Models)

All internal connections are shown dotted and the cable ends are identified by means of coloured sleevings, as indicated on the diagram.

of acid is not caused, but undercharging is definitely harmful and eventually causes sulphated and permanently damaged plates. This time should only be increased if the period of night running is considerable, or when the battery is found to be in a low state of charge (if the specific gravity of the acid solution is 1·210 or below). The chief ill-effect of overcharging is loss of acid by gassing.

The battery must never be left in a fully-discharged condition, and unless some long runs are to be taken, it is advisable to have the battery removed from the machine and charged up from an independent electrical supply.

HINTS FOR DETECTING ELECTRICAL FAULTS
(1932-7) (" MAGDYNO ")

Although every precaution is taken to eliminate all possible causes of trouble, failure may occasionally develop through lack of attention to the equipment or damage to the wiring. The most probable faults are tabulated according to the symptoms which are displayed in the fault-finding tables on pages 114 and 115.

A few hints are given for the best way to make use of these tables, as the sources of many troubles are by no means obvious.

Much evidence can be gained from observation of the ammeter. If, for instance, no reading is indicated when the engine is running at, say, 20 miles per hour with the switch in the C position, the dynamo is failing to charge. To ensure that the ammeter is not at fault, the engine should be stopped and the switch turned to the H position, when a reading on the discharge side of the scale should be observed. Again, if the needle fluctuates when the engine is running steadily, an intermittent dynamo output can be suspected. The dynamo may have been neglected, and the trouble could be caused by, say, worn brushes or a dirty commutator.

First disconnect the Positive Battery Lead as a precaution against Short Circuits. Then see that all terminals on the switch are tight, move the switch through its four positions, and see that the spring triggers make good electrical contact with the terminals. Occasionally one of the leads fouls the trigger or a portion of the insulation gets clipped between the contact and terminal. Slight adjustment of the wire or cutting back the insulation will remedy matters.

A possible cause of the dynamo failing to charge is the reversal of its polarity due either to the headlamp being ineffectively earthed, or to the accidental "shorting" of a terminal or "live" part of the cut-out, perhaps with a screwdriver, when making adjustments without having taken the precaution of removing

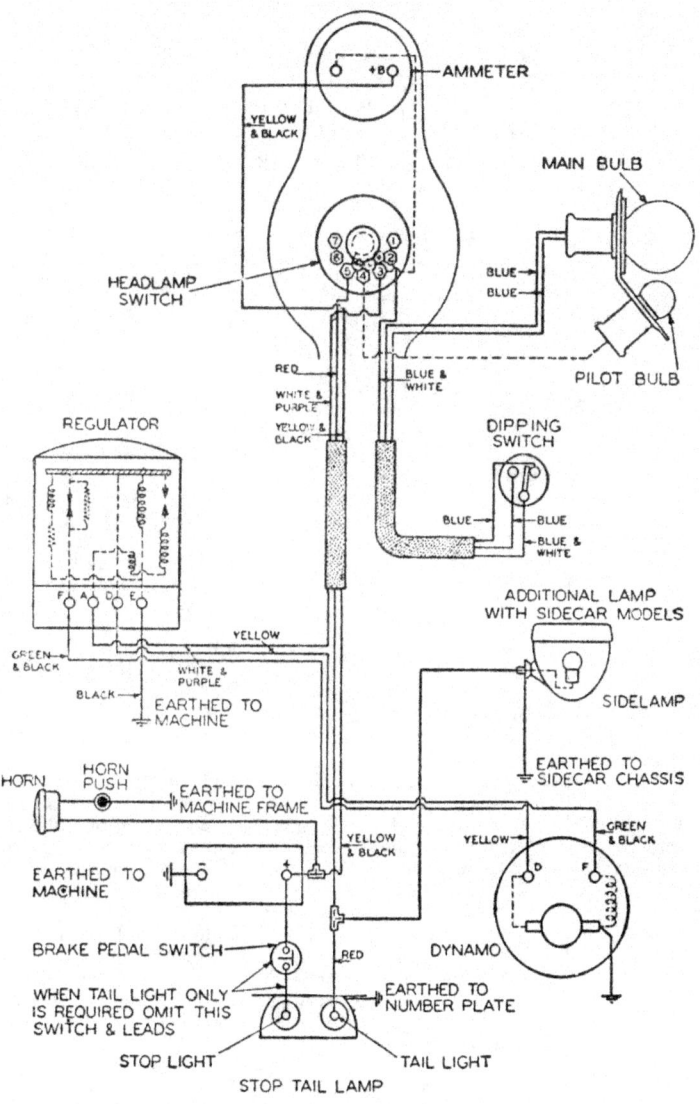

(*Joseph Lucas, Ltd.*)

Fig. 52a. Wiring Diagram for "Magdyno" Lighting Equipment with Automatic Voltage Control (Applicable to all 1938-9 Models)

All internal connexions are shown dotted and the cable ends are identified by coloured sleevings. The panel light is not shown.

the positive battery lead. Examine the connections of the "earthing" lead from the headlamp switch to the earthing terminal on the "Magdyno" or to some part of the cycle frame. The bolt on the frame which clamps the one end of the cable may have become loose, or the cable end may not be making good contact due to dirt or enamel.

TABLE I (LIGHTING)

Condition	Possible Causes and Methods of Detection	Remedy
Lamps give dim, flickering, or no light when the engine is not running	Bulb filament broken	Replace with new bulb
	Bulb discoloured with use	Replace with new bulb
	Bulb out of focus	Focus by moving the bulb until the best illumination is obtained. (See page 109)
	Dirty reflector or bulb	Clean dirty reflector with chamois leather or a soft cloth
	Severed or worn cable, or loose connections at headlamp switch, dynamo, or battery	Tighten loose connection and replace faulty cables
	Faulty earthing of headlamp. The end of the earthing cable may not be making good contact with the frame due to dirt or enamel	Tighten the bolt on the frame which clamps the end of the cable from switch terminal E, and see that it makes good contact
	Faulty earthing of battery. The end of the cable from the negative battery terminal may not be making good contact with the frame	Tighten the bolt in the frame which clamps the end of the cable from the negative battery terminal, and see that it makes good contact
	Battery exhausted. Take hydrometer readings when acid level is correct ($\frac{1}{4}$ in. above plates) and after a run when electrolyte is thoroughly mixed. When half discharged, readings are 1·150-1·250; when fully discharged, readings are below 1·150	Machine should be taken on the road for a long daytime run with switch in C position, or battery charged from independent electrical supply

CARE OF THE ELECTRICAL EQUIPMENT 115

TABLE II (LIGHTING)

Condition	Possible Causes and Methods of Detection	Remedy
After carrying out examination on Table I, lamps still give dim, flickering, or no light when the engine is running	Dynamo not charging, or Charging intermittently. Ammeter should give a reading on the charge side when the machine is running at, say, 20 m.p.h. with switch in C position. Possible causes of dynamo trouble are—	
	Worn or dirty brushes	Clean dirty or greasy brushes with a cloth moistened with petrol. Badly-worn brushes must be replaced
	Dirty commutator	To clean a dirty commutator, remove one of the main brushes from its holder, and insert a fine duster, holding it pressed against commutator surface by means of a suitably-shaped piece of wood, at the same time slowly turning the engine. If commutator has been badly neglected, clean with very fine glass paper
	Reversed polarity of dynamo	To correct polarity of machine, run engine slowly, put switch in C position, and then press cut-out contacts momentarily together

Having examined all cable connections, the polarity of the machine can be corrected by running the engine slowly, putting the switch in the C position, and then pressing the cut-out contacts momentarily together when the machine should begin to generate again.

If the dynamo still does not function satisfactorily, look for the trouble elsewhere.

Should the intensity of the lights vary or should they fail entirely, it is probably due to the battery terminals being allowed to corrode, and the consequent breaking of a connection, or to a defective earth connection. If the cause of the trouble is not located at the battery, the switch should next be examined to see that all the terminals are tight. If one particular lamp does not light, look for a broken filament, a broken connection between the lamp and the switch, or a defective electrical contact between the lamp body and the machine frame.

THE 1938-9 LIGHTING SYSTEM

Most of the preceding instructions are applicable to 1938 models, but a somewhat altered "Magdyno" is used in conjunction with a voltage control unit.

The Latest "Magdyno." The ignition portion now has a face cam type contact-breaker (Fig. 55) and the correct gap is 0·012 in. The cam is lubricated by a wick in the base of the contact-breaker and a few drops of thin machine oil should be added about every 5,000 miles. By removing the spring arm carrying the moving contact the wick screw can be withdrawn. The dynamo maintenance instructions given on pages 103-6 hold good, but it should be noted that both the third brush and the cut-out have been removed from the instrument. About every 4,000-5,000 miles a few drops of thin machine oil should be put into the lubricator on the commutator end bracket (see Fig. 50).

The Automatic Voltage Control Unit. This ingenious device comprises a cut-out and voltage control neatly housed in a box separate from the dynamo and sees to it that the battery is kept properly charged by varying the dynamo output according to the load and state of charge of the battery. The unit should not be tampered with, the only possible trouble, and a remote one, being oxidization, or perhaps welding together, of the points due to accidental crossing of the dynamo field and positive leads. Be careful with the leads at the dynamo end.

The Battery. The automatic voltage control prevents boiling away of the distilled water, but the level and S.G. of the electrolyte should occasionally be checked. Follow the advice on pages 109-10 except the paragraph relating to charging. The 1938 headlamp switch has only three positions—"Off," "L," and "H" and the half charge resistance is omitted. During daylight running with the battery in good condition the dynamo gives only a trickle charge and the ammeter should show only 1 or 2 amperes.

CHAPTER IX

MAINTENANCE AND OVERHAULING (1932–8)

IN this chapter the author has aimed at putting in a convenient form all that information and data necessary to enable the Ariel owner to keep his machine and engine in first-class trim, and this it is hoped will be of value both to novices and experts. All motor-cycles, and for that matter all mechanical contrivances, require periodic lubrication, minor adjustments, and occasional overhauling; at regular intervals the I.C. engine requires to be decarbonized and the valves ground-in if a reasonable degree of efficiency is to be maintained.

The accessibility and straightforward design of the Ariel makes adjustments and overhauling a very simple matter, and decarbonization is by no means a tedious proposition if the rider gets to work in a methodical manner and uses the right tools for the job. Lubrication has already been dealt with in a separate chapter.

There are a number of minor adjustments which it is desirable that the Ariel rider should attend to every few hundred miles, or when circumstances necessitate these adjustments being made. If the rider values his machine, however, he will not wait until adjustment *has* to be made, but will carefully inspect his machine as a matter of routine and make the necessary adjustments before they become essential. By doing this, much time and money is in the long run saved, and the performance of the machine will be kept at its maximum.

ROUTINE ADJUSTMENTS

Cleaning. It requires a considerable amount of time to keep a motor-cycle in anything approaching "showroom" condition, but it is the author's opinion that, unless a machine is kept reasonably clean, the fullest pleasure and maximum efficiency cannot be obtained from it. Apart from the question of pride of ownership, it is an undoubted fact that dirt covers a multitude of defects and greatly accelerates depreciation in respect of market value. This is, of course, obvious. If neglected, a motor-cycle rapidly becomes shabby and an eyesore. After a ride in dirty weather, cleaning may take at least an hour. It entails the use of stiff bristle brushes and paraffin for removing the filth from the lower extremities, together with cloths, leather, and polish for the enamelled parts. On no account should a machine be left wet overnight, or a serious amount of rusting may ensue. If the rider is so busy that he cannot spare the time for cleaning, the machine should be thoroughly greased all over before use.

It should be noted that chromium-plating does not require and should not be treated with metal polish, for it does not oxidize in the same manner as nickel-plating. The chromium-plated parts should be treated similarly to the enamel, and the surfaces will then improve with cleaning. Polish with a *soft* cloth.

Periodical Inspection of Nuts. One of the most important points in connection with the care of a motor-cycle is to look over

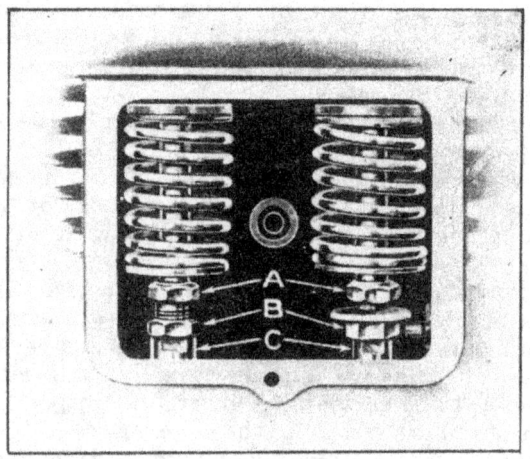

FIG. 53. TAPPET ADJUSTMENT (S.V. ENGINES)

the machine frequently and apply a spanner to any nuts which have worked at all loose.

Valve Clearances. It is very important to maintain the correct valve clearances on all Ariel engines, and the clearances should periodically be checked, especially in the case of new engines where considerable bedding down of the parts occurs, and after grinding in the valves. It should be noted that incorrect valve clearances interfere with both the lift of the valves and also the valve timing. Excessive clearances result in undue noise and loss of efficiency due to reduced valve lift and late opening of the valves, but no damage to the valves is likely to be caused. Insufficient valve clearances, besides resulting in loss of compression, flexibility, and power, may cause distortion and perhaps burning of the exhaust valve due to gas leakage past it during the power strokes.

MAINTENANCE AND OVERHAULING

The correct clearances with the engine *cold* are as follows—

Model	Inlet (in.)	Exhaust (in.)
S.V.	·002	·004
O.H.V.	Nil	Nil
O.H.C. (4F)	Nil	Nil
O.H.V. (4F, 4G)	·006	·008

To adjust these clearances, proceed as follows—

1932-8 S.V. and 1932 Lightweight O.H.V. Models. Remove the valve chest cover and set the engine with the piston somewhere near the top of the cylinder with both valves fully closed. To adjust the tappets, the tappet C (Fig. 53) should be held while the lock nut B is loosened. Then rotate A, holding the tappet C until the desired clearance is obtained. Now secure the lock nut B and recheck the clearance several times whilst rotating the engine from the position where the inlet valve closes until the exhaust valve opens.

On the 1932-8 S.V. engines the clearance is measured with a feeler gauge between the top of the tappet head and the end of the valve stem. Do not be confused by there being no clearance for a few degrees just after the inlet valve closes and just before the exhaust valve opens: this is quite correct. In the case of some 1934-5 S.V. engines, however, the cupped tappet head (Fig. 6) receives the ball end of the valve stem cap and consequently it is quite impossible to use a feeler gauge to measure the valve clearance. Therefore the correct procedure is to adjust the tappets with the engine *hot* so that each tappet rotates freely but has no perceptible vertical play.

On the 1932 lightweight O.H.V. engines when adjusting the tappets, check the clearances between the rocker arms and the hardened caps on the valve stems, as in the case of all other O.H.V. models which have an overhead valve clearance adjustment instead of adjustable tappets.

All 1932-8 O.H.V. Models except 1932 Lightweights. On 1934-8 O.H.V. singles the overhead rocker adjustment is enclosed by quickly detachable valve spring covers or by caps, and these must first be removed by pressing back the spring clips or unscrewing the caps (1938). On the 1932 four-valve engines and the 1933 engines the adjustment is not enclosed. To adjust the valve clearances set the engine with both valves fully closed and the piston at the top of the compression stroke. Then loosen the lock-nut on the adjuster screw which passes through the end of the rocker arm and bears on the hardened cap slipped over the end of the valve stem. Now rotate the adjuster screw until there is just no clearance. Make sure that the rocker return springs are keeping the inner ends of the rockers fully in contact with the push-rods, and that there is sufficient back-lash at the exhaust valve lifter.

On the O.H.V. models the clearance must be checked between the adjuster on the end of the rocker arm and the hardened steel cap on the end of the valve stem. A most practical way of checking the adjustment is to make sure the clearance is practically nil by seeing that it is impossible to depress the end of the rocker arm, and then testing for compression. If this is satisfactory, it is clear that the valves are seating correctly. If there is no compression, either a valve is being held off its seat through too close adjustment, or there is a serious leakage elsewhere. In either case the cause must be found and rectified.

O.H.C. Model 4F. Adjustment on this model is extremely simple and is carried out as follows.

Remove the cover from the rocker-box, and unclip the distributor from the end of the rocker-box. Regard the back plate, on to which the distributor cover fits, as a clock face. Rotate the engine until the insulated distributor arm on the end of the camshaft is pointing to half-past seven. Both valves of No. 1 cylinder are now closed and adjustment can be carried out. Slack off the lock nut X (Fig. 54) and rotate the adjuster Y until the desired clearance is obtained; then holding Y lock up X dead tight. Similarly adjust the clearance for the inlet valve. The clearance is easily measured between the valve stem end-cap and the end of the adjuster screw. Now rotate the engine a little more until the distributor arm Z (Fig. 60) points to half-past four. Adjust the valve clearances of No. 2 cylinder. The valve clearances of Nos. 3 and 4 cylinders are adjusted in a similar manner.

Keep the rocker adjustment so that with the engine cold there is just no clearance between the valve stem end cap and adjuster. If the adjustment has been made correctly, the rocker should slide back freely along the spindle after being pushed against the spring distance washer between adjacent rockers.

Exhaust Valve-lifter Adjustment. It is important that there should not be an entire absence of backlash at the exhaust valve-lifter lever with the exhaust valve fully closed, which would inevitably prevent the exhaust valve from seating properly, and thus cause loss of compression and burning of the valve and its seating, accompanied probably by intermittent banging in the exhaust pipe and silencer. There should be about $\frac{1}{16}$ in. backlash at the handlebar control, and the desired adjustment may be made by loosening the lock-nut on the cable adjuster stop and screwing the adjuster in or out as required a few turns. After adjusting re-tighten the locknut. Always check the exhaust

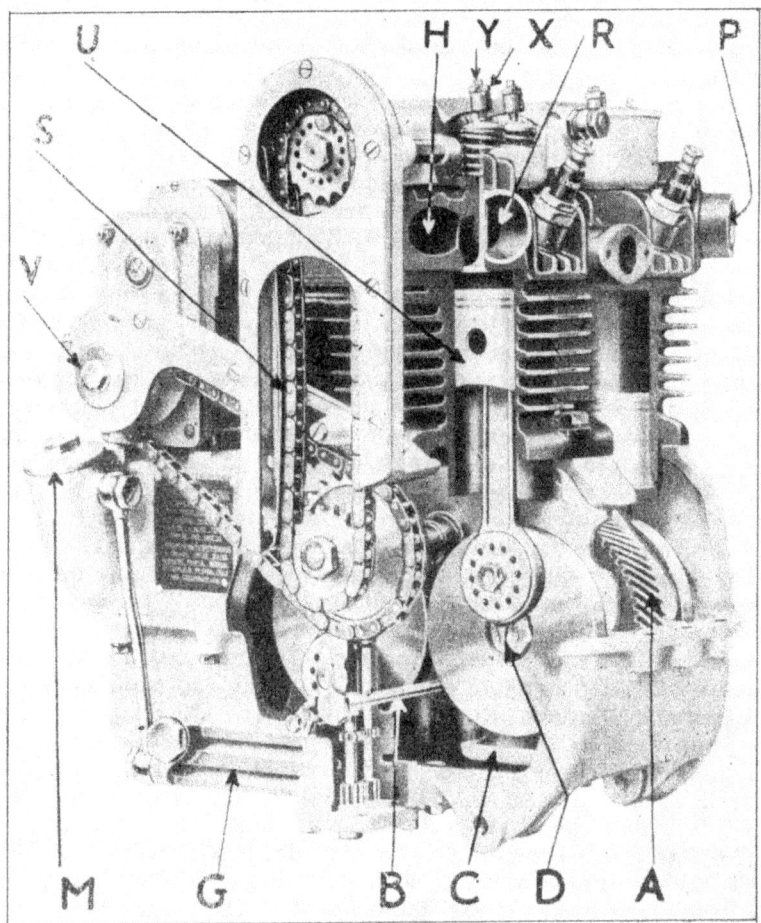

FIG. 54. THREE-QUARTER FRONT VIEW OF PARTLY SECTIONAL 1932 5·97 H.P. FOUR-CYLINDER OVERHEAD CAMSHAFT ENGINE (4F)

The later engine (see Fig. 15) is similar in general design, but incorporates several improvements, particularly in regard to the lubrication system.

KEY TO FIG. 54

- A = Main crankshaft gears
- B = Oil delivery tube to centre gearcase
- C = Oil trough for connecting rod dipper D
- D = Dipper on connecting rod, for splash lubrication
- G = Return oilway from engine sump to oil reservoir
- H = Exhaust gas passage from No. 2 cylinder to port R
- M = Oil reservoir filler cap
- M = Exhaust port for Nos. 3 and 4 cylinders
- R = Exhaust port for Nos. 1 and 2 cylinders
- S = Automatic spring tensioning device for camshaft chain
- U = Slot for gudgeon pin circlip removal
- V = Inspection plug for magneto sprocket and fixing
- X = Rocker adjuster screw lock-nut
- Y = Rocker adjuster screw

valve lifter adjustment before and after adjusting the valve clearances.

A further means of adjustment is to alter the setting of the exhaust lifter arm on the eccentric spindle. This is only held by a nut and taper. To slack off the taper joint, undo the nut a couple of turns, and give the face of the nut a light, sharp blow, so as to drive the eccentric spindle inwards. Set the arm as required and retighten the nut. 1938 O.H.V.'s have no cable adjustment.

The Sparking Plug. Difficult starting or occasional misfiring can usually be traced to a dirty or defective sparking plug. The life of a good plug is considerable, but the points of the electrodes gradually burn away and eventually the gap becomes enlarged considerably, and it is necessary to reset the points with the aid of a feeler gauge. The correct gap is ·018 in. (i.e. about twice the contact-breaker gap). Excessive gap at the plug points means that the voltage required from the magneto is higher; and this not only renders starting difficult, but—what is worse—causes brush discharge inside the magneto. This discharge eventually causes internal corrosion, and the efficiency of the magneto is impaired. From time to time the plug should be removed and thoroughly cleaned with petrol, both inside and outside. All deposits of soot or charred oil must be eliminated, as these are apt to cause leakage and bad running. The insulation should be examined for cracks or flaws, and in very humid weather should be wiped dry with a rag before starting-up. The accepted method of testing for current at the plug terminal is to place a wooden-handled screw-driver, with steel blade, across the terminal and just touching the cylinder fin, when a spark should be visible on rotating the engine. To test the plug itself, remove it with the H.T. lead still affixed, clean it, lay it on the cylinder, and note whether it sparks satisfactorily when the engine is rotated. If it does not, scrap it. Always fit the correct type of plug recommended by the manufacturers. On S.V. engines fit a Lodge H.1. For the standard O.H.V. engines a Lodge H14 plug is quite suitable for touring, but the author recommends a Lodge R14 or K.L.G. 831 for hard driving. On the "Red Hunter" engines a K.L.G. LKS5 should be used for running-in and slow touring, and a Lodge R14 or K.L.G. 831 for harder driving. In the case of the 350 c.c. and 250 c.c. "Red Hunter" engines with high compression pistons a good heat-resisting plug such as the Lodge R14 or K.L.G. 831 should be used, and the same applies to the 500 c.c. "Red Hunter" engine when the H.C. piston is fitted.

It is advisable occasionally to dismantle the sparking plug in order to clean the inside thoroughly. This is most easily accomplished by clamping the gland nut (small hexagon) in a vice and

MAINTENANCE AND OVERHAULING

removing the plug body (large hexagon). Be careful not to scrape the mica on the centre electrode, or this may flake off and cause pre-ignition. Clean the carbon from inside the body with an old pen-knife, and on reassembly do not overlook the copper washer.

The Contact Breaker. The magneto should not be interfered with unnecessarily, for it is a very delicate instrument, and functions best when left well alone; but at regular intervals, say every 1,000 miles, the contact-breaker cover should be removed and the contacts (see Figs. 49 and 55) examined, and their gap

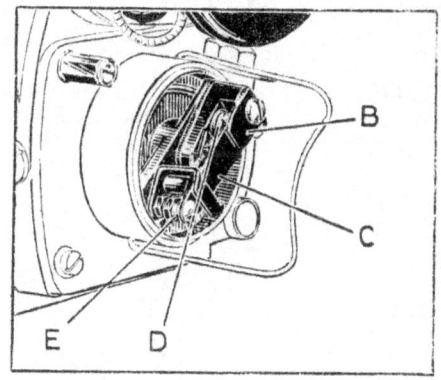

(*Joseph Lucas, Ltd.*)
FIG. 55. FACE CAM CONTACT-BREAKER ON LATEST "MAGDYNO"
B = Backing spring　　D = Screw for wick
C = Contact spring　　E = Contacts

checked with a 12 thou' feeler gauge. If the clearance is excessive, the timing will be advanced and the primary circuit will not be closed for the correct period, and occasional misfiring is very likely. Provided the contacts are kept clean and, above all, *free from oil*, they will probably need adjustment only at long intervals. It is not desirable to alter the setting unless the gap varies considerably from that of the magneto spanner gauge. If adjustment is necessary, rotate the engine round slowly until the points are seen to be fully opened, and then, using the magneto spanner, slacken the lock-nut and rotate the fixed contact screw by its hexagonal head until the correct gap is obtained, as indicated by the feeler gauge; then screw up the lock-nut firmly.

If, when the contact points are examined, it is found that they have become burned or blackened (owing probably to the presence at some time or other of dirt or oil), they may be cleaned with very fine emery cloth, and afterwards with a cloth damped with petrol. All dirt and metal dust must be wiped away entirely. Where the contacts are found to have become seriously pitted, it may be advisable to go over the surfaces with a dead smooth file and only the very smallest amount of metal should be removed. Removing the contact breaker unit will assist filing the contacts quite true, which is imperative.

Any sign of incipient rusting of the contact-breaker spring should be checked immediately, as rust and corrosion are frequent causes of broken contact-breaker springs.

In the case of the "Maglita" contact-breaker, it is as well occasionally to examine the plunger and control spring, and to grease these thoroughly. On a face cam contact-breaker (Fig. 55) to render the contacts accessible for cleaning, remove the spring arm carrying the moving contact by detaching the fixing screw.

Engine Shaft Shock Absorber. The spring pressure is *not* adjustable and the two locknuts must be kept tight against the shoulder on the main shaft. If by any chance they are removed, do not forget to replace the tab washer *between* them, turning one tab washer over on to each nut. The hardened steel washer between the inner locknut and sprocket must also not be omitted.

Magneto Chain (S.V. and O.H.V.). The chain driving the magneto or "Magdyno" is entirely enclosed and automatically lubricated and rotates at only half engine speed. Wear, therefore, takes place very slowly indeed. After a big mileage has been covered, however, the chain-case cover should be removed and the chain inspected. If it is found that there is more than about $\frac{3}{8}$ in. up and down movement in the centre of the chain with the chain in its tightest position, the chain should be tensioned by slackening the two bolts holding the magneto or "Magdyno" on its platform and sliding the instrument back the necessary amount. Afterwards be careful to screw up the retaining bolts thoroughly tight and see that the magneto is held close up to the back of the chain cover, otherwise oil leakage may occur due to displacement of the oil-retaining washers.

Timing Chains (4F, 4G). No adjustment of the magneto and camshaft driving chains is necessary as both chains are automatically spring tensioned.

The Primary Chain. Since this is automatically lubricated and totally enclosed, stretching takes considerably longer than is the case with the secondary chain, which is much more exposed to harmful influences. However, it will stretch in time, and it must be retensioned correctly. If a chain is too slack, it is apt to "whip," which intensifies the wear and tends to break the rollers, especially in the case of the front chain. On the other hand, if it be too tight, a crushing stress is produced on the rollers, and the whole chain is subjected to unfair stresses, and the sprockets

MAINTENANCE AND OVERHAULING

wear quickly. The chain should be adjusted and kept adjusted, so that it can be given midway by pressure with the fingers a total and maximum deflection of about ⅜ in.

Adjustment on some 1932 models is effected by slackening the four sleeve nuts retaining the gearbox to the bottom bracket, and by means of the drawbolt pulling the box rearwards gradually until the correct tension is arrived at. After making an adjustment, see that the gear control has not been upset.

Adjustment on all 1933-8 models and some 1932 models involves swinging the pivot-mounted Burman gearbox backwards or forwards as required by means of the adjusting device situated at the top rear extremity of the offside engine plate. (On recent models an eccentric adjusting device is replaced by a drawbolt. Chain adjustment is effected as described, except that the gearbox is swung by rotating the nut on the drawbolt.) First slack off the pivot bolt which is below the gearbox and also slack off the clamp bolt above the gearbox. Then loosen the large locknut of the eccentric adjusting device and slightly rotate the hexagon-ended centre. This swings the gearbox about the pivot bolt and so varies the chain tension. After making the necessary adjustment retighten the eccentric locknut, the clamp bolt, and the pivot bolt; finally check over the gear control (hand) setting.

The Secondary Chain. The secondary chain requires to be tensioned at regular intervals, depending upon the mileage of the machine and how the rider has treated the chain. This chain should undergo a total maximum deflection of about ⅝ in. when properly adjusted. To adjust, loosen the rear wheel spindle nuts E (Fig. 27) and screw up the two adjuster screws K in the fork ends, after loosening the nut securing the brake anchor bar. See that wheel alignment is not put out when tightening the adjusters, and also that the brake operation is not affected. Make whatever further adjustments are found necessary. A method of testing a chain for wear is to hold a length between the hands and observe to what extent the chain will bend sideways.

Coupling-up Chains. It greatly simplifies chain replacement if the obvious precaution be taken of uniting the two ends behind the vertical diameter of the large sprocket, in which case the whole of the tension is resisted by the sprocket teeth, and it is unnecessary to stretch the chain by hand. When replacing the spring link, see that the closed end faces the direction of motion, for when rapidly accelerating the inertia of the spring-fastening tends to make it lag behind. Uncoupling of a secondary chain or jumping off the sprockets at high speed is liable to cause a serious accident. When using a machine for racing it is wise to use a rivet instead of a spring link for joining the two ends of the chain together.

Gear Control Adjustment. The adjustment of the hand control should be checked over if difficulty is experienced in selecting any of the gears and also whenever the primary chain is adjusted because movement of the gearbox, even if only slight, interferes with the proper adjustment. The gear lever should be *centrally* placed in the second-gear gate of the tank quadrant with second gear engaged. Should it not be central, adjust by removing the joint

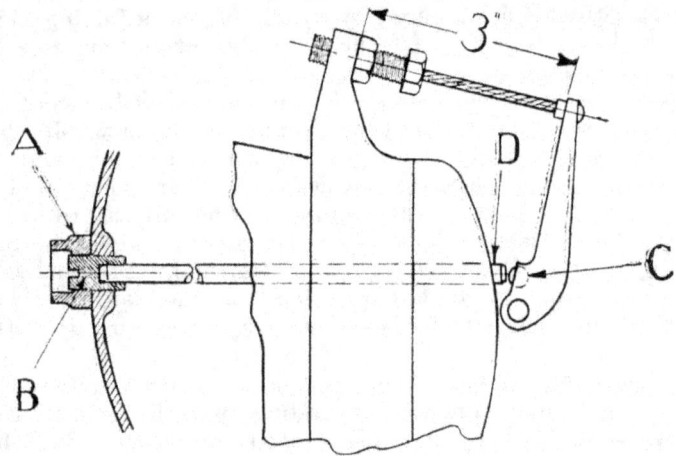

FIG. 56. CLUTCH ADJUSTMENT
(Provided on many 1932-4 models.)

pin in the fork end at the lower end of the control rod and rotating the fork end. Slip the joint pin into position and check the gear lever in each of the other gears. It should not be hard against the end of the quadrant with top and bottom gears engaged.

On the 1932-8 models with foot gear control no adjustment of the control is, of course, necessary after retensioning the primary chain, as the whole of the control is attached to the gearbox itself.

Clutch Adjustment. Adjustment of the clutch is rarely necessary, and all is correct as long as the spring nuts stand level with the face of the spring plate. After adjusting the clutch, see that the spring plate lifts equally; if not, the nuts should be eased off on the low side and tightened on the high side until it does.

1932-4 Adjustment. To ensure freedom from clutch slip it is essential that there is always about $\frac{1}{64}$ in. clearance between the ball C in the clutch-operating lever (see Fig. 56) and the end of the operating plunger D. The end of the actuating lever must

MAINTENANCE AND OVERHAULING

be set by means of the cable adjuster so that its end is approximately 3 in. (2½ in. on 1932 three-speed gearboxes) from the face of the cable adjuster lug on the gearbox. This setting gives equal movement of the actuating lever on each side of the centre line of its pivot with a minimum of bending of the wire cable. This position of the lever is obtained by adjusting *A* and *B* to give the necessary clearance. Slack off the locknut and rotate the adjuster (slotted end) with a screwdriver. To get at these parts it is, of course, necessary to take off the outer half of the primary chain cover (except on oilbath models where an inspection hole is provided in the clutch dome), but as the correct setting is given to the lever when the machine is assembled it will rarely be necessary to make this adjustment. In general, maintain at least $\frac{1}{64}$ in. clearance between the ball and the operating rod by adjusting the cable adjuster and give as straight a pull to the cable as possible.

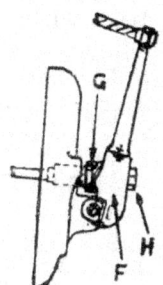

FIG. 57. CLUTCH ADJUSTMENT (1935–8)

1935-8 Adjustment. On a few Ariel models made since 1934 the spring plate adjustment described in the preceding paragraph is retained, but in the majority of cases the adjustment illustrated in Fig. 57 is used. A clearance of approximately $\frac{1}{64}$ in. should be maintained between the two thrust points on the lever *F* and the face of the plunger *G* which slides through the cover of the gear-box. To adjust the clearance, the top end of the operating lever should be pushed in and the Bowden cable slipped off. Then allow the lever to fall down and rotate the screw *H* through the plunger anti-clockwise to increase the clearance or clockwise to decrease it. The cable may now be reconnected and the clearance carefully checked. If by any chance the plunger is removed, be very careful not to lose the small ball inserted between the end of the clutch rod and the adjuster screw *H*. To remove the rubber protecting cover on 1938 models, pull the top end down along the operating lever, after which the lever can be pushed in and the cable released.

Clutch Troubles. The two chief sources of trouble to which a clutch is prone are (*a*) clutch slip, and (*b*) clutch drag. The former can quickly be detected, as on opening the throttle suddenly the engine revolutions increase but the speed of the machine is not increased proportionately; also the clutch becomes very warm due to slip between the plates. Clutch slip may be due to oil getting on the clutch plates by over filling the chaincase on pre-1936 oilbath models or adjusting the needle valve on the other models to give an excessive oil supply (see page 97). The remedy is to dismantle and clean the plates with petrol, and reduce the oil supply to the primary chain. Another possible cause of slip is insufficient clearance between the clutch operating lever and the plunger in the gearbox mainshaft. This trouble which sometimes develops as the friction inserts become worn, can easily be rectified by adjusting the clutch as described in the preceding paragraphs.

Clutch drag, or difficulty in releasing the clutch, is also sometimes caused by oily plates, but the most likely cause of the trouble is incorrect clutch adjustment with excessive clearance between the operating lever and the plunger. A clutch which sticks when the machine has been left standing can be freed by depressing the kick-starter with the clutch raised before starting up the engine. A tipping spring plate due to non-uniform spring pressure, and a worn clutch sprocket bearing are other possible causes of clutch drag, and the remedies are obvious.

Handlebar Adjustment. All 1932–3 Ariel machines have handlebars of a type which may be readily adjusted for reach by undoing two nuts. Full advantage should be taken of this to obtain a really comfortable riding position suited to the owner's stature, and there is no need to adopt a "sit-up-and-beg" position nor a road-hog crouch. A happy medium should be struck.

In the case of the late models with the new design of resilient rubber-mounted handlebars (Fig. 2), it is not advisable to adjust the angle of the bars, and the two locking plugs must always be kept screwed up *hard*, otherwise the full benefits of the shock absorbers will not be obtained and the steering may be spoilt.

Steering-head Adjustment. This should be such that it allows perfect freedom without up-and-down play. To test this, stand astride the machine and grip the bars. Lift them to ascertain if any movement is felt. Play in the steering head is liable to damage the ball races, and also causes a tendency for instability on grease, as does play in the wheel bearings.

Before adjusting the steering-head bearings it is advisable to remove the weight from the front wheel by supporting the crankcase with a suitable block. The steering damper should also be slackened right off. Now loosen the bolt passing through the ball-head clip and unscrew a few turns the thin lock nut placed over the adjuster nut above the clip. The adjuster nut can then be screwed up until all "shake" in the handlebars is eliminated, but avoid over-tightening the nut. Finally, lock the adjustment by means of the lock nut and check the adjustment once again.

Front Forks. A new type of fork adjustment was introduced in 1932 and it is now possible easily to take up wear in the links,

MAINTENANCE AND OVERHAULING 129

as well as to set the friction discs which are provided to damp out oscillations and fork rebound.

To make an adjustment of the spindles, slacken the two hexagon lock nuts, one at each end of the spindle, and re-tighten the spindle by means of a spanner placed on the squared end. An anti-clockwise rotation tightens the links. It should be noted that re-tightening the lock nut at the end which is not squared will tighten up the adjustment, therefore adjust a little at a time, screw up the lock nut, and test. If the adjustment is not right, it is necessary to repeat the process until the correct adjustment is reached. Finally re-tighten the locknut at the squared end.

The reason that the tightening up of the lock nut affects the adjustment is that the spindle at this end is stepped, the shoulder bearing up against a corresponding shoulder in the hole through the link. When the lock nut is loosened, the link moves away from the shoulder on the spindle and extra clearance therefore develops. For correct spindle adjustment the forks should move freely with the dampers out of action, and with no side play on the links. On 1934–8 models the knurled washers near the side links serve as a good guide to correct adjustment. These should just rotate easily.

To bring the fork dampers into action, adjust the spindle which passes through the damper discs, as already described, then in the case of 1932 models loosen the lock nut, give the spindle a partial turn in an anti-clockwise direction and re-tighten the lock nut. If the damping action is then insufficient the spindle has not been rotated far enough.

On 1933–8 models the fork dampers are adjusted by means of the hand nut on the off-side lower front spindle only. Maintain the spindle screwed right home in the near-side link and the lock nut tight.

For the best results the forks should have a free action, with just sufficient friction to prevent excessive fork bounce on bad roads. But however carefully adjusted, forks will never work properly unless they are kept well greased (see page 98).

Wheel Bearings. Taper roller bearings are used for both wheels, the outer race being pressed into the hub and the inner one a light sliding fit on the spindle. The bearing adjustment should be such that there is just the *slightest amount of play as measured at the wheel rim.* Fig. 27 shows the adjustment. The detachable wheel has no adjustment.

Brake Adjustment. A fulcrum adjuster is provided for the rear brake and all normal brake adjustments must be effected by rotating the square-ended fulcrum spindle (Fig. 5) in the brake anchor plate diametrically opposite to the lever bearing. Rotate the spindle clockwise to compensate for wear of the brake linings. The hand adjuster on the front end of the brake rod must be slacked off while making the fulcrum adjustment. When the fulcrum spindle will turn no further, re-tighten the hand adjusting nut until the brake pedal has only the barest amount of idle movement. Use the rod thumbscrew only for countering chain wear.

Adjust the front brake by means of the hand adjuster on the lower end of the brake rod.

CARBURETTOR MAINTENANCE

Tuning the Amal Carburettor. Should the setting of this instrument not give entire satisfaction for particular requirements, there are four separate ways of rectifying matters as given herewith, and the adjustment should be made in this order: (*a*) Main jet (three-quarters to full throttle); (*b*) Pilot air adjustment (closed to one-eighth throttle); (*c*) Throttle valve cut-away on the air-intake side (one-eighth to one-quarter throttle); (*d*) Needle position (one-quarter to three-quarters throttle). The diagram (Fig. 58) clearly indicates the part of the throttle range over which each adjustment is effective.

(*a*) To obtain the correct main jet size, several jets should be experimented with, and that selected should be the *smallest which gives maximum power and speed on full throttle.*

(*b*) To weaken slow-running mixture, screw pilot air adjuster outwards, and to enrich screw pilot air adjuster inwards.

Screw pilot air adjuster home in a clockwise direction. Place gear lever in "neutral." Slightly flood the float chamber by gently depressing the tickler until fuel begins to escape from the mixing chamber. Set magneto at half advance, throttle approximately one-eighth open, close the air lever, start the engine, and warm up. After warming up, reduce the engine revolutions by gently throttling down. The slow-running mixture will prove over-rich unless air leaks exist. Very gradually unscrew the pilot jet adjuster. The engine speed will increase, and must again be reduced by gently closing the throttle until, by a combination of throttle position and air adjustment, the desired "idling" is obtained. It is occasionally necessary to retard completely the magneto before getting a satisfactory tick-over, especially when early ignition timing is used. If it is desired to make the engine idle with the throttle quite closed, the position of the throttle valve must be set by means of the throttle stop-screw, the throttle lever during this adjustment being pushed right home. Alternatively, if the screw is adjusted clear of the throttle valve, the engine will be shut off in the normal way by the control lever.

MAINTENANCE AND OVERHAULING

(c) Given satisfactory "tick-over," set the magneto control all half-advance with the air lever fully open. Very slowly open the throttle valve when, if the engine responds regularly up to one-quarter throttle, the valve cut-away is correct.

A weak mixture is indicated by spitting back through the air-intake with blue flames and hesitation in picking up, which disappears when the air lever is closed down. This can be remedied by fitting a throttle valve with less cut-away. A rich mixture is shown by a black, sooty exhaust, and the engine falters when the air valve is closed. The remedy for this is a throttle valve with

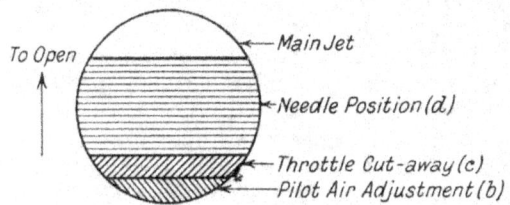

FIG. 58. RANGE AND SEQUENCE OF ADJUSTMENTS—AMAL CARBURETTOR

greater cut-away. Each Amal valve is stamped with two numbers, the first indicating the type number of the carburettor, and the second figure the amount of cut-away on the intake side of the valve in sixteenths of an inch, e.g. 6/4 is a type 6 valve with four-sixteenths in a $\frac{1}{4}$ in. cut-away.

(d) Open air lever fully and the throttle half-way. Note if the exhaust is crisp and the engine flexible. Close the air valve slightly below the throttle, when the exhaust note and engine revolutions should remain constant. Should popping back and spitting occur with blue flames from the intake, the mixture is weak, and the needle should be slightly raised. Test by lowering the air valve gently. The engine revolutions will rise when the air valve is lowered slightly below the throttle valve.

If the engine speed does not increase progressively with raising of the throttle, and a smoky exhaust is apparent with heavy laboured running, and tendency to eight-stroke, the mixture is too rich and the needle should be lowered in the throttle valve. Having found the correct needle position, the carburettor setting is now complete, and it will be found that the driving is practically automatic once the engine is warmed up. For speed work the main jet may be increased by 10 per cent, when the air lever should be fully open on full throttle.

Cleaning the Amal Carburettor. Periodical cleaning is necessary to maintain efficient functioning of the carburettor, and should be carried out in the following sequence.

Disconnect petrol pipe. Unscrew holding bolt Q (Fig. 38) and remove float chamber complete. With box or set spanner, slacken the mixing chamber union nut E. Mixing chamber complete may now be removed from engine, either by unscrewing the clip pin (if outlet) or the bolts (if flange fitting). Unscrew mixing chamber lock ring, and pull out throttle valve needle and air valve. Remove main jet P and needle jet O. Mixing chamber union nut E may then be removed and jet block complete pushed out. If this is obstinate, tap gently, using a wooden stump inside the mixing chamber. Unscrew float chamber cover W and slacken lock screw X. Withdraw the float by pinching the clip V inwards, and at the same time pull gently upwards.

Generally it is sufficient to wash all the parts in clean petrol, but if the carburettor has had extended service, check the following.

(a) FLOAT CHAMBER NEEDLE U. If a distinct shoulder is visible on the point of seating, renew this as soon as convenient.

(b) THROTTLE VALVE. Test in mixing chamber, and if excessive play is present it is advisable to renew this without delay.

(c) THROTTLE NEEDLE CLIP. This part must securely grip needle. *Free rotation must not take place*, otherwise the needle groove will become worn and necessitate a new part being fitted. *Be sure to refit the clip in the same groove.*

(d) JET BLOCK. If trouble has been experienced with erratic "idling," ascertain by means of a fine bristle that the pilot jet J is clear, and that the pilot outlet M in the mixing chamber is unobstructed.

To Reassemble. Refit jet block F with washer on underside, and screw on lightly mixing chamber union nut E. Screw in needle jet O and main jet P. Open air lever $\frac{7}{8}$ in., throttle lever half-way; grasp the air slide between the thumb and the finger; *make sure that the needle enters the central hole in the adaptor top.* Slightly twist the throttle valve until it enters the adaptor guide, when on pushing down the valves the air valve should enter its guide. If not, slightly move the mixing chamber top, when the air valve will slide into place. Screw on mixing chamber lock-nut. *No brute force is necessary.*

Attach carburettor to the cylinder, pushing right home, and examine washer if flange fitting. Insert holding bolt Q, and thoroughly tighten union nut E by means of a fixed spanner. Refit float and needle, holding the needle head against its seating by means of a pencil until the float and the clip V are slipped into position. Make sure that the clip enters the groove provided. Screw on the cover tightly and lock in position by means of the lock screw X. Fit holding bolt in float chamber with one washer above and one below the lug. Screw holding bolt into mixing chamber and lock securely. Clean petrol pipe and filter if fitted, and replace. It will be necessary to re-check the pilot setting if this has been disturbed.

DECARBONIZATION

After 2,000–3,000 miles have been covered (3,000–5,000 on the Square Four), the accumulation of carbon deposits on the piston crown and in various parts of the combustion chamber results in the engine losing its original "kick," and there is a marked decline in general all-round performance, accompanied by a tendency to knocking under the slightest provocation. In addition the exhaust note becomes "woolly." When this happens it is a sure indication that the time has come for undertaking a "top overhaul," or, in other words, for decarbonizing and grinding-in the valves. Carbon deposits are inevitable in internal combustion engines and are due to three things: (a) burnt lubricating oil; (b) carbonization of road dust; (c) incomplete fuel combustion. When decarbonizing it is always worth while inspecting the valve seatings and, *if necessary*, grinding-in the valves. Removal of the valves incidentally facilitates thorough cleaning of the ports.

The Side-Valve Engines. The S.V. engines are perhaps the easiest type to decarbonize, and on all 1933–8 engines with a detachable cylinder head above the level of the valves it is only necessary to remove this in order to decarbonize and grind in the valves. When it is desired to inspect the piston rings and decarbonize the ring grooves and *inside* of the piston, the cylinder barrel must, of course, also be removed. Although the valves can be removed and ground in with the cylinder removed, it is better not to disturb it unnecessarily.

On some 1932 S.V. models the cylinder barrel and cylinder head are cast integral, and the complete cylinder must be removed for decarbonizing.

The Overhead-Valve Singles. All Ariel O.H.V. engines have detachable cylinder-heads, and therefore to decarbonize it is only necessary to remove the head complete with valves, except where it is thought advisable to have a look at the piston, in which case the cylinder barrel has to come off as well. On all 1932–8 Ariel O.H.V. models owing to considerations of space and the method of mounting the rocker-box, this must be taken off together with the push-rods before removing the cylinder-head. On 1935–8 models the oil feed to the valve guides or rockers must also be disconnected.

The Overhead Camshaft Engine. Decarbonizing the "Square Four" engine is quite simple and very similar to decarbonizing the push-rod O.H.V. engines, but the rocker-box or cam box need not be removed. It is necessary, however, to disconnect the camshaft drive and the oil feeds to the cam box and pressure gauge before taking off the cylinder-head complete with cam box and valves. It is then a simple matter to remove the cylinder block itself if desired.

The Overhead-valve " Squariel." The 1937 600 c.c. and 1937–8 1,000 c.c. O.H.V. "Square Four" can be very readily decarbonized. It is quite unnecessary to remove the rocker-box from the cylinder head, it being possible to draw off sideways both of them together with the push-rods after removing a dozen bolts. The cylinder block can then be easily lifted off if desired, although this is not essential for decarbonizing.

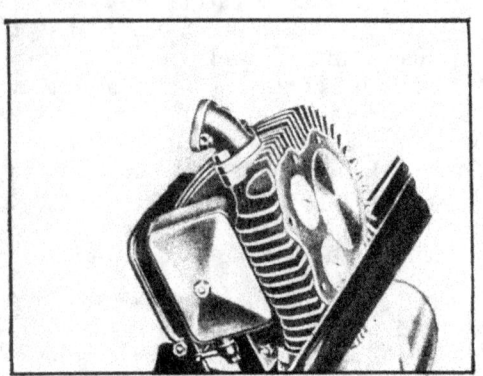

FIG. 59. 1932 S.V. "SLOPER" CYLINDER WITH THE DETACHABLE HEAD REMOVED (MODEL SB)

To Remove Cylinder-Head (1932–8 S.V.). On engines with detachable heads the procedure is to take out the sparking plug, undo the seven set-bolts, securing the cylinder head to the barrel, and lift off the head. Take care not to damage the copper asbestos joint washer. If the head is stuck at all, very gently tap it off and replace the washer if damaged.

Removing the Cylinder (1932–8 S.V.). Remove the sparking plug, valve caps, carburettor, exhaust pipe, and exhaust valve lifter wire in the case of 1932 engines without detachable heads. Where a detachable head is provided, remove it as described above and then undo the carburettor, exhaust pipe, breather pipe from the valve chest (1938), and valve lifter wire.

Now remove the four nuts and spring washers holding down the cylinder, and lift the cylinder up. On the 1932 LB engine there are five holding-down nuts, one of these being inside the valve spring chamber. As soon as the cylinder is clear of the securing studs, incline it forwards and lift up towards the front of the tank. Pull the piston down to the bottom of the stroke and the cylinder will come away. In the case of the 1932 "Sloper"

MAINTENANCE AND OVERHAULING 135

engines (Fig. 59) before removing the cylinder after taking off the detachable head, it is necessary to turn the front wheel to full lock one way or the other so as to give sufficient clearance to enable the cylinder to be drawn off between the two front tubes.

Be Careful with Valve Stem End Caps. The 1935 S.V. engines have direct operating tappets (see Fig. 6) similar to push-rods, and when drawing off the cylinder great care must be taken not to drop either of the small ball-ended valve stem end caps, which engage with the cups on the tappet heads, into the timing gear. Fishing out one of these little caps is likely to be an extremely irksome business.

To Remove Cylinder Head (O.H.V.). The rocker-box(es) must first be detached and the procedure on the 1932–8 models is as follows.

All 1938 O.H.V. Models. Lift the petrol tank after undoing the four set-screws and remove the carburettor, sparking plug, and exhaust pipe(s). The exhaust valve lifter wire and the oil feed to the rocker spindles should then be disconnected. Next the caps over the rocker adjusters should be unscrewed and the engine turned until both valves are fully closed.

Now unscrew the four bolts retaining each rocker-box, lift the boxes clear of the valves and swing them outwards until it is possible to lift them clear of the push-rods. The push-rods may then be pulled out. Having done this, undo the four cylinder head bolts and remove the head carefully. If stiff, gently prise off with a screwdriver, being careful not to break the fins or scratch the joint face. Removal of the head frees the push-rod covers, which should be put in a safe place. Do not disturb the cylinder barrel unless the piston is to be examined.

1932 Models LF, MF, and MH. Remove the sparking plug, carburettor, and exhaust pipes. Set the engine with both valves closed.

Fix the two link plates to support the rocker arms; these are the two plates with projecting pegs, supplied in the tool kit. The method of use is to undo the two rocker spindle nuts on the sparking plug side, and slip the plates on to the spindles so that the pegs come immediately under the rocker arms. Replace and tighten up the spindle nuts, and the rocker arms are held in place against the tension of the return springs, when the rocker-box is removed. This greatly facilitates the replacement of the box.

Remove the two cylinder head bolts on the near side of the engine; this also releases the rocker plate on this side. Next unscrew the two set bolts holding the offside rocker plate to the head and lift up the rocker-box complete, so that it is clear of the push rods; then draw it away towards the offside of the engine. Now remove the two offside head-securing bolts and take off the head. If this tends to stick it can be prised up by inserting a screwdriver into the joint. Take care not to damage the joint or break the fins. Before lifting the head, undo the oil pipe connection to the inlet valve guide.

1932 Models VG and VH. The procedure for removing the cylinder on these models is carried out in a similar way, but on account of differences in construction the following notes have been included.

Remove the sparking plug, carburettor, and exhaust pipes. Set the engine so that all four valves are closed, release the oil pipe to the inlet valve guides, and unscrew the special hollow set-bolt which forms the connection for the top end of the pipe, and which also helps to secure the rocker-box. Now remove the other three set-bolts holding the rocker-box to the head; it is desirable to have all valves closed whilst these bolts are being removed. This frees the rocker-box, push-rods, and enclosing tubes, which can all be removed.

Place a clean rag over the two holes at the top of the timing case into which the push rods fit, so as to prevent the ingress of dirt. Undo the five head retaining bolts. These screw *up* into the head through bosses on the side of the cylinder barrel. Now take off the head, taking care not to damage the joint or break fins.

1932 Model SG. The cylinder head is removed in a very similar manner, but it will be noted that the rocker-box is held to the head by means of three ordinary set bolts and one special hollow set bolt; this latter carries the upper end of the oil pipe for inlet valve guide lubrication. The head itself is secured by five set bolts screwing *upwards* through bosses on the side of the cylinder barrel.

All 1933–7 O.H.V. Models. Remove the sparking plug, the exhaust pipe(s), and the carburettor. Then set the engine with the piston on the top of the compression stroke so that both inlet and exhaust valves are closed. On 1935–7 engines remove the "snap on" valve spring covers by pressing back the retaining springs. Also disconnect the exhaust valve lifter cable from the lever on the off side of the rocker-box. The rocker-box can now be removed by undoing the four set bolts retaining it. Lift up the rocker-box and remove it together with the push-rods and

MAINTENANCE AND OVERHAULING

push-rod covers. Be careful not to lose the fibre and rubber washers at the top and bottom ends respectively of the covers.

Having removed the rocker-box, the cylinder head can be removed by unscrewing the four fixing bolts. Before attempting to remove the cylinder head, however, it is necessary to disconnect the oil leads to the valve guides. Should the cylinder head tend to stick to the cylinder barrel it should be gently tapped with a hammer. No washer is used between the barrel and head, and therefore great care must be taken to avoid scratching or otherwise damaging the ground faces, otherwise there will be a tendency for the engine to "blow" at the joint and to lose compression, both of which are very detrimental to engine efficiency.

1937-8 Models 4F, 4G. On the 600 c.c. and 1,000 c.c. "Square Four," preparation for decarbonizing should be carried out as follows.

Remove the exhaust pipes, manifolds, rocker-box lid, carburettor, and sparking plugs. Then disconnect the oil pipe leading to the rocker-box and remove the twelve bolts which secure the head in position. The four bolts passing through the rocker-box near the push-rods should first be removed; their upper ends have nuts which retain the rocker-box lid. After removing these four bolts, remove the four centre bolts, two of which are near the induction pipe and two in front of the rocker-box. The four remaining bolts which pass through the head at the corners of the rocker-box can finally be extracted. This enables the head to be lifted up sufficiently to enable the push-rods to clear the cylinder block and the head to be lifted clear on one side, together with the push-rods which cannot drop out owing to their upper fixing.

If the copper asbestos joint washers are removed, be careful not to damage them. Scrape them clean and lay on one side ready for reassembly. The cylinder block need not be removed for decarbonizing as the piston crowns are amply exposed, but if it is desired to remove the block for inspecting the piston rings, this is very simple. Undo the eight cylinder base nuts and draw the block straight up clear of the pistons, which should be marked as described later before being removed from the connecting-rods.

1932-6 Model 4F. The procedure when preparing the "Square Four" for decarbonizing is as follows.

Remove the exhaust pipes, sparking plugs, and air and throttle slides from the mixing chamber. The carburettor itself can be left bolted to the cylinder head if the petrol pipe is disconnected.

Push back the two clips K (Fig. 60) securing the distributor cover to the rocker-box, and tie up the cover and leads out of the way.

Unscrew the four thumb nuts securing the rocker-box cover, and lift this off. Take care not to damage the joint washer.

Disconnect the oil pipe to the rocker-box by unscrewing the

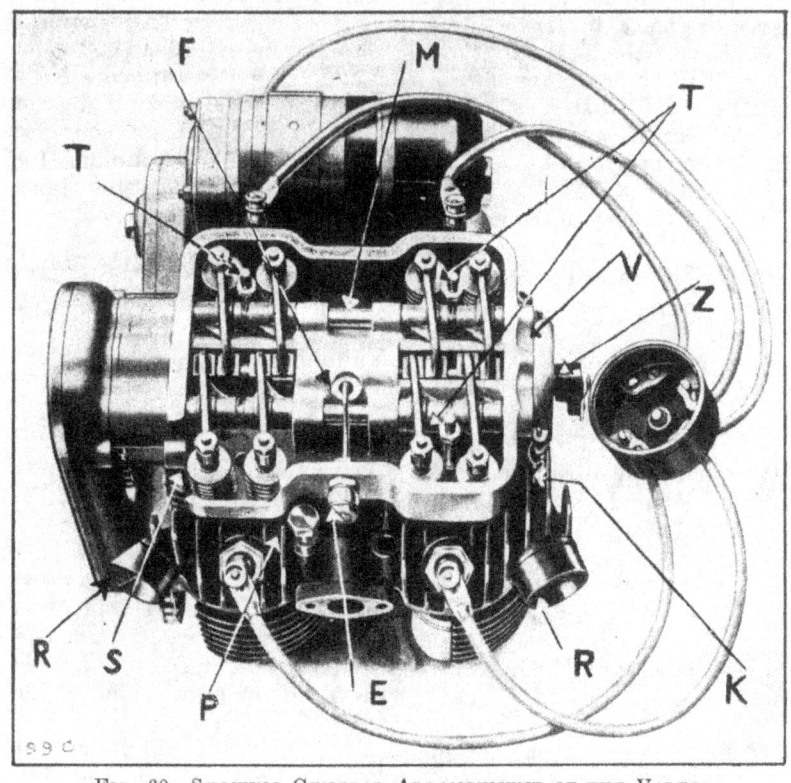

FIG. 60. SHOWING GENERAL ARRANGEMENT OF THE VALVES AND ROCKER GEAR ON THE 1932-6 SQUARE-FOUR

KEY TO FIG. 60

E = Oil delivery union to rocker box
F = Oil delivery hole to camshaft tunnel
K = Spring clip holding distributor cover
M = Rocker lever spindle for Nos. 2 and 3 cylinders
P = Cylinder head securing bolt
R = Exhaust ports
S = Valve spring collar
T = Rocker-box securing studs
V = Distributor cover back plate
Z = Distributor arm

outer nut on the union E (Fig. 60). The oil restrictor piece on the end of the oil pipe can then be slipped free.

Take off the connection in the pressure pipe to the oil gauge. This connection is just above the rocker-box cover.

MAINTENANCE AND OVERHAULING

FIG. 61. REAR SIDE VIEW OF SECTIONED 1932 FOUR-CYLINDER ENGINE

KEY TO FIG. 61. (SEE ALSO FIG. 54)

- A = Magneto pick-up
- C = Oil trough for connecting rod dipper D (Fig. 54)
- F = Delivery oilway from oil reservoir to engine
- G = Return oilway from engine sump to oil reservoir
- H = Oil regulator: (a) Outer hexagon—adjuster screw
  - (b) Centre hexagon—adjuster screw locknut
  - (c) Inner hexagon—regulator body
- J = Screw plug carrying oil delivery tube B (Fig. 54)
- L = Inspection plug for magneto sprocket and fixing
- M = Camshaft sprocket securing bolt
- N = Cylinder head fixing stud nut
- Q = Cheese-head screws holding camshaft chain case to rocker-box
- V = Camshaft sprocket
- W = Plug carrying oil reservoir filter
- Z = Fixing screw for camshaft vernier adjustment

Unscrew the plug in the top of the camshaft chain-case. This is similar to the one *L* (Fig. 61) in the magneto chain-case. This exposes the sprocket securing bolt *M*; unscrew this bolt and remove. Insert into this hole a flanged collar which is provided in the tool kit. This collar is somewhat similar to the plug which has just been removed, but it has no thread, and has a hole through its centre. Through this hole place the extractor bolt and screw this up into the sprocket. This will pull the sprocket off the camshaft, and leave the extractor bolt and collar in position. These, and the false bearing in the back of the chain-case, will hold the sprocket and so prevent the valve timing being upset through the camshaft sprocket coming out of mesh with the chain. Do not touch the vernier bolt *Z*. Remove the two cheese-head screws *Q* on either side of the extractor. These screws hold the chain-case up to the rocker-box.

Now, in the case of the 1932 engine, unscrew the four head-securing nuts. One of these is shown at *N* (Fig. 61). Another nut is just in front of the camshaft chain cover and the other two nuts are in a corresponding position on the other side of the engine. Next remove the four head-retaining bolts, one of which is shown at *P* (Fig. 60). A similar bolt is on the other side of the induction pipe, whilst the remaining two bolts are in a corresponding position at the back of the engine. In the case of the 1933-6 engine remove the eight head-securing bolts.

The head is now perfectly free and can be removed by inserting a screwdriver into the joint face between the barrel and the head, and prising up. The joint is made by means of a copper asbestos washer so that care must be taken not to damage this washer with the screwdriver blade. The head must, on the 1932 engine, be lifted straight up to allow the four studs (on which the nuts screw) to come clear of the cylinder block. It will probably be easier to prise up the block simultaneously from two opposite sides. Lift the head clear and place it carefully on the bench, using care with the distributor arm as this is easily damaged if knocked.

On the 1933-6 engine the cylinder head can be drawn off from the near side as studs are not used. To remove the head from the block it is only necessary to undo the eight bolts. As already mentioned, be careful with the asbestos joint washer and do not try much prising off of the head on the camshaft drive side because the rocker-box is spigoted into the chain-case. Observe how the cylinder head washers are fitted to ensure correct replacement. It is most important to refit the washer so that they conform exactly to the contour of the combustion chambers. After removing the cylinder head it is a simple matter to lift off the cylinder block if it is desired to examine the pistons and piston rings.

MAINTENANCE AND OVERHAULING 141

All that is necessary is to remove the base nuts and lift off the block vertically.

When Removing the Cylinder Barrel or Block. In the case of the S.V., O.H.V., and O.H.C. engines be very careful not to allow the piston or pistons to strike against the edge of the crankcase or the connecting rod. Ariel pistons are made of a special wear-resisting aluminium alloy, and while sufficiently strong for proper conditions of use, they are rather brittle and may readily be cracked or distorted if given a sharp blow. Therefore exercise caution when removing the cylinder and wrap a rag around the connecting rod afterwards to prevent it swaying about and causing damage to the piston. Also handle the piston with great care when removed from the engine.

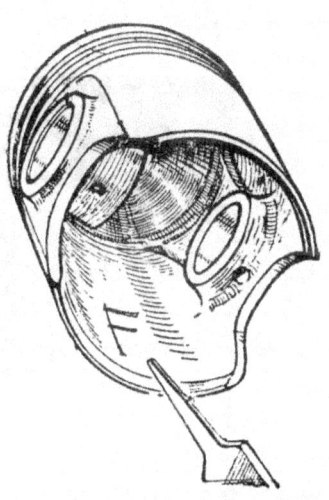

(*From " The Motor Cycle"*)
FIG. 62. MARK INSIDE OF PISTON TO ENSURE CORRECT REPLACEMENT

Piston Removal. The gudgeon pin is of the fully floating type, i.e. free to rotate in the piston and connecting rod bush. The pin is held in position by means of two spring circlips which fit into grooves machined at each outer end of the gudgeon-pin hole through the piston. These circlips can easily be removed by inserting a pointed instrument (e.g. a scriber) in the slot, under the clip, and prising out. Take care not to damage the clip, which should be round and lie flat when removed. On no account interchange the pistons on an O.H.C. model, and mark them on the inside so that they are replaced correctly.

Each piston laps out the cylinder in which it fits in a certain way, depending upon the connecting rod thrust, lubrication, and other factors, and it is *never* advisable to alter its original position on the connecting rod. On the four-cylinder Ariel engine mark the left-hand front piston "LF," the right-hand rear piston "RR," and so on. If the markings are scratched on the inside of the surface which faces the front there will be no doubt as to which is the correct way round to fit the piston on the connecting rod. On all the singles scratch the mark "F" as shown in Fig. 62 to indicate which is the front of the piston.

Piston Rings are Easily Broken. Great care must be taken when removing the piston rings as they are made of cast iron and are exceedingly brittle. It is unsafe to spring them out wider than the diameter of the piston crown, and the best method of removing the rings is shown in Fig. 63. Three strips of sheet tin about 1½ in. long and ⅜ in. wide are inserted under the rings opposite the slots, enabling the rings to be gently eased off one by one. Broken pieces of an old hack-saw blade will answer the same purpose.

The Piston Rings. The rings should be polished round the whole of their surfaces, and if either ring is discoloured or has a black

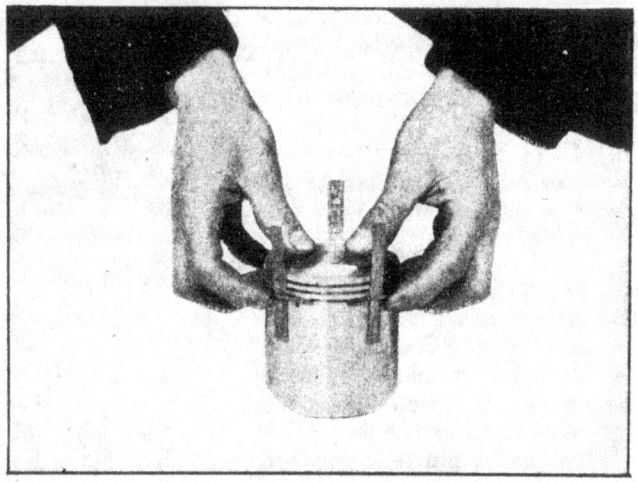

FIG. 63. THE SAFEST METHOD OF REMOVING PISTON RINGS

patch on it it means that gas has been leaking past, and it should therefore be replaced by a new one. With the rings removed the piston should be washed, so that the degree of carbon deposit in the slots may be readily seen. If any is found here it should be scraped away, but extreme care is necessary in order that the surface of the slot is not damaged by the scraping tool. If it is, loss of compression will result, and if the slot is badly cut or dented a new piston will probably have to be fitted for first-class results to be obtained. Any carbon deposit on the inside of the ring should also be scraped away. It is important to note that the rings should be quite free in their grooves, without much up-and-down movement—the actual amount is ·003 in. when new, and the gap between the ends of the ring should be from ·004 in. to ·006 in. on the 4F, LB, and LF models, and from ·006 in. to ·008 in. on the remaining 1932–8 models. On the 1932–6 4F the correct gap between the ends of the lower spring-loaded piston ring is ·010 in.–·014 in. The 4G ring gap is ·010 in.–·012 in.

MAINTENANCE AND OVERHAULING

The word "gap" does not apply here to the distance between the ends of the ring with the cylinder removed; it means the actual gap in working conditions. The only way to test this gap is to push the ring itself into the cylinder bore, making sure that it is square with the walls. To ensure this it is perhaps best to push up the piston ring with the aid of the piston. The gap may then be measured with a feeler gauge, as shown in Fig. 64. If it is less than ·004 in. and ·006 in. respectively, it is advisable to remove a little metal from either one or other end of the ring

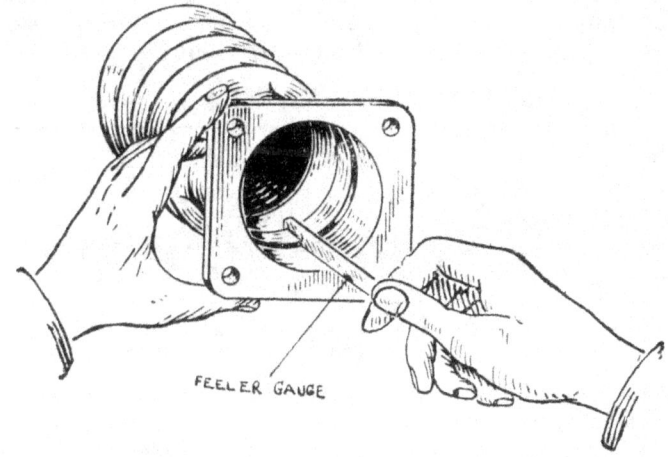

Fig. 64. How to Measure the Piston Ring Gap

until the recommended gap is obtained. The reason for this is that should the gap be too small the expansion of the engine, when it becomes hot, will actually cause the ends of the ring to meet, and may make the ring a very tight fit in the cylinder walls. Renew rings when gap exceeds 0·025 in.–0·030 in.

The piston and rings must again be washed in paraffin, after the carbon deposit has been removed. Refitting the rings is quite a simple matter. Before this is done a few drops of oil should be placed in the slots and the top ring may then be pushed over the top of the piston until it is home, the reverse direction applying to the bottom ring. Alternatively the method shown in Fig. 63 may be used. See that the piston ring gaps are opposite each other. On a two-ring piston they should be spaced at 180 degrees and on a three-ring piston at 120 degrees.

Removing the Carbon. Thoroughness in decarbonizing well repays the labour expended. The more completely the carbon is removed the better will the engine performance be, and the longer will it be before decarbonizing again becomes necessary.

It is inadvisable, however, to decarbonize the piston ring grooves more than about once every alternate decarbonization, when the cylinder as well as the cylinder head should be removed. When undertaking an ordinary top overhaul, the carbon deposits on the piston crown and on the inside of the cylinder head need alone be scraped off. To do this, a moderately sharp penknife, or the end of a screwdriver, should be employed. Be careful, however, not to employ excessive force on the piston, or its comparatively soft aluminium surface will be deeply scratched. When decarbonizing the cylinder head, do not overlook the exhaust ports, which are usually heavily sooted or carbonized, and, as before mentioned, see that the face on the overhead valve

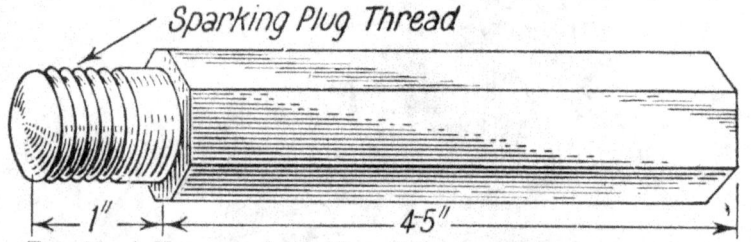

Fig. 65. A Hexagon Steel Bar Turned and Threaded at one End to Hold the Cylinder Head when Decarbonizing

head is not scratched. A good method of holding the head when decarbonizing it is to fit a hexagon steel bar screwed at one end into the sparking-plug hole. Such a bar is shown in Fig. 65. The cylinder head may then be held in a vice by means of the bar. If a bar is unavailable, an old sparking plug makes a good substitute. After the deposits have been removed, clean the surfaces with a calico rag damped in paraffin.

In the case of the 1932 model LB where the entire cylinder has to be removed, the top of the piston may afterwards be rubbed with *very fine* emery cloth until a perfectly smooth surface has been obtained. This method of finishing off may also be used for the detachable heads on all models, but the pistons should not be thus treated except when the cylinder itself is removed, enabling all abrasive particles to be afterwards eradicated. Emery particles which get down on to the rings may cause bad scoring of the cylinder walls. On the 1932 model LB the deposits on the integral cylinder head may be reached through the cylinder mouth. Care should be taken not to allow the screwdriver shank to scratch the part of the cylinder included in the piston stroke. See also that all carbon is removed from the valve caps, which may afterwards be cleaned with emery cloth. On the "Square Four" thoroughly decarbonize all four combustion chambers and also clean the joint washer.

MAINTENANCE AND OVERHAULING 145

When occasion is had to remove the piston or pistons, do not attempt to remove carbon from the outside of the skirt. Only the crown, the inside, and the piston ring grooves should be scraped and cleaned. The latter may be cleaned of all deposits after the rings have been removed by running a small, sharp, flat-ended tool round their circumferences. Only a tool of the right size should be used, or the shape of the grooves may be spoiled. A piece of broken piston ring can be used, but it is better to use a special tool.

Removing Valves (1932-8 S.V.). Place the cylinder on its side—valve spring chamber upwards—on a bench, and remove the

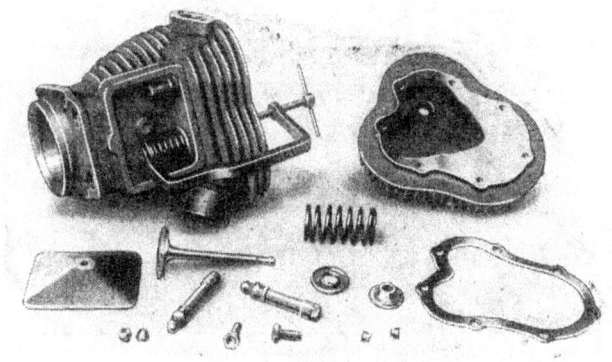

FIG. 66. REMOVING THE SIDE VALVES
(Models VA3, VA4, VB)

valves, using the valve extractor, which may be obtained from any of the Ariel agents. The forked end is placed under the valve collar and the point of the screw in the small centre hole in the valve head. Screw up, compressing the spring, and then remove the split cones. Unscrew the extractor and remove the valve, valve spring, and collars. Both valves are dealt with in this manner. Fig. 66 shows the 1935 S.V. cylinder with the inlet valve removed and the exhaust valve spring being compressed.

If it is intended to grind in the valves without removing the cylinder barrel, block up the bore with a rag, rotate the engine until both valves are closed, slack off the tappets and proceed as described above. After removing the valves be careful to see that they are not subsequently interchanged. The inlet valve is stamped "IN" or "2·S11," while the exhaust valve is stamped "EX," "J.H.3," or "G.2."

146   THE BOOK OF THE ARIEL

1932 O.H.V. The valves are held by the taper cotters and collars as on the side-valve models. The springs are easily removed by means of a special tool.

This tool is used as follows: Drop the square-shaped part through two of the head bolt holes and slip the wire through the small holes in the ends of the tool so that it cannot be withdrawn. Place a small block of wood inside the head so that the valves rest on this, and then hold the head down firmly on the bench or table.

With two studs, which are inside the body of the tool, resting

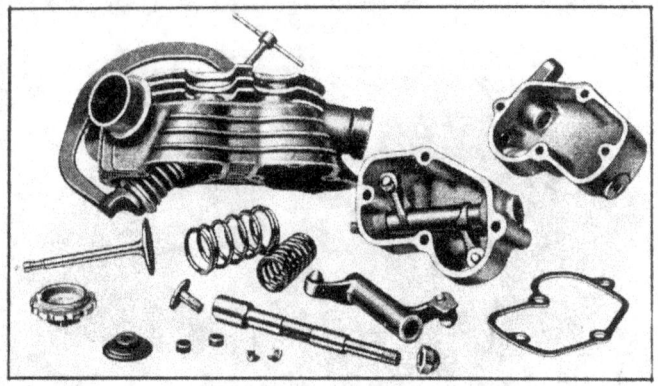

Fig. 67. Showing Redesigned Cylinder Head with one Valve Spring being Compressed and the two Rocker-boxes Removed

These rocker-boxes provide complete enclosure (1933 Models).

on the top spring collar, depress the handle, so compressing the spring, and withdraw the taper cotters. Note that the handle of the tool folds up if used the wrong way round. Having removed one valve (two or four-valve models), place the tool in the other two head bolt holes and remove the remaining valve(s) in a similar manner.

After removing the valves be careful not to mix up the inlet and exhaust valves.

1933–8 O.H.V. Owing to different cylinder-head design, the type of valve spring compressor for 1932 engines is not suitable for compressing the valve springs on the 1933–8 O.H.V. engines. It is necessary to use a screw-type compressor similar to that employed for the 1932–8 S.V. engines. A tool specially designed for the purpose (see Fig. 67) is obtainable for a few shillings from Messrs. Ariel Motors, Ltd., or from any of their agents. The method

MAINTENANCE AND OVERHAULING

of using this tool is precisely the same as in the case of the S.V. models. Place the forked end on the valve spring collar and the pointed end of the screw in the centre of the valve head and screw up until the valve spring is sufficiently compressed to allow of the split cones being removed. If stuck, gently tap them out. The valve, valve spring, and collars can now be removed. Deal with each valve similarly. Fig. 68 shows in addition to the valve spring compressor being used on the inlet valve, details of the 1934–7 rocker-box, the upper half of which has been removed.

As on the other engines, avoid interchanging the valves after

Fig. 68. Showing Overhead Valve Removal and Rocker-box Details
(1934–7 Models.)

removal. The inlet and exhaust valves are stamped "IN" and "EX" respectively.

1932-6 O.H.C. Take off the rocker-box cover and rotate the camshaft until all four valves belonging to the two front cylinders are on their seats. Remove the distributor cover back-plate, held by four screws; examination of the end face of the rocker-box behind the back-plate will show two holes in line with the two rocker spindles. Obtain a ¼-in. diameter bolt screwed 26 thds.-per-inch; insert this into the left-hand and screw it up into the end of the front rocker-spindle. Pulling this bolt outwards will pull the rocker-spindle out of the case and free the rockers, distance shims, and spring washers, etc. Carefully collect these as the spindle is pulled out and lay out each item on the bench in the same order. These parts are all interchangeable, but it is always better practice to replace a part in the same position, and if the items are, therefore, arranged on the bench in the sequence in which they come out, they can be put back into exactly the same order. The rear rocker spindle is dealt with in exactly the same manner. Remove the valve stem end caps and put them in a safe place.

To remove the valves, get a small block of wood, small enough to fit inside the combustion chamber. Lay this block on the bench and place the head over it so that the top end of the block fits into one of the combustion chambers and bears up against two valve heads. Downward pressure on the top spring collar *S* (Fig. 60) will compress the valve spring, when the two split cones, or cotters, can be taken out. This releases the top collar and spring, which can be lifted off. The valve will then drop out as soon as the wood block is removed. Be careful not to interchange the valves.

Note the sequence of numbering the valves. With the cylinder

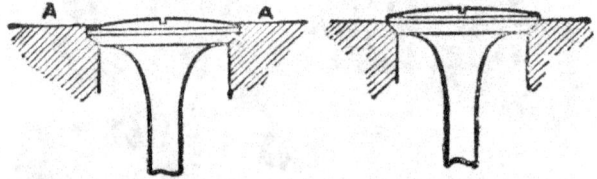

FIG. 69. SHOWING THE BAD EFFECT OF EXCESSIVE VALVE GRINDING
The valve at *AA* has become "pocketed" and this is detrimental to engine efficiency.

head inverted and the ports facing the operator, the front row are 1, 2, 3, 4 right to left, and the back row 5, 6, 7, 8 left to right.

1937-8 Models 4F, 4G. The rockers must be removed. To do this undo the two hexagon spindle bearing plugs at the oil feed end of the rocker box. To withdraw the spindles screw into their ends a $\frac{5}{16}$ in. by 26 T.P.I. bolt (one of the rocker-box bolts) and pull straight out through the end of the box. Collect the rockers, shims and spring spacing washers, etc., as the spindles are withdrawn and lay out on the bench in order. Whilst all these parts are quite interchangeable it is best practice to refit each part in its original position. Note that no shim is used next the bearing plug. Remove the valve stem end caps, draw out the push rods and put with the other parts. Note the sequence of numbering the valves. With head upside down and the front towards operator, the front row are 1, 2, 3, 4 right to left, and the back row 5, 6, 7, 8 left to right.

The valve springs can be compressed with a valve spring compressing tool, when the split cotters can be removed and the valves taken out. Note that the large coil of the inner spring fits next the taper hole collar.

Grinding in the Valves. Should the valve faces or seats show

MAINTENANCE AND OVERHAULING 149

signs of serious pitting, the valves will have to be ground in. Valves of the side-by-side type have, of course, to be *pressed down* on their seatings when using a screwdriver, while those of the overhead type have to be *pulled up* against their seatings.

Only grind in valves when necessary, using a ready-made compound such as Richford's grinding paste; only a small quantity is necessary, and do not revolve the valves round and round, but rotate the valve about a third of a turn in one direction and then an equal amount in the opposite direction. About every six oscillations lift the valve, rotate it $\frac{1}{8}$ to $\frac{1}{4}$ of a revolution and proceed as before, stopping when no "cut" can be felt to redistribute the grinding paste and examine the valve face and seat. Continue grinding in until both the valve face and valve seat are quite bright. It will facilitate grinding-in the valves on the S.V. engines if a small compression spring is inserted under the valve head. This avoids the nuisance of having to repeatedly lift the valve by hand to change it to a new position. A small hand vice will be found a convenient tool for holding the valve stem on O.H.V. engines, and very great care must be taken after this operation to remove all traces of valve-grinding compound. The valve stems may be cleaned with *very fine* or worn emery cloth. Do not use coarse grinding compound for grinding valves in unless the pitting is very extensive. A little fine paste smeared very lightly over the valve face is far better. Care should be taken to avoid burring the valve stems, otherwise unnecessary wear will take place in the valve guides. The same remarks apply to the head itself. This should be polished with very fine or used emery cloth after the deposit has been removed.

Do not grind valves unnecessarily, as this causes them to become "pocketed" (see Fig. 69), but see that all pit marks are removed from the valve face. Finish off with a fine paste. Wash valve seats, valves and springs, etc., with clean paraffin, taking great care to remove all traces of emery or grinding paste. Dry with a clean, smooth cloth. All is now ready for reassembling. When replacing the valves see that the duplex springs, collars, and cotters bed down properly. It will facilitate replacing the valve springs if the recessed portion of the valve stem is greased as this will allow the split cones to be kept in place while the spring is being compressed.

Reassembling (1932-8 S.V.). Before replacing see that all parts are perfectly clean, with no trace of grinding paste from valve grinding and with no particles of carbon or dirt adhering to any of the internal parts.

When reassembling a side-valve engine, which is almost exactly the dismantling process reversed, push gudgeon pin into the piston until it comes flush with inside of boss of piston; slip piston over connecting rod, then push gudgeon pin gently in. Refit the spring circlips. These should be quite firm when in position and should not shake about. The piston rings should be spaced so that the gap of top ring faces front and gap of bottom ring faces rear. Smear piston thoroughly with oil and see that there is plenty behind the rings. Wipe top of the piston clean. The cylinder should be smeared with oil and then refitted to crankcase. If paper washer is torn, fit a new one. Be sure that the oil hole registers correctly. If any difficulty is experienced in getting piston rings to enter cylinder, obtain assistance to hold the cylinder while the rings and piston are eased in.

Before lowering the cylinder on certain models arrange the tappet "feet" fore and aft, and lower the cylinder into position. If the tappet "feet" are not arranged like this, they will not go into position on the cams. On present models if the direct operating tappets have been removed, observe that the locknut with the large collar goes on the exhaust tappet. This collar comes above the nut.

Screw down cylinder nuts, giving each a half turn alternatively and diagonally. Fit the detachable head (all models except 1932 LB), taking care not to omit the copper-asbestos washer, and to see that the joint washer and the joint faces are quite clean. Insert the set bolts and screw these down finger tight until the head of each bolt is down on the cylinder head. Then with a spanner give one bolt a one-eighth turn. Repeat this on the next but one bolt and then on the next but one bolt to the last. Work right round the head in this manner until all the bolts are tight. This ensures that an even pressure is put on the joint. Screw in sparking plug, refit exhaust lifter cable, and the exhaust system. Attach valve cover, valve caps (1932 LB), carburettor, and high-tension wire to plug. The work is now complete. Start engine and run gently until warm. Then check tappet clearances and cylinder and head holding-down nuts and bolts for tightness.

Reassembling (1932 O.H.V. Lightweights). Make sure that the joint faces of the head and barrel are clean, smooth, and have no carbon particles or old jointing compound on them, or a tight joint will not be obtained (no jointing washer is used). See that the engine is on top of the compression stroke. Now refit the cylinder barrel as on the S.V. engines. Smear the joint face on the barrel with a little of one of the special jointing compounds (gold size may be used), place the head in position, and screw down the two offside head bolts finger tight. Replace the rocker-box, seeing that the ball ends on the rocker-arms are in the cups at the top ends of the push-rods, and that the enclosing tubes are

MAINTENANCE AND OVERHAULING 151

located in the holes on the top of the return spring chamber. Insert the two set bolts securing the offside rocker-place and then the two nearside head bolts. See that the four head-retaining bolts are turned down finger tight until the head of each bolt is down on to the cylinder head. Now take a spanner and give one bolt a one-eighth turn, repeat this on the bolt diagonally opposite, and then on the two remaining ones; keep going round in the same order, giving each bolt a one-eighth turn at a time until all are tight. This method ensures that the cylinder head is pulled down evenly so that a good joint is made. Remove the two link plates and then reconnect the exhaust lifter, warm up the engine, go over the nuts and bolts once again, and finally adjust the valve clearances.

Important Note re all O.H.V. Models: *It is important to remember to replace the hardened steel cap ends on the valve stems or considerable damage may be done.*

1932 Heavyweights and all 1933–7 O.H.V. Models. The cylinder barrel is replaced as on the S.V. models. Be careful not to put any strain on the connecting-rod when slipping the barrel over the piston. Rotate the engine until neither cam lever is on the lift, i.e. valves closed. See that all parts are clean and free from grinding paste, make sure that the joint faces of the head and barrel are clean, smooth, and have no carbon particles or old jointing compound on them, or a tight joint will not be obtained (no jointing washer is used). Smear the joint face on the barrel with a little of one of the special jointing compounds (Heldite may be used), place the head in position and screw down the head bolts finger tight, and then give one bolt a one-eighth turn. Repeat this on the diagonally opposite bolt, and so on round the head. Then return to the first bolt and give it another eighth turn and carry on until all the bolts are quite tight.

Insert the two push-rods into their enclosing tubes. Put the rods and covers into position with the ball ends of the rods locating with the cups in the cam levers. If the rubber oil-retaining washers are damaged or perished, fit new ones, or an oil leak will occur. Place the hardened steel caps on the valve stems. Take the rocker-box, replace the exhaust lifter wire if this has been removed, and put the box into position, seeing that the ball ends on the rocker-arms are in the cups at the top of the push-rods, and that the enclosing tubes are located in the recesses at the base of the rocker-box. Be sure to replace the fibre washers in the recesses to prevent oil leakage.

Keep the rocker-box pressed down so as to overcome the resistance due to the compression of the rubber washers at the bottom of the push-rod tubes, and then in the case of the 1932 engines insert the two set bolts which secure the rocker-box to the pillars on the timing side. Make sure that these set bolts are screwed in straight or the thread will be damaged; due to the upward thrust on the rocker-box, it is easy to get the threads crossed if a little care is not exercised. Tighten up these set bolts and secure the other side of the box with the two nuts which screw on the tops of the head bolts.

In the case of the 1933-7 models also keep the rocker-box pressed down to overcome the resistance of the rubber washers and then screw up the two nuts holding the near side rocker-box supporting plate as far down the cylinder head studs as possible by hand. Now insert and screw home the two offside set bolts and finally tighten the near side nuts and reconnect the oil pipe to the inlet valve guide.

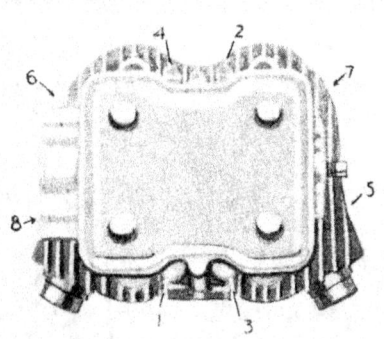

FIG. 70. ORDER OF TIGHTENING HEAD BOLTS AND NUTS, 1932-6 4F

Replace the carburettor, sparking plug, silencing system, etc. Then adjust the valve clearances, warm up the engine and go over the various nuts again.

1932-6 O.H.C. The reassembly of the head, etc., of the Square Four is perfectly straightforward. Assuming that the valves have been replaced and the rocker gear assembled, the head and rocker-box is now complete and ready for replacing on the cylinder block. See that all trace of jointing compound has been scraped away from the joint face on the head, and that the gaskets are in sound condition.

On 1932-6 models, four gaskets are used instead of the one big one on earlier types. These gaskets are copper faced on each side and can therefore be used either way up (on earlier types the steel face should be placed next to the head, with the brass face next to the block). Be particularly careful, however, to see that each gasket is replaced with its greatest diameter truly across the cylinder bore, so that it matches up with the oval shape of the combustion chamber.

Should a gasket require renewing at any time, a complete set of four pieces *must* be used. The gaskets are graded and arranged in sets, which must not be split.

Smear the exposed faces of the gaskets with jointing compound

MAINTENANCE AND OVERHAULING   153

and lower the head down on to the cylinder block, screwing the four nuts on to the head-retaining studs and inserting the four head bolts. To do this, first see that the four head bolt and stud nuts are screwed up so that they are resting on the faces of the bosses.

No cylinder head studs are provided on the 1933–5 engines, eight bolts being used instead. These should be screwed home uniformly.

Screw the head bolts down finger tight, taking care to do the outer bolts first. The correct order of tightening up the bolts and nuts on 1932 machines is as follows: 5, 6, 7, 8, 1, 2, 3, 4. (See Fig. 70.) This tends to bring the greatest pressure on the outer edges of the gaskets, a result which materially assists in getting a good gastight joint.

If the fibre washers which make the joint between the rocker box and the chain case are damaged, they must be replaced before the head is fitted. On 1933–5 engines the rocker-box is spigoted into the chain-case. To re-fit the camshaft sprocket on the camshaft it is necessary, on the 1932–5 models, to take off the outer camshaft chain-case cover. First, unscrew the sprocket extractor bolt and withdraw the bolt and collar; the sprocket will drop down on to the edge of the camshaft bearing housing and will remain there, keeping the chain properly in mesh with the sprockets whilst the chain cover is taken off.

Now press the tension spring up against the side of the chain case, placing the bolt M (Fig. 61) through the sprocket and lightly screw it up into the camshaft. Rotate the engine slowly, pressing the sprocket inwards against the camshaft until the sprocket key engages with the camshaft key-way. Now tighten up the bolt M, and replace the chain cover.

The valve timing cannot possibly be assembled incorrectly if these instructions are carried out, as there is only one key in the sprocket and one key-way in the camshaft. Replace the sprocket inspection plug, the rocker box oil pipe, the rocker box cover and joint washer, and do up the oil gauge pipe connection. Be careful with the cover joint washer, seeing that this is properly in position before doing up the securing nuts tightly, so that a good oil retaining joint may be made. Now fit the exhaust pipes, carburettor, sparking plugs, and distributor cover, and connect the leads to the appropriate plugs. The engine should then be ready for starting. Check over the valve clearance.

When a gasket is first fitted, it will " give," or compress freely as the engine warms up. Therefore, when the engine has been run from 10 to 15 minutes, tighten the head bolts again. Repeat this in about 50 miles and again after a similar distance. This should pull the gasket down to its compression limit. A periodical testing of the holding down bolts will prevent any possibility of a blown gasket. Before pulling down the head, the camshaft case screws Q (Fig. 61) should be slackened off and, of course, subsequently re-tightened.

Reassembling 1938 O.H.V. Models. Refit the piston and cylinder as described for the S.V. models. See that both valves are closed and that all parts are clean, particularly the joint faces of the head and barrel. No jointing washer is used but Heldite (obtainable from Ariel stockists) should be smeared on the joint face of the head before replacing it. New rubber washers should be fitted to the push-rod covers to prevent oil leakage. Now locate the covers round the spigot below the head and lower the head and cover assembly into position. Insert the four head bolts, screw them in a few turns and make sure that the push-rod covers are correctly located at each end and that the head correctly fits the spigot of the cylinder barrel. Screw down the bolts finger tight and then with a spanner put extra tension on the two bolts next the push-rod tubes until the rubber washers have been squeezed down sufficiently to allow the head to make contact with the barrel all round the joint face.

Now give one bolt a one-eighth turn and repeat on the bolt diagonally opposite. Do the same on the two remaining bolts. Return to the first bolt, give it another one-eighth turn, repeat on the opposite bolt and then on the other two, and so on, working round the head from one bolt to another until all are perfectly tight. This will ensure a good gas-tight joint. Insert the two push-rods.

See that the rocker-box joint faces are clean, both on the head and on each box, and examine the joint washers. If these are damaged fit new ones, or an oil-tight joint will not be obtained. Lay the washers in position on the head and take one of the boxes and the *long* bolt which passes through the push-rod end of the box. Slip this bolt through the box and then put the box in position, but hold it about half an inch above the head. Start the bolt by two or three threads and then, using the bolt as a guide, slide the box down on to the joint face. If this is done carefully the ball end on the rocker will drop into the push-rod cup; check this by testing the rocker for up and down play through the adjustment cover hole, whilst holding the box down firmly with the hand. When the rocker and push-rod have engaged, insert the three short bolts and carefully tighten all four, pulling down each bolt a little at a time as was done for the head. Now fit the other rocker-box in a similar manner.

Replace the carburettor, sparking plug, silencing system, etc., and secure the petrol tank.

MAINTENANCE AND OVERHAULING

IGNITION AND VALVE TIMING

Why Correct Ignition Timing is Important. Unless the spark occurs at a certain interval *before* the piston reaches the top of the compression stroke the engine will not develop full power, especially when running fast, because the piston will have travelled an appreciable part of its firing stroke before the pressure generated by the combustion of the explosive gases has reached its maximum. In other words, the ignition must be advanced. This advance, however, must not be excessive because if it is the maximum pressure generated by the burning gases will occur before the piston is on top dead centre and this gives rise to knocking and severely stresses the engine, particularly the connecting-rod bearings. To obtain the best performance and get the longest life from an engine always run it with the ignition timing correctly set. It is necessary to reset the timing whenever the magneto or "Magdyno" chain is removed or the instrument itself is detached.

To Ascertain the Piston Position. For the purpose of retiming the magneto it is only necessary on the majority of the 1932 models to find the top dead centre position of the piston. To do this is quite simple. Gently rotate the engine until both valves are closed and the piston is at the top of its compression stroke. Then insert a piece of stiff wire or a pencil through the sparking-plug hole so that the end rests on the piston (on detachable head models removal of the head will enable the piston position to be readily ascertained). By slowly revolving the engine backwards and forwards, the position of the piston when no motion is imparted to the wire or pencil can be determined. This is, of course, the top dead centre (T.D.C.) position.

When retiming the magneto on some 1932 models and all 1933–8 single-cylinder models it is necessary to set the piston so that it is a fixed distance, say $\frac{3}{8}$ in., below T.D.C. To do this, scratch a mark on the pencil or wire to indicate T.D.C., and then scratch another mark $\frac{3}{8}$ in. (or whatever the maximum ignition advance happens to be) above it. Now rotate the engine *backwards* until the top mark occupies the position of the lower mark. Clearly the piston will have descended a distance equal to that between the two marks. The ingenious type of rider will have no difficulty in devising a suitable indicator from an old sparking plug, a spring, and a piece of steel rod. T.D.C. indicators are also obtainable from accessory dealers.

Retiming the Magneto (1932 Models LB, LF, MB, MF, MH, VB, VG, VH). Remove the sparking plug and release the magneto sprocket from the taper on the armature shaft. Rotate the engine until the piston is at top dead centre and both valves are closed. Set the ignition control " full retard." Move the contact-breaker in the direction of rotation until the points are just separating, and tighten up the chain sprocket, taking care that this operation does not alter the setting. It is advisable to check the setting because of its importance. This setting gives approximately $\frac{7}{16}$ in. advance before top dead centre.

With the models MH, VG, and VH give slightly more advance. Set the contact-breaker points just separating with the cam ring at full advance, and the piston approximately $\frac{1}{2}$ in. or $\frac{9}{16}$ in. before top dead centre.

If a Maglita, running at engine speed, is fitted, time as follows: Set the piston $\frac{7}{16}$ in. *before* top dead centre with the piston coming up the compression stroke; this brings both valves closed. Set the contact-breaker cam ring at *full advance* and the points just breaking.

1932 Models SB, SG. Remove the sparking plug and take off the timing cover (do not forget to disconnect the oil gauge pipe at the top of the cover). Release the magneto pinion from the taper on the armature shaft. Rotate the engine until the piston is at top dead centre and *both valves are closed*. Set the ignition control to "full retard." Move the contact-breaker in the direction of rotation until the points are just separating, and tighten up the pinion, taking care that this operation does not alter the setting. This should be checked. This setting gives approximately $\frac{7}{16}$ in. maximum advance before top dead centre.

1933–8 Single-cylinder Models. To retime the ignition on all the 1933–8 S.V. and O.H.V. models proceed as follows. First remove the sparking plug and take off the magneto or "Magdyno" chain-case cover. Then without removing the chain undo the nut securing the sprocket to the armature shaft. The sprocket may then be released from the shaft taper. If necessary, use the extractor, but be careful not to impose any strain on the armature. Now rotate the engine until the piston is the correct distance below T.D.C. with both valves closed ($\frac{5}{16}$ in., $\frac{3}{8}$ in., and $\frac{5}{8}$ in. in the case of the S.V., O.H.V., and the "Red Hunter" engines respectively), and set the ignition-lever to the full advance position. Have a look at the contact-breaker cam ring and make sure that the handlebar lever is pulling it right round against the stop. The contact breaker should next be rotated clockwise until the contacts are just commencing to "break." Perhaps the easiest way of checking this is to open the contacts and slip a very thin piece of paper between them (cigarette paper is about right). By pulling on the paper and slowly revolving the contact

MAINTENANCE AND OVERHAULING   157

breaker, the commencement of the "break" (which releases the paper) can be accurately noted. With the contact breaker and armature in this position, fit the sprocket on the taper and retighten the lock nut, being careful not to upset the timing while doing so. Finally check over the setting once again and replace the chain-case cover and the sparking plug.

1932–6 Model 4F. To retime the magneto on this model, take out the sparking plug from No. 1 cylinder and remove the plug V (Fig. 54). Undo the nut holding the magneto sprocket to the armature. Screw the extractor into the thread cut in the sprocket box and then screw the set pin through the centre of the extractor. As soon as this pin comes up against the end of the armature shaft it will free the sprocket from the taper. The extractor can be withdrawn and the sprocket will remain in position on the armature. Now, rotating the engine in its normal direction, bring the piston of No. 1 cylinder up to within $\frac{5}{16}$ in. of top dead centre with both valves closed. The distributor centre piece on the end of the camshaft should be pointing to approximately 7 hr. 30 min. Remove the magneto contact-breaker cover, see that the ignition control is in the fully advanced position, and rotate the magneto contact-breaker anti-clockwise (looked at from the contact-breaker end) until the points just begin to separate. Take a box spanner, place it up against the face of the magneto sprocket and give the outer end of the spanner a sharp tap. This will drive the sprocket up on to the armature taper and will hold the sprocket in position whilst the retaining nut is being done up tightly. Replace the sparking plug, and the plug V in the chain cover. It is always a sound plan to check the timing after tightening the sprocket securing nut, just to make quite certain that the sprocket has not slipped during the tightening up operation.

Do not Interfere with Valve Timing. Whilst correct ignition timing is, as already mentioned, very important, correct valve timing is still more important. The exact moment when a valve opens and closes vitally affects engine performance and even an alteration in valve timing to the extent of one tooth only will produce a pronounced effect. Ariel engine designers know their job and it is, to say the least, a foolish and ignorant rider who would seek improved performance by "messing about" with the valve timing. To ensure correct replacement of the timing gear after a general overhaul, the manufacturers have adopted a system of marking the meshing timing gears on the S.V. and O.H.V. engines. On the O.H.C. engine the arrangement of the camshaft drive is such that it is almost impossible to interfere with the valve timing if reasonable care is taken when reassembling.

Removal of the camshaft chain and sprockets will not upset the valve timing so long as the sprockets are kept in mesh with the chain. Each sprocket is fitted to its shaft with one key, and consequently it always fits in the same relative position. Small variations in valve timing can be obtained by means of the vernier mounting of the camshaft sprocket on the driving boss. Instructions for dismantling and reassembling the timing gear on the various 1932–8 engines are given below.

Dismantling the Timing Gear (1932 Models LB, LF, MB, MF, and MH). Undo the ten cheese-headed screws securing the chain cover and remove this. Undo the nuts holding the magneto driving sprockets and withdraw the sprockets with the extractor provided. It is unnecessary to remove the oil pump, and this is best left in position. Now undo the single cheese-head screw by the magneto driving sprocket, and withdraw the gear cover, pressing on the ends of the camshaft spindles to prevent these being pulled out and the timing upset. Note that the cover is located on the crank case face by means of two hollow pegs.

If the cams are removed, it is perfectly easy to reset the timing. Rotate the engine until the piston is towards the top of the cylinder. The timing pinion will be seen to be centre-punched in two places: one dot towards the top left and two dots towards the top right; take the inlet cam, lift the tappet, and insert the cam wheel so that the centre dot marked on this coincides with the single dot on the pinion. Similarly, insert the exhaust cam, which has two dots on the timing pinion.

Note that the dots on the timing pinion are sometimes covered up by the securing nut; this nut has a left-hand thread. It is impossible to get the timing wrong if these instructions are carried out carefully. The timing pinion has one keyway and the mainshaft is keyed to the fly-wheel.

Be careful to replace all joint washers, renewing these if damaged, and securely screw up all nuts, etc., or an oil leak may occur. It is most important to note that, when securing the timing cover, the paper washer must be replaced in position, and that there is an *additional paper washer* ·005 in. thick at the joint connection to the sump.

1932 Models VB, VG, and VH. Undo the seven set-screws securing the chain cover and remove this. Remove the oil pump by taking out the two cheese-headed screws. Next undo the nuts holding the magneto driving sprockets and withdraw the sprockets with the extractor provided. Before removing the sprocket behind the oil pump, slip the small adaptor on to the eccentric on the end of the spindle. This prevents damage to this part. Undo the two

MAINTENANCE AND OVERHAULING 159

oil pipes to the oil tank, that to the chain, and the small one to the oil gauge. This latter is at the front of the case. Now slack off the set-bolt holding the magneto platform and remove the five set-screws securing the timing cover. Withdraw the gear cover, pressing on the end of the camshaft spindle to prevent this being pulled out and the timing upset.

If the cams are removed, the timing is perfectly easily reset. Rotate the engine until the piston is at top dead centre. The timing pinion and cam wheel will be seen to be centre-punched.

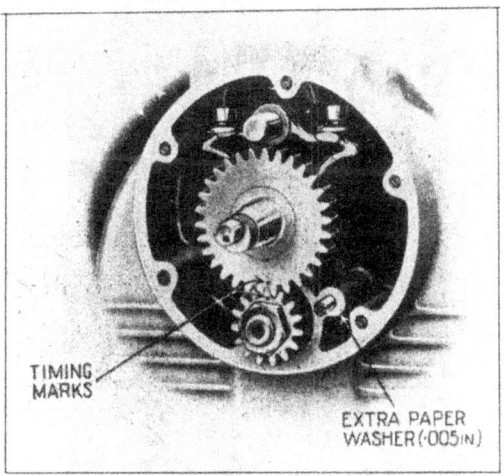

Fig. 71. 1932 Single-cylinder Timing Gear
The 1933-8 timing gear is similar.

Take the cam wheel, lift the cam levers, and insert the cam wheel so that the centre dot marked on this coincides with the centre dot on the pinion (see Fig. 71). Sometimes the dot on the timing pinion is covered up by the nut (left-hand thread).

When fitting the cam levers, insert that for the inlet valve first, and then that for the exhaust valve. The small hole in the lever for lubricating the cam lever pin bearing comes on top.

It is impossible to get the timing wrong if these instructions are carried out carefully. The timing pinion has one keyway and the mainshaft is keyed to the fly-wheel.

Be careful to replace all joint washers, renewing these if damaged, and securely do up all nuts, screws, etc., or an oil leak may occur. Here again it is most important to note that when replacing the timing cover, the paper washer must be in position and that there is an *additional paper washer* ·005 in. thick at the joint connection to the sump. Do not forget the set bolt supporting the magneto platform.

1932 " Sloper " Engines. Disconnect the oil gauge pipe and then take off the timing cover after undoing the ten set-screws holding the cover to the case. Undo the nut which secures the magneto sprocket to the armature shaft and draw the pinion off the paper on the shaft by means of the extractor provided in the tool kit.

FIG. 72. TIMING GEAR, SHOWING DECOMPRESSOR, AS FITTED ON THE 1932 "SLOPER" ENGINES
(The engine here depicted is the SG.)

The idler wheel simply slides off the spindle. If the engine is rotated so that both the valves are closed, the cam wheel can also be pulled out.

The timing pinion is a light driving fit on the mainshaft and is tightened up by means of the locking nut—left-hand thread—against a shoulder. The pinion is keyed so that it can only be fitted in one position. The radiused end of the hole through the pinion goes up against the shoulder on the shaft. A centre-punch mark will be noted by one of the teeth on the timing pinion, and there is a corresponding mark on the cam wheel. When the teeth

MAINTENANCE AND OVERHAULING

are meshed so that these two dots come opposite one another, the valve timing is correct (see Fig. 72). When fitting the cam levers, insert that for the inlet valve first, and then for the exhaust valve. The small hole in the lever for lubricating the cam lever pin bearing comes on top.

When replacing the cover, see that the joint washer is not damaged or broken, and securely do up the retaining screws or an oil leak will occur.

The Decompressor. The 1932 "Sloper" Ariel machines have decompressors fitted to the timing case to facilitate starting. The decompressor cam, which lifts the exhaust valve during a part of the compression stroke, is mounted on the engine mainshaft at the back of the timing pinion. The decompressor lever is mounted on an eccentric and can be brought into action by the partial rotation of the eccentric spindle.

The spindle is actuated through the medium of the outer lever and is held in position by friction. This friction is obtained by the compression of a coil spring mounted on the spindle and compressed between the end of the eccentric and the inner end of the timing cover bearing.

It will probably be found that when the machine has been on the road some little time, parts will bed down, so reducing the friction, with the result that the outer lever will drop instead of remaining in the " up " position, when the engine is kicked over with the decompressor in action. This is easily rectified by fitting a packing washer on the eccentric spindle between the spring and the bearing. To fit this washer, undo the nut holding the outer lever and take this off. Do not disturb the flange bearing plate. Now take off the timing cover, pressing on the end of the eccentric spindle, in order not to upset the lifter parts, etc. Fit the washer and replace the cover.

1933–8 S.V. and O.H.V. Models. To dismantle the timing gear it is necessary first to undo the seven set screws which secure the magneto chain-case cover and remove the cover. The complete oil pump can now be removed by detaching the two cheese-headed fixing screws holding the pump body (Fig. 45). Next remove the two magneto drive sprockets with the sprocket extractor provided after first removing the two armature and camshaft nuts. As a precaution against damaging the camshaft eccentric (which operates the pump) the small cupped adaptor should be slipped over it before attempting to remove the camshaft sprocket. After removing the two sprockets proceed to remove the delivery and return oil pipes and also the small pipe leading to the oil pressure gauge (O.H. rockers, 1938). On the steel chain-case models the pipe from the engine breather to the secondary chain must also be detached. Now slack off the set bolt holding the magneto platform and remove the five set screws securing the timing-case cover. Withdraw the cover and while doing so press against the end of the camshaft to prevent it being pulled out of its bush and the timing upset. If it is desired to examine the cams, the cam wheel can be pulled out and also the cam levers or toggles. It is a simple matter to reset the valve timing when reassembling.

Do not interfere with the small timing pinion on the mainshaft as the removal of this pinion is rarely necessary. It is keyed to the mainshaft and the locknut has a left-hand thread. The key ensures that the pinion is always refitted in exactly the same position on the shaft. To reset the valve timing after removing the cam wheel, rotate the engine until the piston is on top dead centre, take the cam wheel, lift the cam levers and insert the cam wheel so that the centre dot punched on it coincides with a similar dot punched on the engine pinion (see Fig. 71). The valve timing will then be correct. When fitting the cam levers, fit the inlet one first and then the exhaust. Note that the small hole in the lever for lubricating the cam lever pin bearing comes on top. After refitting the sprockets and tightening up the securing nuts firmly, see that the magneto driving chain is properly retensioned (see page 124). Before securing the armature sprocket, however, the magneto must be retimed as described on page 155. Be careful to replace all joint washers and if any of them are damaged they must be renewed, or oil leakage may occur. When replacing the timing-case cover see that the paper washer is replaced and also be sure that there is an *additional paper washer* ·005 in. thick at the joint connection to the sump (see Fig. 71). Do up all nuts, screws, etc., thoroughly tight and do not forget the set bolt which supports the magneto platform.

1932 VALVE TIMINGS

Model	Inlet Opens	Inlet Closes	Exhaust Opens	Exhaust Closes
LB, LF	$\frac{1}{64}$ in. or 5° before T.D.C.	$\frac{7}{16}$ in. or 50° after B.D.C.	$\frac{33}{64}$ in. or 55° before B.D.C.	$\frac{7}{64}$ in. or 20° after T.D.C.
MB, MF, MH	5° before T.D.C.	$\frac{15}{32}$ in. or 50° after B.D.C.	$\frac{17}{64}$ in. or 55° before B.D.C.	$\frac{1}{4}$ in. or 20° after T.D.C.
VG, VH, SG	$\frac{9}{64}$ in. or 22° before T.D.C.	$\frac{15}{16}$ in. or 70° after B.D.C.	$\frac{15}{16}$ in. or 70° before B.D.C.	$\frac{3}{16}$ in. or 25° after T.D.C.
VB, SB	$\frac{1}{64}$ in. or 5° before T.D.C.	$\frac{17}{32}$ in. or 50° after B.D.C.	$\frac{1}{4}$ in. or 55° before B.D.C.	$\frac{5}{32}$ in. or 20° after T.D C
4F	$\frac{1}{32}$ in. or 10° before T.D.C.	$\frac{11}{32}$ in. or 50° after B.D.C.	$\frac{13}{32}$ in. or 55° before B.D.C.	$\frac{3}{64}$ in. or 15° after T.D.C.

1932-6 O.H.C. Model. The timing gear for this model is perfectly simple, and absolutely straightforward in replacement if a few simple instructions are carried out. The actual 2 to 1 reduction

MAINTENANCE AND OVERHAULING

between the engine crankshaft and the camshaft is brought about by the small gear on the front crankshaft meshing with the larger gear on the half-time shaft. The large gear engages with the boss up against the shoulder on the half-time shaft. These two gears are inside the centre gearcase. The half-time shaft has one plain bearing in the wall at this centre gearcase, and the other bearing (a ball) in the wall of the outer gearcase. Keyed on to the outer end of the half-time shaft is the magneto driving sprocket and then the camshaft driving sprocket. The large sprocket, i.e. the magneto driving sprocket, fits with the small boss inside, while the camshaft driving sprocket should also be put on with the boss inwards.

1933–7 VALVE TIMINGS

Model	Inlet Opens	Inlet Closes	Exhaust Opens	Exhaust Closes
S.V.	$\frac{3}{64}$ in. or 5° before T.D.C.	$\frac{17}{32}$ in. or 50° after B.D.C.	$\frac{5}{8}$ in. or 55° before B.D.C.	$\frac{5}{64}$ in. or 20° after T.D.C.
O.H.V. Standard	$\frac{3}{64}$ in. or 5° before T.D.C.	$\frac{19}{32}$ in. or 55° after B.D.C.	$1\frac{1}{16}$ in. or 60° before B.D.C.	$\frac{5}{32}$ in. or 20° after T.D.C.
O.H.V. "Red Hunter"	$\frac{3}{64}$ in. or 22° before T.D.C.	$1\frac{5}{8}$ in. or 70° after B.D.C.	$1\frac{5}{8}$ in. or 70° before B.D.C.	$\frac{3}{32}$ in. or 25° after T.D.C.
4F (1933–6)	$\frac{1}{32}$ in. or 10° before T.D.C.	$1\frac{1}{4}$ in. or 50° after B.D.C.	$1\frac{3}{8}$ in. or 55° before B.D.C.	$\frac{3}{64}$ in. or 15° after T.D.C.

The camshaft sprocket is keyed and bolted to the end of the camshaft and has the same number of teeth as the driving sprocket, the reduction having already been brought about by the half-time gears. These two timing pinions inside the main gearcase are keyed to their respective shafts, whilst the two sprockets already mentioned are also keyed to their shafts. The valve timing is therefore fixed, except for the variation brought about by altering the mesh of the interior timing gears, or by altering the mesh of the two chain sprockets with the camshaft chain. To get accurate adjustment of the valve timing when first assembling the engine, a vernier arrangement is incorporated in the camshaft sprocket. During the ordinary course of reassembly, that is to say so long as the reduction gears inside the centre gearcase are not disturbed, it is quite unnecessary to disturb the vernier setting. Assemble the half-time shaft sprocket, rotate the engine until No. 1 piston is at top dead centre, and then turn the camshaft clockwise, when looked at from the driving end, until the inlet valve of No. 1 cylinder has just commenced to open (this valve commences to open with the crank 10° before top dead centre). Slip the camshaft sprocket into position on the end of the camshaft so that the key is engaging with the keyway, slip the chain on to the lower sprocket, taking care not to rotate the engine, and pull the chain up into position. It will then be found that the teeth on the camshaft sprocket are in line with the side-plates on the chain; that is, the chain and the sprocket are ready to mesh. Mark one of the teeth of the camshaft sprocket and the corresponding side-plate of the chain, slip the sprocket off the camshaft, insert it into the chain, so that the marked tooth is in mesh with the marked link, and then slip the sprocket back on to the camshaft and tighten up with the centre bolt. If the instructions have been followed out correctly, the timing will be right.

Reassembling in this manner, without touching the vernier adjustment means that the timing will either be correct, or one or more complete teeth out. Following the instructions as given brings the timing correct.

1938 VALVE TIMINGS

Model	Inlet Opens	Inlet Closes	Exhaust Opens	Exhaust Closes
VB	$\frac{5}{32}$ in. or 22° before T.D.C.	1 in. or 70° after B.D.C.	1 in. or 70° before B.D.C.	$\frac{7}{32}$ in. or 25° after T.D.C.
NG	$\frac{1}{64}$ in. or 5° before T.D.C.	$\frac{19}{32}$ in. or 55° after B.D.C.	$1\frac{1}{4}$ in. or 60° before B.C.D.	$\frac{5}{32}$ in. or 20° after T.D.C.
VG				
LG, LH	$\frac{3}{64}$ in. or 22° before T.D.C.	$1\frac{5}{16}$ in. or 70° after B.D.C.	$1\frac{5}{16}$ in. or 70° before B.D.C.	$\frac{3}{32}$ in. or 25° after T.D.C.
NH, VH				

When Reassembling the Oil Pump (S.V. and O.H.V.). Be careful to place the joint washer correctly in position and tighten up the set screws securely. If the washer is damaged, fit a new one. It is of the greatest importance that a good joint is made between the pump face and the cover. The author does not advise removal of the pump unnecessarily. When replacing the duralumin block (Fig. 45) make sure that the chamfered hole which engages the camshaft eccentric faces *inwards*.

Dismantling Flywheel Assembly not Advised. Only those having expert mechanical knowledge and experience should attempt to dismantle the flywheel assembly, as this is a delicate operation, requiring considerable skill and precision. The flywheels must run *dead true* when reassembled. For the benefit of those who feel competent to undertake the task of dismantling the flywheels and subsequently truing them up the following brief notes are given.

1. First undo the crankpin nut on the driving side, holding by the driving side flywheel only. Then support this flywheel and press out the crankpin complete with timing side flywheel, etc.

2. Both mainshafts and crankpin are secured by the usual taper fixing. The mainshafts are also keyed, while the crankpin

MAINTENANCE AND OVERHAULING 165

has a key which engages with a keyway in the timing side flywheel. This ensures the correct registering of the oilways between the timing side shaft and the flywheel and between the flywheel and the crankpin. It also ensures that the valve timing will be correct if the cam wheel is properly refitted.

3. Both crankpin nuts and driving side mainshaft nuts have right-hand threads. Both timing side mainshaft nuts have left-hand threads.

4. The connecting-rod has a double row roller bearing big-end, the hardened steel crankpin constituting the inner member, while the hardened steel outer member is a press fit in the connecting-rod eye and can be renewed together with the crankpin when worn.

5. When truing up the flywheel assembly it is more imperative to get the mainshafts to run dead true than it is for the flywheels themselves, although with proper alignment both should run true.

6. When fitting the flywheels into the crankcase, see that they have from ·008 in. to ·012 in. end-play. Hardened packing washers or shims of various thicknesses can be supplied for adjustment within reasonable limits. These washers may be inserted on either mainshaft as necessary in order to keep the flywheels centrally located in the crankcase.

7. Having reassembled the flywheels, it is advisable to check the register of the various oilways. The simplest way to do this is to force oil into the hollow mainshaft and then to watch for it exuding at the big-end bearing.

To Dismantle the Burman Clutch. On pre-1936 oilbath models remove the outer half of the chain-case. On later models remove the clutch cover. Then undo the five spring retaining nuts which project through the spring plate. This enables the clutch plates to be withdrawn. When reassembling be careful to refit the plates in the correct order. First replace the thick plain plate, then a fabric insert plate, and a plain plate alternately finishing with a plain plate. Finally readjust the clutch (see page 126).

To Remove the Clutch Centre. Remove the clutch plates, undo the nut on the end of the mainshaft, and pull off the clutch centre, which is splined on the mainshaft. The clutch sprocket (with roller bearing) and the outer clutch housing are then left in position on the mainshaft. Pull the clutch sprocket away, taking care to lose none of the rollers as they fall out. When reassembling, fit first the plain washer, then the inner roller race, rollers, and sprocket. Next fit a plain washer, the clutch centre, and finally the securing nut.

How to Remove Wheel Bearings. Having removed the wheel from the frame, take off the brake anchor plate (see next paragraph). Then screw off the two thin lock nuts and tap the wheel spindle gently out towards the brake-drum side. Prise off the dirt-excluding cover and the inner bearing with rollers and cage will then come out out complete. Both sides are the same. The outer bearing race is pressed into the wheel hub and no attempt should be made to remove it unless it is damaged.

Brake Anchor Plate Removal. To remove the anchor plate complete with brake shoes and fittings, remove the spindle nut on the brake-drum side. Then insert a thin spanner on to the hexagon between the fork end and brake plate and loosen this nut half a turn. Disconnect the brake rod or cable (the chain also in the case of the rear wheel), undo the other spindle nut, and remove the wheel. If dealing with a front wheel, also disconnect the anchor bar holding the plate. It is only necessary to unfasten it at the top end. If the brake anchor plate locking nut (already slackened) is removed, the anchor plate will slip straight off the spindle.

To Take off the Brake Pedal. On some oil-bath models the spindle for the pedal is pressed in the chain-case, and to remove the pedal it is only necessary to undo the nut on the spindle. On the earlier steel chain-case models the brake pedal is mounted on a tapered shaft carried in a bearing tube welded to the engine plate. In order to remove the pedal slack off the retaining nut and drive the shaft inwards. This will free the taper. To avoid damaging the greaser nut on the shaft it is wise to interpose a short distance piece. The jaws of a set spanner will answer the purpose. On 1938 models the brake pedal is carried on a pin fixed to the frame stay behind the gearbox fixing.

If you wish to Dismantle the Steering Damper. First support the front wheel off the ground by placing a box beneath the engine. Then unscrew the damper knob and remove the anchor plate bolt and star washer fixing-nut. Now remove the lower rear fork spindle and take out the tie rod which passes through the steering column. When reassembling the damper, note that the nut securing the star washer screws up against a small shoulder, leaving the washer free to revolve. Be careful not to trap the washer.

Footrest Adjustment (1938). Slack off one nut on the end of the footrest rod until the spring washer is just free. With a heavy hammer or mallet give the inner end of the footrest a smart blow

MAINTENANCE AND OVERHAULING 167

to release the taper; the direction of the blow must be such as to rotate the rest about the support. Strike the other rest in the same manner.

Removing Detachable Wheel. To remove the detachable wheel, put the machine on the rear stand. Undo the 3 wheel nuts holding the hub to the brake drum, slacken the two plated stay nuts and unscrew and withdraw the spindle bolt on the offside. Tap out the distance piece between the hollow wheel spindle and the fork end, if it has not already fallen out, pull the wheel to the side clear of the driving pegs and studs, lift up the hinged guard and roll the wheel out. The wheel is replaced by reversing the procedure.

To Take off Petrol Tank. The petrol tank is secured by four set-screws, each having two rubber washers and one plain steel washer and locked with a wire. The thick rubber washer goes next to the tank. The set-screws should not be screwed up too tightly.

If the tank has to be taken off, the cross pipe connecting the two sides must be removed, and the tank should therefore be emptied. Note: As this pipe comes below the tank, it is liable to choke with sediment, etc. If, therefore, the petrol capacity of the tank appears to diminish take off this pipe and clean, so that there is a free petrol flow between the two sides of the tank. Also disconnect the petrol feed pipe, oil gauge pipe at rocker-box union and the speedometer flex at gearbox.

Dismantling Rocker-boxes (1938). If it is required to dismantle the rockers at any time, the rocker-box is taken off as already described and the flat large-headed screw is removed from the end of the rocker spindle next the sparking plug. The spindle is then pressed or tapped out towards the same end, thus freeing the rocker. When reassembling, see that the small distance washer is fitted on the spindle between the rocker and the box itself. This washer prevents the rocker rubbing the soft aluminium and also forms an abutment against which the spindle is pulled when the outer oil union retaining nuts are screwed up. The flat headed screw at the other end in conjunction with the fibre washer is nothing but an oil seal and must be tightened *after* the oil union nuts have been done up.

CHAPTER X

CARE OF 1939 MODELS

New Models. The 1938 Models VB, VG, NG, NH, VH, 4G have been retained in improved form at reduced prices and Models LG, LH have been replaced by Models OG, OH which are similar. The new models consist of another 1000 c.c. Square Four (Model 4H) similar to Model 4G, but with somewhat less luxurious equipment; a 600 c.c. Square Four (Model 4F) of similar design to the 1000 c.c. models, and last but not least a 500 c.c. side-valve (Model VA) designed on the lines of Model VB.

MAINTENANCE HINTS (SINGLES)

Most of the advice given in the 1938 edition is up to date and the maintenance and overhauling instructions for the 1938 machines apply also to the 1939 models. Owners of 1939 Ariels should, however, note the following.

Suitable Engine Oils. The following brands and grades of lubricants are suitable for Ariel single-cylinder engines: Patent Castrolaero, Mobiloil D (BB during winter), Golden Shell Extra Heavy (Triple Shell during winter), Price's Motorine B De Luxe, and Essolube Racer. The lubrication system is entirely unchanged and the instructions in Chapter VII hold good.

Ignition and Valve Timing. Ignition timings remain unaltered and the advice on page 156 is unaffected. Valve timings, however, have been changed considerably and the correct timings for the 1939 singles are tabulated below. As hitherto, the timing gears are punch-marked.

1939 VALVE TIMINGS

Model	Inlet Opens	Inlet Closes	Exhaust Opens	Exhaust Closes
NG, VG	3° after T.D.C.	47° after B.D.C.	52° before B.D.C.	12° after T.D.C.
VA, VB, OG	14° before T.D.C.	62° after B.D.C.	62° before B.D.C.	17° after T.D.C.
NH, OH, VH	18° before T.D.C.	68° after B.D.C.	63° before B.D.C.	23° after T.D.C.

The above valve timings should be checked with a tappet clearance of ·010 in. (both valves closed).

Care of New Models. Note that Model VA is similar to the 1938–39 S.V. Model VB except that de luxe equipment is not provided and the 500 c.c. engine has a bore and stroke of 81·8 mm. × 95 mm. Models OG, OH are for practical purposes identical to the 1938 250 c.c. O.H.V. Models LG, LH respectively.

CARE OF 1939 MODELS

The corresponding maintenance and overhauling hints therefore apply.

Gearbox Lubrication. All Burman gearboxes should be replenished every 1000–1500 miles with 2–3 oz. of Wakefield's Castrolease Medium, Gargoyle Mobilgrease No. 2, Shell Retinax Grease, Price's Belmoline C or Esso Grease. For sprint work, wash out and replenish with thin oil. Always keep the gearbox approximately **one-third full**.

To Adjust Clutch (250 c.c. Models). An improved form of Burman lightweight gearbox (type H.P.) with completely enclosed clutch operation is fitted on Models OG, OH. In addition to the usual cable stop adjuster at the top of the casing (partly hidden from view), there is a fulcrum adjustment of the enclosed lever. To adjust, remove the small raised plate secured to the gearbox end cover by two screws and then turn the sleeve nut exposed **anti-clockwise** to decrease back-lash and clockwise to increase backlash which at the handlebar lever should be not less than ½ in.

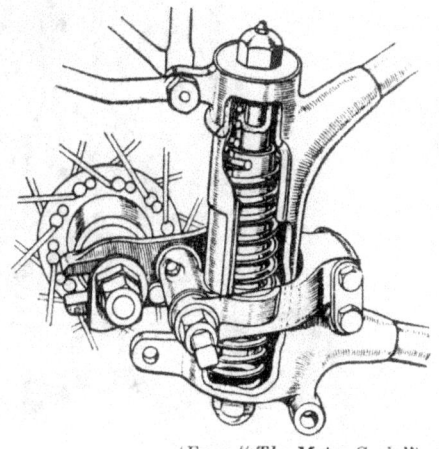

(*From "The Motor Cycle"*)

Fig. 73 Cut away View of Off-side Spring Frame Assembly

The Ariel spring frame, which comprises two assemblies and costs £10 extra, is designed to provide maximum unsprung weight, constant chain tension and perfect lateral stability.

Spring Frame Maintenance. As may be seen in Fig. 73, each spring frame assembly has two grease nipples provided and to obtain maximum benefit from the springing it is important to apply the grease-gun to the near- and off-side nipples about every 250 miles. No adjustment is needed, but after an extensive mileage bush renewal may be desirable.

MAINTENANCE HINTS (SQUARE FOURS)

The instructions given previously for the 1937 600 c.c. and 1938 1000 c.c. Square Fours (Models 4F, 4G) are in general applicable to the 1939 Square Fours (Models 4F, 4G, 4H) which are of similar design and engine capacity.

Engine Lubrication. The brands and grades mentioned on page 168 for the singles are suitable for the four-cylinder models during the summer, but different grades are advised for winter use. During the winter use Patent Castrol XL, Mobiloil A, Double Shell (Medium), Price's Motorine M, or Essolube "30." For running-in (500–1000 miles) it is sound policy to mix some Acheson's Colloidal Graphite (see page 63) with the fuel. Keep the oil pressure at 40–45 lb. per sq. in. and occasionally check the circulation by removing the tank filler cap and observing the oil which should return in bubbles after a preliminary gushing on starting up. Do not forget to drain the tank and sump every

Fig. 74. The Square Four Cylinder Head and Rocker-box with Manifold and Valve Components Removed

1000–1500 miles (see page 95). After draining the tank it may be necessary to slacken off temporarily (10–15 seconds) the relief valve in order to restore correct oil pressure.

When Decarbonizing. Stripping down for decarbonizing (every 5000–8000 miles) is fully described on page 137. If it is necessary to remove the cylinder block (not advised unless essential) the "Magdyno" must first be removed by detaching the driving sprocket, loosening the clamping strap nut and taking out the base bolt. Do not remove the carbon which forms around the top of each cylinder bore above the piston stroke, as this provides an excellent oil seal.

Grinding-in the Valves. Valve removal and grinding-in are fully dealt with on pages 148–149.

Suitable Sparking Plugs. On the 600 c.c. and 1000 c.c. engines fit a Lodge C14, or if a hotter plug is required, a Lodge H14 or a K.L.G. LKS5 or 831.

Correct Valve Clearances. The correct clearances **with a cold engine** for all Square Fours are: ·006 in., inlet; ·008 in., exhaust. Adjust by means of the overhead rocker screws and lock-nuts.

Ignition Timing. The recommended ignition timings are $\frac{5}{16}$ in. and $\frac{3}{16}$ in. before T.D.C. on *full advance* in the case of the 1000 c.c. and 600 c.c. engines repectively. To retime the ignition, remove No. 1 plug, turn over engine until piston is the correct distance before T.D.C. (on the compression stroke) and fully advance ignition lever. Now release the "Magdyno" sprocket from its taper, turn contact-breaker in the direction of rotation until it is just "breaking" and retighten the "Magdyno" sprocket. The position of the rotor arm relative to the contacts in the distributor body should be checked. When the rotor is turned **anti-clockwise** to take up drive back-lash, the marks on the rotor and on the base should be in line. If they are not, pull off the rotor, slacken the screw in the shaft centre and tap sideways the top of the shaft to free the taper fixing. Now the sleeve at the top should be rotated until the marks come into line and the screw may then be retightened. Replace the rotor and again check the ignition timing.

The Contact-breaker and Distributor. The 180° "Magdyno" runs at **engine speed** and has a contact-breaker of the type shown in Fig. 49. Keep the gap at ·012 in. and the contacts clean (see page 123). To clean thoroughly, unscrew the centre fixing screw and remove the contact-breaker from the tapered shaft to which it is keyed. The contact arm may then be readily taken off. Current from the H.T. pick-up is led to the centre of the distributor and to ensure correct firing (order, 1, 2, 3, 4), the distributor leads must be properly connected. Beginning from the centre (H.T. "Magdyno") in a clockwise direction, the distributor connexions are 3, 2, 1, 4. No. 1 cylinder is the front one on the timing side.

Square Four Valve Timing. The correct timing is: Inlet opens $\frac{3}{16}$ in. (25°) before T.D.C.; Inlet closes $\frac{1}{2}$ in. (55°) after B.D.C.; Exhaust opens $\frac{19}{32}$ in. (60°) before B.D.C.; Exhaust closes $\frac{1}{8}$ in. (20°) after T.D.C. The timing sprockets are marked and the timing should be correct when the line scribed on the rear crankshaft sprocket is in line with the two holes in the camshaft sprocket.

The Cycle Parts. The instructions already given in regard to the cycle parts such as gearbox, clutch, engine shock absorber, chains, wheel bearings, steering head, forks, etc., apply also to the "Fours."

INDEX

ALIGNMENT, wheel, 64–66
Amal carburettor, 76–77, 130–133
Ammeter readings, 105
Automatic voltage control, 116

BATTERY, care of, 109–112, 116
Brakes, 53, 56, 99, 129, 166
Brushes, dynamo, 103
Burman clutch, dismantling, 165
—— gearbox, 81

CARBON, removing, 143
Chain adjustment, 124
—— lubrication, 97–98
Clutch, 97, 126–127, 169
Commutator, care of, 105
Contact-breaker, 123
Cut-out, 105
Cylinder removal, 134–140

DECARBONIZING, 133, 170
Detachable wheel, removing, 167
Dry sump lubrication, 86
Dynamo maintenance, 103–106

ENGINE lubrication, 86
—— oils, 54, 91, 168
—— principles, 71
Exhaust valve-lifter, 120

FILTERS, oil, 94
Flywheels, dismantling, 164
Footrest adjustment, 167
Front forks, 98, 128

GEAR changing, 55
—— control adjustment, 126
Gearbox lubrication, 95, 169
Grinding-in valves, 148

HANDLEBAR adjustment, 128

IGNITION timings, 155, 168, 171
Instrument panel, 3

LAMPS, 106–109
Lighting faults, table of, 114–115
Lubrication chart, 96

"MAGDYNO," 95, 100, 116,
"Maglita," 95, 102
Magneto, retiming, 155–157

NUMBER plates, 48

OIL pump, 87, 164
—— purifier, 93

PETROL tank removal, 167
Pillion riding, 51, 61
Piston removal, 141
Pressure gauge, oil, 89, 92

REASSEMBLY, engine, 149
Regulator, oil, 89
Rings, piston, 141–143
Rocker-box, 92, 99, 167
Running-in, 61, 63

SPARKING plug, 122
Starting engine, 54
Steering damper, 56, 167
—— head, 98, 128

TOPPING-UP battery, 109
Timing gear, dismantling, 158–162
Tyre pressures, 66, 68
—— removal, 69

VALVE clearances, 118–120
—— timing, 157–164, 168, 171
Valves, removing, 145–148

WHEEL bearings, 98, 129, 166,
Wiring diagrams, 111, 113

OTHER CLASSIC MOTORCYCLE MANUALS CURRENTLY AVAILABLE

ARIEL WORKSHOP MANUAL 1933-1951:
All single, twin & 4 cylinder models

ARIEL (BOOK OF) MAINTENANCE & REPAIR MANUAL 1932-1939:
LF3, LF4, LG, NF3, NF4, NG, OG, VA, VA3, VA4, VB, VF3, VF4, VG, Red Hunter LH, NH, OH, VH & Square Four 4F, 4G, 4H

BMW FACTORY WORKSHOP MANUAL R27, R28:
English, German, French and Spanish text

BMW FACTORY WORKSHOP MANUAL R50, R50S, R60, R69S:
Also includes a supplement for the USA models: R50US, R60US, R69US.
English, German, French and Spanish text

BSA (BOOK OF) MAINTENANCE & REPAIR 1936-1939:
All Pre-War single & twin cylinder SV & OHV models through 1939
150cc, 250cc, 350cc, 500cc, 600cc, 750cc & 1,000cc

DUCATI OHC FACTORY WORKSHOP MANUAL:
160 Junior Monza, 250 Monza, 250 GT, 250 Mark 3, 250 Mach 1, 250 SCR & 350 Sebring

HONDA 250 & 305cc FACTORY WORKSHOP MANUAL:
C.72 C.77 CS.72, CS.77, CB.72, CB.77 [HAWK]

HONDA 125 & 150cc FACTORY WORKSHOP MANUAL:
C.92, CS.92, CB.92, C.95 & CA.95

HONDA 50cc FACTORY WORKSHOP MANUAL: C.100

HONDA 50cc FACTORY WORKSHOP MANUAL: C.110

HONDA (BOOK OF) MAINTENANCE & REPAIR 1960-1966:
50cc C.100, C.102, C.110 & C.114 ~ 125cc C.92 & CB.92
250cc C.72 & CB.72 ~ 305cc CB.77

NORTON FACTORY TWIN CYLINDER WORKSHOP MANUAL 1957-1970: *Lightweight Twins:* 250cc Jubilee, 350cc Navigator and 400cc Electra and the *Heavyweight Twins:* Model 77, 88, 88SS, 99, 99SS, Sports Special, Manxman, Mercury, Atlas, G15, P11, N15, Ranger (P11A).

NORTON (BOOK OF) MAINTENANCE & REPAIR 1932-1939:
All Pre-War SV, OHV and OHC models: 16H, 16I, 18, 19, 20, 50, 55, ES2, CJ, CSI, International 30 & 40

SUZUKI 200 & 250cc FACTORY WORKSHOP MANUAL:
250cc T20 [X-6 Hustler] ~ 200cc T200 [X-5 Invader & Sting Ray Scrambler]

SUZUKI 250cc FACTORY WORKSHOP MANUAL: 250cc ~ T10

TRIUMPH (BOOK OF) MAINTENANCE & REPAIR 1935-1939:
All Pre-War single & twin cylinder models: L2/1, 2/1, 2/5, 3/1, 3/2, 3/5, 5/1, 5/2, 5/3, 5/4, 5/5, 5/10, 6/1, Tiger 70, 80, 90 & 2H. Tiger 70C, 3S & 3H, Tiger 80C & 5H, Tiger 90C, 6S, 2HC & 3SC, 5T Speed Twin & 5S and T100 Tiger 100

TRIUMPH 1937-1951 WORKSHOP MANUAL (A. St. J. Masters):
Covers rigid frame and sprung hub single cylinder SV & OHV and twin cylinder OHV pre-war, military, and post-war models

TRIUMPH 1945-1955 FACTORY WORKSHOP MANUAL NO.11:
Covers pre-unit, twin-cylinder rigid frame, sprung hub, swing-arm and 350cc, 500cc & 650cc.

VESPA (BOOK OF) MAINTENANCE & REPAIR 1946-1959:
All 125cc & 150cc models including 42/L2 & Gran Sport

VINCENT WORKSHOP MANUAL 1935-1955:
All Series A, B & C Models

COMING SOON IN THIS SAME SERIES

BRIDGESTONE FACTORY WORKSHOP MANUAL: 50 Sport, 60 Sport, 90 De Luxe, 90 Trail, 90 Mountain, 90 Sport, 175 Dual Twin & Hurricane

BRITISH MILITARY MAINTENANCE & REPAIR MANUAL:
Service & Repair data for all British WD motorcycles

BRITISH MOTORCYCLE ENGINES: AJS, Ariel, BSA, Excelsior, JAP, Norton, Royal Enfield, Rudge, Scott, Sunbeam, Triumph, Velocette, Villiers & Vincent ~ a compilation of 1950's articles from *The Motor Cycle* dealing with engine design.

CEZETTA 175cc MODEL 501 MANUAL & PARTS BOOK

LAMBRETTA (BOOK OF) MAINTENANCE & REPAIR:
All models through 1958 (Except Model 48)

VILLIERS ENGINE WORKSHOP MANUAL:
All Villiers engines and ancillaries through 1947

PLEASE CHECK OUR WEBSITE FOR AVAILABILITY
~ WWW.VELOCEPRESS.COM ~